Accounting in Context

Roy Dodge
Leonard T. Brown

CollinsEducational

Collins
Educational

National Extension College Trust Ltd

NEC
NATIONAL
EXTENSION
COLLEGE

Acknowledgements

Authors: Roy Dodge, Senior Lecturer in Accountancy, University of Westminster
Leonard T. Brown, Passmaster

Consultants: Brian John, Principal Lecturer in Accounting and Finance, University of Westminster
John Morley, Senior Lecturer, University of Brighton
Joe Baggott, B.Sc. (Econ.), FCMA, FSCA

Project manager: Janette Edwards

Design and illustration by Vicky Squires.

We are grateful to: the Central Statistical Office for permission to reproduce the extracts from the General Index of Retail Prices; the Office of Population Censuses and Surveys for permission to reproduce Tables 2.1 and 2.2 in Appendix 1; Marks and Spencer for permission to reproduce an extract from their Annual Report 1991; Sainsbury's and ICI for permission to reproduce balance sheet details from 1984 and 1985; the Association of Accounting Technicians for permission to reproduce a question from the Intermediate exam, 1992; the Controller of Her Majesty's Stationery Office for permission to reproduce an extract from the Customs and Excise VAT Guide and the VAT Return (VAT 100), both of which are Crown copyright.

Printed in Great Britain at the University Press, Cambridge

ISBN   0 00322 358 2

The National Extension College is an educational trust and a registered charity with a distinguished body of trustees. It is an independent, self-financing organisation.

Since it was established in 1963, NEC has pioneered the development of flexible learning for adults. NEC is actively developing innovative materials and systems for distance learning opportunities on over 100 courses, from basic skills and general education to degree and professional training. NEC has prepared a distance learning route to Accounting NVQ levels 2 and 3 (AAT Foundation and Intermediate). Accounting in Context Workbook and Accounting in Context Simulations for Devolved Assessment are available from NEC.

National Extension College Trust Ltd
18 Brooklands Avenue
Cambridge
CB2 2HN
Tel: (0223) 358295/450214
Fax: (0223) 313586

Collins Educational
HarperCollins Publishers
FREEPOST GW2446
Bishopbriggs
Glasgow G64 1BR
Tel: 041 306 3269 Fax: 041 306 3750

NATIONAL
EXTENSION
COLLEGE

Collins
Educational

Accounting in Context

Contents

Introduction to Part 1: Capital Transactions

This is the first of two modules on financial accounting. It will lead you step-by-step through all the basic principles, concepts, and practical aspects of capital transactions.

In particular, we will be looking at the depreciation and disposal of fixed assets and the regulations covered by Statement of Standard Accounting Practice 2 (SSAP 2) and SSAP 12.

In designing this course it was recognised that the students who use it might have some previous knowledge of accounting, or they might be complete beginners. The level of material chosen is intended to work for both types of student.

Good luck with your studies. If you complete this first part of the course satisfactorily, you will be able to proceed to the second part with a firm foundation in the basic knowledge.

Chapter 1

The nature and control of capital transactions

Introduction

This chapter considers a matter of considerable practical relevance to the practising accounting technician. You may already be aware of the importance to any organisation of:

- properly recording all assets (items of value or 'future economic benefit') and liabilities (debts or obligations) to register a measure of the net worth (or value) of the organisation

- periodically measuring performance ('profit and loss' or 'net income') by properly grouping and matching period incomes against period costs or expenses

- safeguarding its assets and other interests.

For many organisations, the largest amounts of expenditure are incurred in respect of fixed assets, i.e. assets of continuing longer-term use. They will include items such as land and buildings, machinery and equipment and motor vehicles. They are often substantial assets of relatively high value.

Fixed assets are of great significance to the evaluation of organisational worth. As they are used, (or 'employed') they generate costs which must be included in any calculation of the organisation's performance or profit and loss. As fixed assets are of material value, records and registers of them are maintained to aid internal control and ensure they are not stolen or abused.

This chapter deals with maintaining the records and accounts relating to capital items and expenditure, and looks at the accounting regulations covered by the Statement of Standard Accounting Practice 2 (SSAP 2).

Objectives

After you have completed this chapter, you should be able to:

- describe and explain the application of the four fundamental accounting concepts to accounting for capital transactions

- explain the concept of accruals as it applies to capital expenditure

- distinguish capital transactions from revenue transactions

- distinguish the specific expenditure that may be included as capital or fixed asset expenditure in the balance sheet and compute relevant balance sheet figures

- relate the materiality concept to the size and nature of an organisation

- record various items, including capital expenditure, in the balance sheet

- operate procedures for the planning and control of capital expenditure

- explain the principles of internal control and check and use them in the design of systems for the planning and control of capital expenditure

- explain the need for effective coding systems for capital expenditure and for the production of asset registers.

1 The fundamental accounting concepts

The accounting profession identifies four fundamental accounting concepts. These concepts are so fundamental to the preparation of financial statements that you can always presume they have been observed unless there is a note in the financial statements stating that they have not.

We will state them here so that you will be aware of them. The descriptions may contain terms that you have not yet met – don't worry too much about that now, but try to remember to look back at these concepts once you have read through Part 1.

The fundamental accounting concepts are identified and defined in SSAP 2 of the Accounting Standards Board (ASB) and are also required by the Companies Act 1985. They are:

- going concern

- accruals

- consistency

- prudence.

These apply to all aspects of accounting. In this chapter we will relate them to accounting for capital transactions.

The fundamental concepts can only be overridden if not to do so would produce something less than a true and fair view to accounts users.

Going concern

This concept is particularly relevant to the presentation of fixed asset figures in the financial statements. Accountants preparing the statements are required to do so under the assumption that the organisation will 'continue in existence for the foreseeable future'. Fixed asset values should not be written down below net book values. The figures are determined on the basis that the business will not be sold (or liquidated) in the near future. Assets are not, therefore, shown at their realisable values, i.e. the values at which they might be sold. The amounts are based, under usual practice, on historical cost.

Accruals

This concept aims to match the income of a period with the expenditure 'used up' in the process of generating that income. As fixed assets are used up over their estimated useful life, their cost must be spread into profit and loss accounts over that life. In this way, a fair charge for the asset's use is made in each year of its life.

Consistency

Organisations are generally required to treat similar fixed assets in a similar way within each financial period and from one period to the next. Consistency means that similar assets should not be depreciated using different depreciation methods, nor should they be depreciated over different anticipated economic lives, unless the organisation genuinely feels that their economic lives will be different.

Prudence

Any permanent decrease or 'diminution' in the value of a fixed asset should result in a writing down of that asset, with a charge to profit and loss, to reflect prudence.

Accounting policies

SSAP 2 requires disclosure of accounting policies in the financial statements and, in particular, the 'accounting bases' or methods chosen to apply the fundamental accounting concepts to the transactions of the organisation. There are several choices of accounting bases for recording capital transactions. Choice of one depreciation method rather than another would represent one such choice. Once adopted, a particular basis or method of calculating depreciation becomes part of the organisation's accounting policy and, as already stated, must therefore be applied consistently.

2 Capital vs. revenue expenditure

The word 'expenditure' relates to any type of cost incurred for which a benefit of some kind is received. This expenditure can be classified either as capital expenditure or as revenue expenditure. Some expenditure may provide the business with long-term benefits, such as when it buys a delivery van that will be used in the business for several years. This type of expenditure is referred to as *capital expenditure*. The assets acquired through capital expenditure are referred to as *fixed assets*.

Other forms of expenditure result in benefits that are used up ('consumed') immediately, such as the payment of wages for the services of an employee. This type of expenditure is referred to as *revenue expenditure*.

When calculating business profits for a period, the trading revenues and other incomes earned in the period must be matched against the costs of earning that revenue. So, if a benefit (resource or 'asset') has been consumed in earning sales revenues of a period, the cost of that benefit is treated as an expense and will be matched against sales incomes in the profit and loss account.

Fixed assets, such as buildings and equipment, will be gradually consumed over a period of years. According to the concept of accruals, or 'matching', the costs of using fixed assets, including the initial expenditure on acquisition such as purchasing and installing it, must therefore be matched against the revenues the assets help to earn over their full period of use in the organisation. This process involves spreading the net costs of capital expenditure into profit and loss over the years of economic use of each asset, a process called 'depreciation'.

Capital and revenue transactions – why the distinction is important

It is important to distinguish between capital and revenue items because revenue items have an immediate impact on the measure of performance of an organisation. They are dealt with immediately in the profit and loss account, whereas capital items are dealt with in the balance sheet.

The profit and loss account attempts to present a true and fair view of business performance. It reflects revenue transactions, such as receipts from the sale of goods and the costs of earning that revenue, for example, buying the goods and paying the day-to-day expenses. It is prepared using the accruals (matching) concept.

The balance sheet shows fixed assets at their depreciated historical cost or net book value (i.e. cost less accumulated depreciation). It is not intended to show what a business is 'worth' if it is sold or taken over. Capital transactions, dealt with in the balance sheet, alter the make-up of the business capital (net assets) rather than increase or decrease the total. If a business spends £100,000 on buying a factory:

- one of the assets (cash) is reduced by £100,000

- another asset (the value of the buildings) has increased by £100,000

  but

- the total capital of the business, which is equal to net assets, has remained the same.

Even if the business borrows money, there is no change in the business capital at the time the money is received: the asset of cash has increased and liabilities (a loan creditor) have increased by the same amount.

Being able to distinguish between capital and revenue items is one of the most important skills you will use when preparing financial statements.

Activity 1	In each case, indicate whether the transaction is a capital or revenue one. Payments:

In each case, indicate whether the transaction is a capital or revenue one.
Payments:

1   Purchase of a delivery van by a vegetable retailer: ....

2   Purchase of a car by a car dealer: ....

3   Payment of wages to employees: ....

4   Payment for electricity: ....

5   Purchase of goods for resale: ....

Receipts:

1   Sale of trade goods: ....

2   Sale of a fixed asset: ....

3   Rent received on sub-letting part of the business premises: ....

4   Further cash introduced into the business by the proprietor: ....

3 Classification as capital expenditure

Fixed assets are those:

■ of continuing, longer-term use in an organisation

■ not classified as current assets – i.e. not classified as stocks of raw materials, work in progress and finished goods, debtors, prepayments or cash and bank balances.

Fixed asset accounts are created or adjusted to reflect additional capital expenditure costs as they are incurred. The balances of such accounts are shown in the balance sheet.

The question of which costs to include in fixed asset balances has been one of much debate within the accounting profession. Regarding a cost as an element of capital expenditure means that it will be reflected as part of fixed asset costs in the balance sheet. This means that the whole cost will not be written off immediately in the profit and loss account and, as a result, immediate profit figures will be comparatively improved.

There is a danger that company directors will reach subjective decisions to portray the profit and loss account and balance sheet in the best possible light. Accounting regulation therefore specifies which costs may be classified as capital expenditure. The rule is that any costs incurred in bringing an asset into usable condition and location may be 'capitalised', i.e. recorded in the balance sheet.

The next Activity is designed to test your ability to distinguish whether costs should be capitalised. Before working this Activity, note that it is usual when recording capital costs to 'be sensible' and recognise the accounting principle of materiality. This provides reasonable discretion to those accounting for business transactions.

For example, if a large international business purchased a calculator for general office use at a cost of £100, it would be highly impractical to record the calculator as a fixed asset and to calculate full depreciation on the asset. From a balance sheet point of view, the amount is likely to be so small as to make no material difference whatsoever to interpretation by accounts users of the figures presented for fixed assets. On the other hand, a small business spending a similar amount might well consider it material enough to capitalise.

Materiality would dictate that the larger business could decide not to show the cost of the calculator as a fixed asset in the balance sheet and could instead simply charge the cost to profit and loss. You will notice just how beneficial this may be when working through the sections on depreciation; avoiding the work involved on depreciating such a small asset will clearly be of advantage.

Most organisations specify a minimum financial figure below which assets would not be classified as fixed assets and would therefore not be shown in the balance sheet. A typical figure would be £200, although some large organisations apply much higher figures.

The main points of materiality are that as long as there is no material effect on the interpretation of the financial statements, you need not:

■   capitalise new fixed assets in the balance sheet if of very small value

■   open fixed asset accounts for assets of very small value nor calculate depreciation for the accounting period

■   make charges to profit and loss in the event of permanent diminution of a fixed asset.

Activity 2	Crabtree Ltd has recently taken delivery of some new machines, resulting in the expenses listed below. Tick the appropriate box to show whether each amount should have been charged to profit and loss (P&L) or capitalised in the balance sheet (BS) as fixed asset expenditure:

	P&L	BS
Initial cost of the machinery	☐	☐
Inward delivery costs (Paid to the supplier)	☐	☐
Fitting and installation costs	☐	☐
Maintenance costs (First three months following acquisition)	☐	☐
Small repairs	☐	☐
Replacement of a major part (Straight replacement)	☐	☐
Replacing a component by a new high technology component with much greater production capacity	☐	☐
Cost of operator time for initial set-up of the machinery	☐	☐
Cost of 20 small shelving units (£15 each)	☐	☐

Capitalised expenditure may also include interest costs on any borrowing used to finance acquisition and installation of a fixed asset; specifically, on any such costs incurred up to the point of the asset being in 'location and condition' for use.

New expenditure on existing assets will be capitalised if it produces improved performance by those assets, either from extended economic life or greater capacity to provide earnings for the entity.

4 Double-entry principles

Double entry simply recognises that every transaction has a twofold aspect. You have already seen some examples of this when trying to make sense of capital and revenue expenditure – for example, on buying a building, the two aspects of the transaction were:

1   the cash balance was reduced, and

2   the fixed assets (buildings) were increased.

Every transaction has this twofold aspect.

In the following series of activities, you are going to prepare a balance sheet after each transaction for a fictional business. In practice, there are literally thousands of transactions during any one period and it would be pointless to produce a balance sheet after each one. One of the reasons a business needs an accounting system is to classify, collate, and record all its transactions for a period. This enables a single balance sheet to be produced at the end of the period that gives expression to the total transactions for that period.

The format and layout of balance sheets can vary, depending on the preferences of those who prepare them, unless the entity is a company. The Companies Act 1985 prescribes the format and layout of balance sheets for companies. It is more helpful for beginners to start with a 'two-sided' balance sheet, that is, one where the assets are shown on the left hand side, and the liabilities are shown on the right.

Here is an example of a two-sided balance sheet of a sole trader business:

Assets			Liabilities		
Fixed assets:			**Current liabilities:**		
Delivery van:		28,000	Creditors		1,000
Current assets:			**Long-term liabilities:**		nil
Stock	2,000				
Debtors	2,500				
Cash	1,500		**Capital:**		
		6,000	Cash introduced	12,000	
		____	Retained profits	21,000	
		34,000			33,000
					34,000

You should notice the following points:

Group headings: On each side of the balance sheet, figures are grouped together under specific headings (i.e. fixed assets, current assets, current liabilities, long-term liabilities, and capital). Where there is more than one item under a group heading (as with current assets and capital) the figures are inset and a sub-total is shown in the total column.

Assets: These are divided into two groups – fixed assets and current assets.

Liabilities: There are three groups – current liabilities, long-term liabilities, and capital. The distinction between current liabilities and long-term liabilities is based on the length of time between the balance sheet date and when the money is due to be paid to the creditor. If payment has to be made during the next 12 months, the amount due is classified as a current liability. If payment is due to be made after 12 months (e.g. a loan), it is classified as a long-term liability.

Capital: Note that this is a different meaning of the word capital from the one we have been using so far. In this case, it is the balance of £33,000 which represents the proprietor's investment in the business. You may find it difficult to think of this as a liability. The proprietor will not be asking for this amount to be paid back while the business continues to operate. You should note that the business could not afford to pay off the £33,000 without selling all its assets and going into liquidation (and this assumes that the assets can be sold for their balance sheet values).

It is in the context of liquidation that you have to think of it as a liability. It represents a residual amount owed by the business to the proprietor, residual in the sense that it would be the last amount to be paid out by the business after all the assets were sold and the real creditors had been paid.

The total amount invested in the business by the proprietor (£33,000) arises from two sources, namely:

1   cash put into the business (usually to get it started)

2   profits earned by the business that have not been withdrawn by the proprietor.

The profits belong to the proprietor. If these profits are left in the business instead of being withdrawn, they must be treated as increasing the proprietor's investment. In effect, the same thing would happen if the proprietor withdrew all the profits in the form of cash and then paid some of the money back into the business in order to finance expansion. But this would be an unnecessary movement of funds; the proprietor might just as well not withdraw the amount which is needed to finance expansion.

The figure for retained profits is cumulative, in the sense that it represents all the profits that the proprietor has left in the business since it began.

Below (in Activities 3–11) you will find blank outline balance sheets in which you can enter the descriptions and figures after each transaction. Some of the group headings will not necessarily be applicable to your answers, in which case you should leave them blank. They are included to help you become familiar with the format of a balance sheet, and to make sure that you enter items in the appropriate place.

Activity 3

Mr Chileshe has set up business as a computer dealer. His first transaction is to put £10,000 of his own private savings into a separate business bank account. Set out the balance sheet of his business (in the form provided) following this transaction.

BALANCE SHEET

after completing Transaction 1

Assets	Liabilities
Fixed assets:	**Current liabilities:**
Current assets:	**Long-term liabilities:**
	Capital:

Activity 4	The second transaction was to purchase a delivery van, for use in the business, at a cost of £3,000.
	Before doing the new balance sheet, think about the following question: Will Mr Chileshe's capital alter as a result of this transaction?

BALANCE SHEET

after completing Transaction 2

Assets	Liabilities
Fixed assets:	**Current liabilities:**
Current assets:	**Long-term liabilities:**
	Capital:

Activity 5	Mr Chileshe realised that the money he had invested in the business would not be enough and so his third transaction was to get his friend, Mrs Kateka, to lend £1,000 to the business. Mrs Kateka agreed that the loan could be interest-free and repaid at any time during the next five years.
	Show the new balance sheet after this third transaction. (Make sure you are showing the loan in the right place.)

BALANCE SHEET

after completing Transaction 3

Assets	Liabilities
Fixed assets:	**Current liabilities:**
Current assets:	**Long-term liabilities:**
	Capital:

Activity 6

The fourth transaction was to buy two computers (intended for resale) at a cost of £3,500 each. Mr Chileshe paid for them by a cheque drawn on the business bank account.

Set out the new balance sheet.

BALANCE SHEET

after completing Transaction 4

Assets	Liabilities
Fixed assets:	**Current liabilities:**
Current assets:	**Long-term liabilities:**
	Capital:

You will notice that Transactions 2 to 4 have not affected the total of Mr Chileshe's capital; all that has happened is that the composition of the net assets of the business has changed.

Activity 7	See if you can think of four types of transaction that will cause the proprietor's capital to alter in total. Make a note as to whether the transaction mentioned will increase or decrease the capital.

Transactions that will increase or decrease the proprietor's capital:

Transaction	Effect on capital
1	increase/decrease
2	increase/decrease
3	increase/decrease
4	increase/decrease

Activity 8	Mr Chileshe's fifth transaction was to sell the two computers bought in Activity 6 for £5,000 each (£10,000 in total). The customers paid for them in cash which Mr Chileshe put into the business bank account. How much gross profit has Mr Chileshe made, and where will you show this profit in the balance sheet?

Activity 9	Set out Mr Chileshe's balance sheet after completing this fifth transaction.

BALANCE SHEET

after completing Transaction 5

Assets	Liabilities
Fixed assets:	**Current liabilities:**
Current assets:	**Long-term liabilities:**
	Capital:

Activity 10	Mr Chileshe now carried out the following additional transactions:
	1 Paid his assistant £200 for wages.
	2 Withdrew £500 for himself.
	3 Paid back £200 to Mrs Kateka as a part repayment of the loan.
	One of these transactions will not affect Mr Chileshe's capital. State which one, and explain why. Explain why the other transactions do affect Mr Chileshe's capital.

Activity 11	Show what the balance sheet would look like after the transactions in Activity 10 have been completed.
	(You should think of the £500 withdrawn by Mr Chileshe as a withdrawal of profit, and therefore as something that will reduce the retained profits; we will discuss this in more detail later.)

BALANCE SHEET

after completing the transactions in Activity 10

Assets	Liabilities
Fixed assets:	**Current liabilities:**
Current assets:	**Long-term liabilities:**
	Capital:

That is as far as we will take this series of transactions. In Part 2 we will go on to look at profit and loss accounts and appropriation accounts.

5 Control of capital expenditure

Capital expenditure decisions have far more serious consequences than those relating to working capital (current assets less current liabilities). Capital expenditure is long-term and the effects of bad decisions might influence the company's results for a considerable time.

Investment in working capital is different; it is typically under daily control and can be changed quickly should any decision turn out to be bad.

It is not surprising therefore, that capital expenditure is typically subjected to a high level of management control; capital expenditure must be properly planned for, justified, and authorised and fixed asset performance must be monitored and controlled. The performance of fixed assets must be compared to plans; ensuring that deviations are noted and that appropriate management action is taken – either to ensure performance improvements or to incorporate any information gained into cost-benefit analyses supporting future planning decisions.

Expenditure on fixed assets might be authorised by adoption into the organisation's plans and budgets. Plans and budgets should be formulated in advance of each financial period. The process should follow a full review of all possible lines of business action, and the selection of the best line in the light of the main corporate objectives (e.g. maximisation of profit).

Functional budgets are typically produced for each area of organisational activity including capital expenditure. If top-level management approve the budgets, they approve and authorise everything within them; approval of the capital expenditure budgets will authorise the capital investment programmes they contain.

Additional capital expenditure that is not specified in period plans and budgets must be subjected to formal procedures that should include:

- formal justification and requests to management

- authorisation by those carrying authority for such expenditure

- monitoring and control during implementation

- post-audit reviews designed to monitor resultant performance of the fixed assets acquired compared with those in the plans, with a view to improving future decisions.

Formal justification and requests to management

Standardised forms should be used where possible to support the request for capital expenditure to the managers and/or committees with authority to authorise them. People submitting requests should fully justify those requests – setting out costs, benefits and revenues and any other quantitative or qualitative information that might support approval.

Authorisation

There should be a clearly defined organisational structure that specifies the authority levels of particular managers and/or committees for taking capital investment decisions. This authority should relate to the responsibilities of those concerned, ensuring they feel an obligation or accountability for the decisions they take.

Approval of capital expenditure should be given following a review of the justification for that expenditure. Where possible, decisions should be taken well in advance of implementation so that the expenditure may be included in formal plans and budgets for a period.

Monitoring and control

Standards and targets should be set following capital expenditure authorisation. Timings for implementation and project completion and detail of anticipated costs and revenues should be clearly set out. Actual performance will then be compared to the standards and targets to evaluate progress and ensure management action where necessary, e.g. providing for prompt corrective action in event of performance below that expected.

6 Internal control and capital expenditure

Internal control is the whole system of controls, financial or otherwise, that provides for proper maintenance of the accounting records and safeguards the organisation's assets.

Internal check is concerned with the separation of employee duties in such a way as to support internal control.

The fundamental requirement of internal control and check in the area of capital expenditure is, where possible, giving separate individuals responsibility for authorisation and control of expenditure, physical control of assets and accounting and control of the capital expenditure records.

Those employees dealing with the justification and authorisation of capital expenditure should be independent of those whose responsibility it is to receive the fixed assets and maintain control of them. The employees dealing with the justification and authorisation of capital expenditure should also raise the entries to the accounts following acquisition.

The accounts department should record capital expenditure from the information given by those who authorised that expenditure. The accounts department should ensure that the accounting entries are supported by receipts and/or delivery notes from the employees having physical control of the assets, thereby ensuring that the assets are properly received. The accounts department should also make payment for such assets.

'Three-way division of duties' in this way provides for internal control in a highly effective way. If you consider the position of each of the parties referred to, you can see that it would be extremely difficult for any individual to carry out fraud or theft of fixed assets. Problems should be avoided unless the individuals involved are acting together.

Coding of capital expenditure and assets

Capital expenditure and fixed assets should be appropriately coded to ensure proper classification and control. Coding systems should allocate expenditure and assets to cost centres, departments, or functions of the organisation – thus providing for allotment of responsibility to those same areas for the expenditure and/or assets of the organisation.

Expenditure and assets could then be grouped under the coding system by generic type (e.g. all office equipment in the administrative department) and finally by individual item or type of item.

Such coding systems are dealt with fully in Part 3. Use of a coding system provides for full classification of the capital expenditure and assets attributed to particular areas or segments of the organisation, thereby providing a full record of the assets held and attributing responsibility for them to the managers of the areas or segments involved.

Maintaining fixed asset registers

Registers that record assets by area or segment of responsibility, generic group and then actual asset (or asset type) can be used as a basis for periodic audit checks on the existence and condition of fixed assets. Further checks can also be made to ensure that assets are beneficially owned, that title or ownership documents are properly maintained. Such checks can also provide for judgement on the proper presentation of fixed assets in the financial accounts. Asset registers can be simply generated from any database that incorporates an effective asset coding system.

Summary

In this chapter you have been working with the underlying principles that apply when preparing the financial statements and distinguishing profit and loss account items from balance sheet items. In particular, you should be:

- able to describe the application of the fundamental accounting concepts to capital transactions

- able to explain the concept of accruals (or matching) as it applies to capital expenditure

- aware that capital transactions are those that affect the organisational position in the balance sheet; revenue transactions are those to be charged or credited to profit and loss

- able to identify the specific costs that may be classified as capital expenditure in the balance sheet as those incurred to bring the fixed asset to a usable condition and location

- aware that new expenditure on existing fixed assets may be capitalised when it improves asset performance

- able to compute all relevant balance sheet figures for fixed assets

- able to explain the materiality concept

- able to explain procedures for planning/controlling capital expenditure

- able to explain the principles of internal control and internal check and apply those principles appropriately in the design of systems for the planning and control of capital expenditure

- able to explain the need for effective coding systems for capital expenditure and for the production of asset registers⁺

- able to show the effect of transactions on a balance sheet.

Key to Chapter 1 activities

Activity 1   Payments:

1 Capital; 2 Revenue – it is part of the stock of the business. It is a current (not fixed) asset; 3 Revenue; 4 Revenue; 5 This is a little awkward. If you have put revenue, you can consider your answer correct. But strictly speaking it depends on whether or not the goods have been sold. It is only the cost of those sold that will be treated as a revenue item – as cost of sales.

Receipts:

1 Revenue; 2 Capital; 3 Revenue; 4 Capital.

Activity 2   Here are our answers:

	P&L	BS
Initial cost of the machinery		✓
Inward delivery costs (Paid to the supplier)		✓
Fitting & installation costs		✓
Maintenance costs (First 3 months following acquisition)	✓	
Small repairs	✓	
Replacement of a major part (Straight replacement)	✓	
Replacing a component by a new high technology component with much greater productive capacity		✓
Cost of operator time for initial set-up of the machinery		✓
Cost of 20 small shelving units (£15 each) (as £15 is likely to be below the minimum figure set by the organisation for capitalising assets)	✓	

Activity 3

BALANCE SHEET

after completing Transaction 1

Assets		Liabilities	
Fixed assets:		**Current liabilities:**	
Current assets:		**Long-term liabilities:**	
Bank	10,000		
		Capital:	
		Cash introduced	10,000
	10,000		10,000

Activity 4

No, not in total. But the composition of the business assets will change; some of the cash has been changed into a delivery van.

BALANCE SHEET

after completing Transaction 2

Assets		Liabilities	
Fixed assets:		**Current liabilities:**	
Delivery van	3,000		
Current assets:		**Long-term liabilities:**	
Bank	7,000		
		Capital:	
		Cash introduced	10,000
	10,000		10,000

Activity 5

BALANCE SHEET

after completing Transaction 3

Assets		Liabilities	
Fixed assets:		**Current liabilities:**	
Delivery van	3,000		
Current assets:			
Bank	8,000	**Long-term liabilities:**	
		Loan – Mrs Kateka	1,000
		Capital:	
	11,000	Cash introduced	10,000
			11,000

Activity 6

BALANCE SHEET

after completing Transaction 4

Assets			Liabilities	
Fixed assets:			**Current liabilities:**	
Delivery van		3,000		
			Long-term liabilities:	
Current assets:			Loan – Mrs Kateka	1,000
Stock	7,000			
Bank	1,000		**Capital:**	
		8,000	Cash introduced	10,000
		11,000		11,000

Activity 7

(1) introducing more cash into the business: capital increase; (2) making a profit: capital increase; (3) making a loss: capital decrease; (4) proprietor withdraws cash from the business: capital decrease.

Activity 8

£3,000, i.e. Sales £10,000; less Cost of sales £7,000. The profit will be shown as an item under 'Capital' called 'retained profits'. This will be added to the cash introduced in order to arrive at the total capital.

Activity 9

BALANCE SHEET

after completing Transaction 5

Assets			Liabilities		
Fixed assets			**Current liabilities:**		
Delivery van		3,000			
Current assets:			**Long-term liabilities:**		
Stock	nil		Loan – Mrs Kateka		1,000
Bank	11,000				
		11,000	**Capital:**		
			Cash introduced	10,000	
			Retained profits	3,000	
					13,000
		14,000			14,000

Notice that the capital of the business has increased by £3,000 because you have replaced an asset that was previously in the balance sheet at £7,000 (the stock) with another asset worth £10,000 (the cash banked).

Also, as none of the profit has yet been withdrawn by the proprietor, the figure of £3,000 can be referred to as retained profits.

Activity 10

Item 3. The decrease in an asset (cash) is compensated by a decrease in a liability (Mrs Kateka's loan) and so the net assets will stay the same.

Item 1 is an expense of the business, and so capital decreases.

Item 2 is a withdrawal of capital by the owner, and so capital decreases.

Activity 11

BALANCE SHEET

after completing remaining transactions

Assets			Liabilities		
Fixed assets:			**Current liabilities:**		
Delivery van		3,000			
			Long-term liabilities:		
Current assets:			Loan – Mrs Kateka		800
Stock	nil				
Bank	10,100		**Capital:**		
		10,100	Cash introduced	10,000	
			Retained profits	2,300	
					12,300
		13,100			13,100

Workings:

Retained profits: 3,000 – 200 – 500

Bank: 11,000 – 200 – 500 – 200

Chapter 2

Depreciation and disposal

Introduction

Fixed assets are resources and the use of any resource involves cost. Depreciation is the accountant's representation of the cost of use of fixed assets over the number of years for which that asset is in use. Depreciation methods attempt to spread capital costs into the profit and loss account over periods that extend over those years.

The application of depreciation methods results in depreciated historical cost (unexpired cost) being shown in the balance sheet. This balance sheet figure is arrived at by subtracting all the depreciation (accumulated depreciation) charged in the profit and loss accounts over the asset's life from its cost.

Objectives

After you have completed this chapter, you should be able to:

■   explain the concept of depreciation

■   recognise the figures on which to base depreciation calculations

■   calculate depreciation and include the figures in the accounting records

■   deal with asset disposals and the accounting for asset disposals

■   deal with revisions of useful economic lives of fixed assets and the resulting depreciation effects

■   deal with the effects of additional expenditure on existing fixed assets and the resulting depreciation effects

■   deal with the accounting for depreciation fully and prepare journal entries for depreciation amounts appropriately

■   describe the relevance of SSAP 12 to depreciation accounting.

1 Depreciation

The nature of depreciation

Most fixed assets have a finite useful life. It is unlikely that any asset created by humans will last for ever. Some of them, such as buildings, may last for a very long time; others, such as motor vehicles, have a relatively short life. All bring with them a cost for their use, and depreciation is the cost attributed to fixed asset use and charged to the profit and loss account.

Activity 1	There is one asset that might be owned by a business which can be thought of as having an infinite life. It is a natural asset – not one created by human beings. Can you think what asset this is?

In the previous chapter, we simply treated the cost of a fixed asset as capital expenditure and broadly discussed the allocation of this cost to the profit and loss account. The cost of a fixed asset is just as much a cost of earning sales revenue as is the cost of wages, rent, electricity, and so on. The only difference is that the benefits derived from buying a fixed asset are consumed over several accounting periods, whereas the benefits derived from paying wages, rent, and so on, are consumed in the specific accounting period during which they are paid.

The fundamental concept of accruals ('matching') requires that we recognise the capital costs of fixed assets in the profit and loss account by matching them against the sales revenues those costs have helped to generate. A proportion of fixed asset costs will therefore have to be treated as an expense in the profit and loss account each year. This expense is called depreciation. At any particular accounting date, the proportion of original fixed asset cost which has not yet been treated as an expense (unexpired cost) is carried forward in the balance sheet, and is referred to as the 'net book value' of the asset.

Depreciation defined

The current definition of depreciation has been adopted by the Accounting Standards Board (ASB) in the accounting standard SSAP 12. It can be paraphrased as follows:

The measure of wearing out, consumption, or other reduction in useful economic life of a fixed asset; whether through use, passage of time, or obsolescence. Obsolescence may be a result of market or technology changes.

Notice that the word 'value' is not used anywhere.

'Useful economic life' is defined in SSAP 12 as: the period over which the *present owner* will derive economic benefits.

Calculations of depreciation charge are based on the length of time that the business intends or expects to use an asset and not on its total expected life. A new computer system might be expected to last eight years given its quality and reliability but be depreciated over three years if it is anticipated that changing technology will necessitate replacement three years after acquisition. Its useful life in the organisation will be three years.

Activity 2

Read the definitions again and then answer the following question: Do you think it will be necessary to calculate depreciation for an asset that is gaining in value, such as a building? Give reasons for your answer.

Activity 3

As mentioned earlier, the expression 'net book value' refers to the proportion of expenditure on a fixed asset which has not been transferred to the profit and loss account as an expense at the accounting date. Why do you think the term 'net book value' is used?

Depreciation measurements

Depreciation must be provided on all assets which have a finite useful economic life by:

allocating the cost less estimated residual value fairly to the accounting periods expected to benefit from use of the asset (SSAP 12).

In practice, several methods are used in order to do this. SSAP 12 does not insist on any particular method; it simply states that the method chosen should be the most appropriate for the type of asset and its use.

The two most popular methods used in practice are referred to as:

1   The straight line method

2   The reducing balance method.

The fundamental accounting principle of consistency, supported by SSAP 2 and the Companies Act 1985, dictates that once a business has chosen a particular depreciation method for a particular asset, it should consistently apply the same method to the asset, and to other similar assets over subsequent accounting periods. SSAP 12 allows for a change in depreciation method only if the new method gives a 'truer and fairer' view of the organisation's position via the profit and loss account.

The straight line method

This method simply calculates depreciation as an equal amount for each year. The annual amount is found by dividing the cost of the asset less its estimated residual value (called 'the depreciable amount') by the estimated number of years of economic use in the business.

Activity 4

A businessman buys a van for £8,000 at the beginning of his first year of trading. He intends to use it in the business for four years and estimates that the van can be sold for £2,000 at the end of the fourth year. Calculate the annual depreciation expense.

| Activity 5 | What will be the 'net book value' of the van (in Activity 4) at the end of the trader's second year? |

The net book value appears in the balance sheet together with a record of the original costs of assets and the accumulated depreciation to date.

The straight line depreciation charge is often expressed as a percentage of original cost. Expression as a percentage enables accounting personnel to compute the total depreciation amounts to be passed to profit and loss for any period by simply applying the percentage to the original costs of assets as they would appear in the balance sheet.

| Activity 6 | What will be the straight line depreciation percentage for the van in Activity 4 over the years of economic life with the trader? |

The reducing balance method

This method calculates depreciation for each financial period as a fixed percentage of the net book value at the start of the period. As each period passes, the net book value will gradually reduce. Consequently, the amount taken as depreciation each year will gradually decrease.

| Activity 7 | The trader in Activity 4 decides to use the reducing balance method for calculating depreciation. Calculate depreciation for years 1 to 4 using a rate of 30%. You can do this by completing the figures in the following outline computation (work to the nearest £1 in year 4): |

Cost at start of year   £8,000

Depreciation for year 1 (30% of £8,000)

Net book value at start of year 2

Depreciation for year 2

Net book value at start of year 3

Depreciation for year 3

Net book value at start of year 4

Depreciation for year 4

Net book value at end of year 4

You will notice that the net book value at the end of year 4 is not equal to the estimated residual value of £2,000 mentioned in the details for Activity 4. If the trader had intended to reduce the net book value to £2,000 by the end of year 4, the rate of 30% was set a little too high.

The percentage to be used for depreciation calculations under the reducing balance method would probably be given to you by your managers, or by the assessors for NVQ central assessment. The figure is, however, easily derived using the formula:

$$1 - \left[\sqrt[n]{\frac{\text{Estimated residual value of the asset}}{\text{Original cost of the asset}}} \right] \quad \text{multiplied by 100}$$

n is the number of years over which the asset is to be written down to its estimated residual value (4 in our example).

Activity 8	What will be the reducing balance depreciation percentage for the van (in Activity 4) over the years of economic life with the trader?

The calculation reveals, as suggested in the above text, that the percentage depreciation rate should be a little less than 30%.

Pro-rating depreciation charges with time

Depreciation is designed to reflect the accruals concept and to charge the capital costs of assets appropriately to the profit and loss account, i.e. matching costs over the years of use with the revenues that the assets have helped to generate.

Full annual depreciation charges are computed, but depreciation is concerned with matching and charging costs to the profit and loss account based on the length of time for which the asset was owned and used during each period.

In the example you have been working on, the asset was acquired at the beginning of the first year of trading. It therefore made sense to calculate depreciation for the whole of the first year and to suggest a full annual charge to profit and loss. If the asset had been purchased halfway through the first year, the depreciation for that year would have been one-half of the amount suggested for the whole year.

Accurate (and 'true and fair') working of annual depreciation charges would suggest that pro-rating of the charge for each asset to period of ownership within the year would be a good idea. Pro-rating is the most appropriate method in practice.

Nevertheless, you must check the policy of your organisation in such matters. Some organisations will provide a full year's depreciation for an asset in the year of acquisition (as the charge to profit and loss) even though the asset may have been owned for only a very small fraction of the year. They will probably then make no depreciation charge at all for any usage for the part of the year of disposal. This is generally accepted, even though it does not properly support the fundamental accruals concept.

Activity 9	A trader purchases an asset for £8,000 on 1st August 1991 and decides to use the reducing balance method for calculating depreciation. Calculate depreciation for years 1991 to 1993 using a rate of 30% and assuming the asset is sold on 31st May 1993. The trader's year end is 31 December.

Revision of anticipated fixed asset lives

SSAP 12 states that: if the anticipated life of a fixed asset changes, the remaining net book value (NBV) should be written off to profit and loss over the remaining portion of that anticipated economic life *unless* to do so would provide something less than a true and fair view of organisational performance to users of the financial statements (i.e. the accounts would be materially distorted).

If such treatment leads to a view that is less than true and fair, the organisation should:

■ register a depreciation charge in profit and loss for the present financial period that reflects figures as they would have been had the revised period of life been adopted and consistently applied for working depreciation since the asset was first acquired, and

■ register a separate charge or credit in profit and loss for the adjustment to depreciation for earlier years, making reference to this charge or credit separately in the notes to the financial statements.

For example, Rambotrop Ltd has depreciated a particular asset for five full years using straight line depreciation. The asset cost was £120,000 and has been depreciated using a nil anticipated scrap value and an eight-year life. Rambotrop Ltd now feels the asset will only remain of use to the organisation for another two years.

The NBV after depreciation at the end of year 5 is £45,000 (£120,000 less 5 x £15,000 depreciation). The rule in SSAP 12 on revision of the asset life suggests that the depreciation for the final two years might be £45,000/2 = £22,500 p.a. This, of course, increases the previously recorded annual depreciation charge on the asset by 50%.

If, in the opinion of the directors, this would cause the view of the present year profit (or loss) to be less than true and fair, Rambotrop Ltd could:

- recognise a present year depreciation figure based on original cost of £120,000 but reassess the economic life to be a total of seven years (five years already depreciated plus the two years to the anticipated end of asset life). The present year charge would thus be:

$$1/7 \times £120,000 = £17,143$$

- separately disclose the 'undercharge' of depreciation for earlier years – reporting this figure separately and independently to enable proper interpretation of the accounts. The figure adjusted for earlier years would be :

'Undercharge' = 5 x (£17,143 – £15,000) = £10,715

Rambotrop Ltd would make it clear in the notes to the accounts that this latter figure of £10,715 was due to the adjustment of earlier year depreciation and is not to be strictly regarded as part of the present year performance figures.

So the balance sheet would show:

£120,000 less (5 x £15,000) less £17,143 less £10,715 = £17,142.

This is a figure for transfer to profit and loss as the depreciation charge in the final year. It is the same as that which would result from a seven-year life being assumed from the beginning, i.e. £120,000/7= £17,143.

If the remaining NBV had been simply written off over remaining years of life following the general SSAP 12 suggestion, the remaining charge for the final year of asset use would be a further £22,500.

The advantage of the alternative treatment given under SSAP 12 is that it helps the users of the financial statements by clearly identifying a further charge for earlier years rather than simply an increased charge for the latest year. The general approach in SSAP 12 would cause material distortion in this case.

Permanent loss or diminution of fixed asset values

If a permanent loss in the value of an asset is experienced, for example, by a major breakdown that can only be partially repaired, the value of the asset should be immediately written down to the estimated recoverable amount, i.e. the maximum the organisation could expect to get by either using the asset over its remaining economic life or by selling it.

SSAP 12, following the Companies Act 1985, allows any provision or charge made for such diminution or loss in value to be written back (debiting the fixed asset value in the balance sheet and crediting profit and loss) if the situation changes and the reasons for writing the asset value down no longer apply.

New expenditure on existing fixed assets

New expenditure on existing fixed assets should be capitalised to the extent to which that expenditure increases the performance, and therefore the 'earning capacity' or economic worth, of existing fixed assets. This increased performance may be an increase in projected asset lives or increased ability or capacity to perform.

If there is additional capitalised expenditure on existing fixed assets the addition to remaining net book values (NBVs) for the assets concerned should be written off to profit and loss over the anticipated remaining period of economic lives.

For example, Rambotrop Ltd has another fixed asset with NBV £23,000 at 31st December 1991. Over 1992, it spends £15,000 on improvements to the asset. The improvements mean the asset will now have a projected useful life in the organisation of six years and will have greater capacity, in that the asset will be able to process more products.

The company would simply add the £15,000 to the fixed asset value in the fixed asset cost account and then depreciate the increased net book value of £38,000 over six years if straight line depreciation is used – i.e. depreciate at £6,333 per annum.

If the company uses another method of depreciation, the other method would be used exactly as before but using the revised expected life.

Fixed assets that need not be depreciated

SSAP 12 recognises that there may be circumstances in which it is inappropriate to depreciate a fixed asset.

It states that freehold land and 'assets maintained to such a standard that depreciation does not arise' are beyond its scope and therefore will not require depreciation. An example of an exception to this would be freehold land that is subject to loss of value through depletion by, for example, the extraction of minerals.

SSAP 12 further recognises two situations in which it may be inappropriate to depreciate a fixed asset:

■   where anticipated residual value is greater than present net book value (NBV) – see the key to Activity 2

■   where the anticipated useful economic life of the asset is either infinite or such that any depreciation charge would be insignificant.

In either case, a nil depreciation charge would be allowed under SSAP 12.

2 Accounting for depreciation

Balance sheet presentation

You will get a much better idea of how the book-keeping is normally done if we think about the balance sheet first.

The amount carried forward in the balance sheet at the end of each year is actually the net book value, but it is more informative to present the figures so that the user can see how this net book value has been arrived at. This is a legal requirement for companies. This is easily achieved by presenting three figures for each class of fixed asset, namely:

1   the cost

2   the accumulated depreciation

3   the net book value (simply the cost less accumulated depreciation).

Accumulated depreciation at the end of the year represents the total amount of cost which has been charged in the profit and loss account as an expense for all the years since the assets were acquired. In accounting terminology, the accumulated depreciation is referred to as the closing balance on 'provision for depreciation'. Since the word 'provision' is not something that a non-accountant would readily understand, it is usually called 'accumulated depreciation' in the balance sheet. The ledger account in which it is recorded may refer to either 'accumulated depreciation' or 'provision for depreciation'.

The three figures are normally set out in the form of a table, and you will get some idea of how this works in the following two Activities.

Activity 10

Complete the following for the van in Activity 4, where depreciation was calculated on a straight line basis. The first year has been completed in order to get you started, and you should assume that the van was still owned at the end of year 4.

	Cost	Accumulated depreciation	Net book value
At the end of year 1:			
Motor vehicles	8,000	1,500	6,500
At the end of year 2:			
Motor vehicles			
At the end of year 3:			
Motor vehicles			
At the end of year 4:			
Motor vehicles			

Activity 11

Now do the same thing again but using the depreciation amounts calculated under the reducing balance method for Activity 7:

	Cost	Accumulated depreciation	Net book value
At the end of year 1:			
Motor vehicles	8,000		
At the end of year 2:			
Motor vehicles			
At the end of year 3:			
Motor vehicles			
At the end of year 4:			
Motor vehicles			

You can probably appreciate that in most businesses there will be several classes of fixed asset – for example, motor vehicles, freehold premises, office equipment. Each class is shown on a separate line of the table. For example, if the above trader had also purchased office equipment during year 1 for £6,000 and £1,000 of this cost had been charged to profit and loss account as depreciation for that year, the fixed asset section of the balance sheet would be as follows:

Balance sheet at end of year 1

Fixed assets	Cost	Accumulated depreciation	Net book value
Motor vehicles	8,000	2,400	5,600
Office equipment	6,000	1,000	5,000
	14,000	3,400	10,600

Notice how this explanation refers to 'classes' of fixed asset. This involves classifying similar types of asset together under one heading – it would be too unwieldy to show each individual asset in the balance sheet. In practice, the detailed workings to arrive at year-end net book values are shown in the notes to the financial statements.

The book-keeping

The book-keeping is quite simple. There is typically one ledger account to record the cost for each class of fixed asset, and another to record the accumulated depreciation for each class of fixed asset.

The accounts for the motor van from Activity 4 with depreciation being worked at 30% reducing balance would be as follows.

The balance on the provision for depreciation account must be subtracted from the balance on the fixed asset at cost account to give net book value shown on the balance sheet.

Fixed Asset at cost – Motor Vans		Provision for Depreciation – Motor Vans	
Year 1 Bank £8,000		Year 1 P&L £1,500	
(Payment on acquisition)		Year 2 P&L £1,500	

The corresponding debits for these entries are firstly made in a depreciation expense account and then transferred to the profit and loss account.

The ledger account for cost is debited (and the bank account credited) when the assets are purchased. These costs are built up and the balance carried forward from year to year.

The ledger account for accumulated depreciation is called 'provision for depreciation' and this account is credited each year with the annual depreciation figure. The amounts are accumulated and carried forward from year to year.

These two accounts (fixed asset at cost and provision for depreciation) are set out in the balance sheet in order to derive net book value – as demonstrated in Activities 10 and 11.

The amount credited to the provision for depreciation in any particular year will represent the depreciation expense for that year and so the double entry is completed by debiting the profit and loss account. The expense is described as 'depreciation'.

In strict book-keeping terms, an expense should not be debited directly to the profit and loss account. You will recall that expenses such as wages and rent are initially recorded in separate ledger accounts before being transferred to the profit and loss account at the end of the year. We should deal with depreciation in much the same way, and so we need an account called 'depreciation expense'. This account is debited with the depreciation charges for the various classes of asset and the total is transferred to the profit and loss account.

Activity 12	A trader starts up business on 1 January 1990 and prepares accounts to 31 December each year. During year ended 31 December 1990 the following fixed assets were purchased:

1 January	Office equipment	£4,000
1 April	Delivery van 1	£6,000
1 July	Delivery van 2	£8,000

During year ended 31 December 1991 the only transaction on fixed assets was as follows:

1 January   purchased a computer for office use at a cost of £2,000

Depreciation on the office equipment is to be calculated at the rate of 25% per annum on the reducing balance. Depreciation on the delivery vans is to be calculated on a straight line basis. The trader intends to use the delivery vans for five years and at the end of this time the residual values are estimated to be as follows:

| Delivery van 1 | £1,000 |
| Delivery van 2 | £2,000 |

You are required to write up the relevant ledger accounts (below) for the first two years of trading. Be careful with the depreciation calculations in 1990 (some will have to be time apportioned). Balance off the accounts at the end of each year. Assume all assets were paid for by cheque.

Office equipment – cost	Provision for depreciation – office equipment

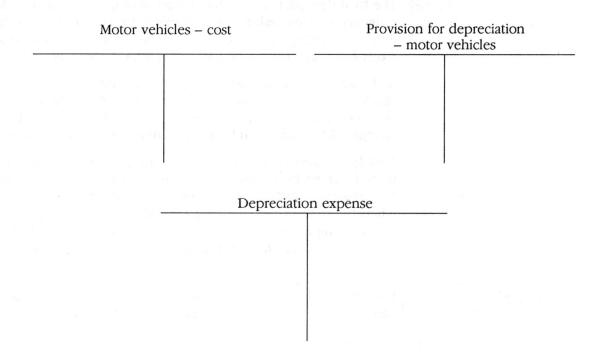

Motor vehicles – cost   Provision for depreciation – motor vehicles

Depreciation expense

3 Disposals of fixed assets

Introduction

When a fixed asset is disposed of, there are two things to deal with:

1   receipt of the cash, and

2   removal of the asset (i.e. its net book value) from the balance sheet. This involves elimination of balances of cost and depreciation provision for the asset.

It is unlikely that the estimates used in calculating the total depreciation of an asset will turn out to be correct. The asset may be sold well before the end of its useful economic life. Even if it were kept for exactly for the same length of time as was originally thought, the amount received on disposal is likely to differ from the residual value estimated at the time of purchase.

Consequently, there will always be a difference between the sale proceeds and the net book value at the time of disposal. This difference is usually described as a profit or loss on disposal, although strictly speaking it relates to depreciation under- or over-provided for in the previous accounts.

It is easy enough to see the end result when figures for the particular asset are known, for example:

if the cost of the asset was	£8,000
and the accumulated depreciation on this asset was	£3,000
then the net book value will be	£5,000
and assuming it is sold for	£6,000
the difference is described as 'profit on sale'	£1,000

The total depreciation of a fixed asset is originally estimated by taking the estimated residual value from the original cost. This total is then allocated to the accounting periods expected to benefit from use of the asset. But we won't know the true total depreciation until the asset is sold.

In the above example, the true total depreciation is £2,000 (i.e. original cost of £8,000 less sale proceeds of £6,000) and yet £3,000 has been treated as an expense in all the accounting periods up to the time of sale. We have charged £1,000 too much for depreciation in those previous periods.

This has arisen simply because the original accounting estimates have turned out to be incorrect. But we cannot go back and revise all the accounts for previous periods and so an adjustment is made in the year when the asset is actually sold (and the true figures are known). In the above example, this would be done by including a credit of £1,000 in the profit and loss account which is described as profit on sale.

Activity 13	It might be a bit confusing to the user of accounts to see this £1,000 credit being described as a profit on sale. Try and describe why.

Some accountants might describe the adjustment of £1,000 as an over-provision of depreciation in previous years – still confusing for the non-accountant, but marginally better than describing it as a profit. However, it is normal to describe these adjustments as profits or losses on sale.

Before we look at the book-keeping, we should consider depreciation in the year of sale. When you were learning depreciation calculations, you saw that annual depreciation is usually time apportioned or 'pro-rated' in the year of purchase in order to relate the expense to the length of time the asset was used in that period. This might suggest that we should do the same thing in the year of sale.

In practice, depreciation is not usually calculated for the year in which the asset is sold. There would be no point; calculating a figure based on estimates which are now known to be wrong does not make any sense. In any event, if a depreciation expense is charged in the profit and loss account for the year of sale, it will only be 'clawed back' through an increased profit on sale, or 'topped up' by an increased loss on sale. You can discover this for yourself by working through the following Activity.

Activity 14	A delivery van which had cost £8,000 is being depreciated at the rate of £1,000 per annum. At the end of the previous period, the accumulated depreciation was £3,000. It was sold half way through the current period for £6,000. Time-apportioned depreciation for the current period (if charged) would therefore be £500.
	Calculate the charges and credits that would appear in the profit and loss account for the current year if:
	1 depreciation is charged in the year of sale
	2 depreciation in the year of sale is ignored.
	When you have done this, compare the two methods and note what effect they will have on the amount of net profit for the year.

In practice, your employer is likely to have an established policy on whether or not depreciation is to be provided in the year of sale. If any assessment is silent on this, you can assume that depreciation should not be calculated for the year of sale. On the other hand, you should always assume that depreciation in the year of purchase is time-apportioned unless you are told otherwise by your employer or by the person setting a work-based assessment.

Book-keeping on the sale of fixed assets

The objective of the book-keeping is to:

1   remove the cost of the asset from the books

2   remove the accumulated depreciation (on that asset) from the books

3   account for the cash received and the profit or loss on sale.

This is quite easily achieved by bringing all the figures together into one ledger account called 'disposal of fixed assets'. The cost of the asset sold is transferred to the debit side of this account, the accumulated depreciation transferred to the credit side, and the cash proceeds are credited. The balance will then be the profit or loss on sale which is transferred to the profit and loss account.

For example, a company buys a motor van for £12,000 at the beginning of a financial year. It has an anticipated scrap value of £3,000 and an estimated life of four years. It is sold for £10,350 three months into the third year of its life. The book-keeping entries would be as follows:

Fixed Asset – Motor van				Provision for Depreciation – Motor van			
Year 1 Bank	£12,000					Year 1 P&L	£2,250
(Payment on acquisition)		Year 3 Disposal	£12,000			Year 2 P&L	£2,250
				Year 3 Disposal	£5,063	Year 3 P&L	£563
	£12,000		£12,000		£5,063		£5,063

Disposal Account – Motor van			
Year 3 Fixed Assets – Motor Vans	£12,000	Year 3 Bank	£10,350
Year 3 Profit and Loss	£3,413	Year 3 Depreciation – Motor van	£5,063
	£15,413		£15,413

The motor van in the above example may have been the only motor vehicle owned, or it may have been one of several which were included in the balance on the motor vehicles account. In either case, the cost and its related accumulated depreciation have now been removed from the books. If it were one of several, the balance remaining on the account for motor vehicles at cost, and on the account for accumulated depreciation, will relate to vehicles still owned.

Fixed asset register – and movements in fixed asset accounts

Since there is only one ledger account for each class of fixed asset (motor vehicles, office equipment, etc.), it would be quite difficult to find the relevant details for any single asset within each group – particularly if there is a large number of assets in that group and several years have passed since the asset was purchased.

To cope with this problem, a subsidiary record is often kept for certain types of fixed asset. This record is called a 'fixed asset register' and it will contain details (date of purchase, cost, identification number, depreciation, etc.) for each individual asset. In a well-organised system, the fixed asset register will show how the balances on the ledger accounts for cost and for accumulated depreciation are made up in terms of individual assets. Otherwise, completed reconciliations are required.

The existence of a fixed asset register helps the auditor when verifying the physical existence of fixed assets and the depreciation charged on them.

Activity 15

A trader makes up accounts to 31 December. The balances in the books for office equipment at 31 December 1989 were as follows:

Cost	£40,000
Accumulated depreciation	£18,000

During year ended 31 December 1990, a computer which had cost £4,000 on 1 July 1987 was sold for £1,000. Depreciation on office equipment is based on the reducing balance method, using a rate of 25% per annum. In the year of purchase, the annual charge is calculated according to the length of time the asset was owned. No depreciation is charged in the year of sale.

There were no other transactions for office equipment during 1990. On a separate piece of paper, calculate the figures for cost and accumulated depreciation that will appear in the balance sheet at 31 December 1990 (work to the nearest £1).

Activity 16

Calipers plc purchases a new computer system on 28th October 1992 for £28,000. The system is felt to have a prospective life of 10 years if used reasonably. However, the business anticipates changing the system in three years' time as changing technology would lead the company to anticipate a need for up-grade at that time.

Expected residual value in 10 years time is £4,500; expected residual value in three years' time is £11,200.

Over which period should the company depreciate the asset?

What is the total charge to be depreciated to the profit and loss account?

Use of the journal

Journal entries are quite typically used to record asset acquisitions, end-of-period adjustments for depreciation and periodic asset disposals.

You may have already studied journal entries in Units 1-3 at AAT Foundation/NVQ Level 2.

Activity 17

Look back to the details given for Activity 15. On the proforma that follows this Activity, show journal entries for:

■ the end-of-period depreciation for those assets remaining in the business as of 31st December 1990

■ acquisition of a new piece of office machinery for £8,000 on 14th February 1991.

Work to the nearest £1.

Journal   **Folio 212**

Date	Account	Debit (£)	Credit (£)

Journal entries provide security to the entries that are passed through the books of account. The person raising the book-keeping entries must check the entries raised, thus providing greater security in the accuracy of the entries raised. Someone will cross-check the entries before they are entered into the books, providing for accuracy of input. Auditors find them useful when tracing transactions.

Summary

The main learning points in this chapter are:

- expenditure on fixed assets is a long-term expense and should be charged against sales revenue over all periods that benefit from using the asset

- this is done by first calculating the estimated total depreciation of each asset – that is, its cost less estimated residual value (called the depreciable amount)

- this total depreciation is then allocated as an expense over the estimated number of years it will be used in the business (useful economic life)

- the two most popular methods of allocation are straight line and reducing balance

- the cost of assets is recorded in a separate account for each class; the accumulated depreciation for each class of asset is recorded in a separate account

- balance sheet figures are presented by deducting accumulated depreciation from accumulated cost for each class of asset – the difference is described as 'net book value'

- when fixed assets are sold, the cost of the asset together with its related accumulated depreciation must be removed from the books

- the cost and accumulated depreciation for the asset disposed of are transferred to an account called 'disposal of fixed assets'

- this account is also credited with the cash received; the resulting balance represents a profit or loss on sale which is transferred to the profit and loss account

- revisions of useful economic lives (of fixed assets) are dealt with by simply spreading remaining net book value (NBV) to profit and loss over the revised remaining life unless this materially affects the view of the business position given to users of the accounts (i.e. the accounts would be materially distorted)

- if the view of accounts users is materially affected, a reworking of depreciation for the present year using amounts and periods as they should have been since beginning to use the assets and then working a special charge or credit for any under- or over-depreciation in earlier years is recommended. Both entries are made in the profit and loss account of the year

- the effect of additional expenditure on existing fixed assets is to increase NBV if performance is enhanced, and the revised NBV is charged to profit and loss over the period to the end of the latest projected useful life

- accounting for depreciation and preparing journal entries for depreciation amounts is in full accord with double-entry principles.

Key to Chapter 2 activities

Activity 1   It is land. This does cause a slight practical problem because the price paid for freehold business premises will relate partly to the land and partly to the buildings on the land. Depreciation must be calculated on the buildings but not on the land unless the land is owned because it contains coal or diamonds that will be extracted, then its value to the business will decrease and it should be depreciated.

Activity 2   According to SSAP 12, yes. Buildings have a finite economic life, and the periodic depreciation measurements will be based on the reduction in useful economic life resulting from the passage of time during the accounting period. However, if its residual value at the end of its useful economic life is greater than its original value, then, by definition, no depreciation has occurred.

Activity 3   There are several acceptable answers. Probably the most pertinent is that the expression is used in order to try and prevent users of accounts from thinking that the figure carried forward in the balance sheet represents the market value of the asset. 'Net' in accounting means that something has been subtracted from a 'gross' figure. Here, net book value merely means original cost less accumulated depreciation.

Activity 4   £1,500, i.e. (£8,000 – £2,000) ÷ 4.

Activity 5   £5,000. The amount transferred to the profit and loss account as depreciation over the two years will be £3,000 (i.e. 2 × £1,500) leaving £5,000 (i.e. £8,000 less £3,000) to be carried forward.

Activity 6   The annual depreciation percentage will be £1,500/£8,000 x 100 =18.75%

Activity 7

Cost at start of year 1	8,000
Depreciation for year 1 (30% × 8,000)	2,400
Net book value at start of year 2	5,600
Depreciation for year 2 (30% × 5,600)	1,680
Net book value at start of year 3	3,920
Depreciation for year 3 (30% × 3,920)	1,176
Net book value at start of year 4	2,744
Depreciation for year 4 (30% × 2,744)	823
Net book value at end of year 4	1,921

Activity 8   The annual depreciation percentage will be:

$$1 - \left[\sqrt[4]{\frac{2000}{8000}} \right] \quad \text{multiplied by 100}$$

which is approximately 29.29%.

Activity 9

Cost at start of year 1	8,000.00
Depreciation for year 1 (30% × 8,000 × 5/12)	1,000.00
Net book value at start of year 2	7,000.00
Depreciation for year 2 (30% × 7,000)	2,100.00
Net book value at start of year 3	4,900.00
Depreciation for year 3 (30% × 4,900 × 5/12)	612.50

Activity 10

	Cost	Accumulated depreciation	Net book value
At the end of year 1:			
Motor vehicles	8,000	1,500	6,500
At the end of year 2:			
Motor vehicles	8,000	3,000	5,000
At the end of year 3:			
Motor vehicles	8,000	4,500	3,500
At the end of year 4:			
Motor vehicles	8,000	6,000	2,000

Activity 11

	Cost	Accumulated depreciation	Net book value
At the end of year 1:			
Motor vehicles	8,000	2,400	5,600
At the end of year 2:			
Motor vehicles	8,000	4,080	3,920
At the end of year 3:			
Motor vehicles	8,000	5,256	2,744
At the end of year 4:			
Motor vehicles	8,000	6,079	1,921

Activity 12

Office equipment – cost						
1 Jan 90	Bank	4,000	31 Dec 90	Balance c/d	4,000
		4,000			4,000
1 Jan 91	Balance b/d	4,000	31 Dec 90	Balance c/d	6,000
1 Jan 91	Bank	2,000			
		6,000			6,000
1 Jan 92	Balance b/d	6,000			

Provision for depreciation – office equipment

31 Dec 90	Balance c/d	1,000	31 Dec 90	Dep'n expense	1,000
		1,000			1,000
31 Dec 91	Balance c/d	2,250	1 Jan 91	Balance b/d	1,000
			31 Dec 91	Dep'n expense	1,250
		2,250			2,250
			1 Jan 92	Balance b/d	2,250

Motor vehicles – cost

1 Apr 90	Bank	6,000	31 Dec 90	Balance c/d	14,000
1 Jul 90	Bank	8,000			
		14,000			14,000
1 Jan 91	Balance b/d	14,000	31 Dec 91	Balance c/d	14,000
		14,000			14,000
1 Jan 92	Balance b/d	14,000			

Provision for depreciation – motor vehicles

31 Dec 90	Balance c/d	1,350	31 Dec 90	Dep'n expense	1,350
		1,350			1,350
31 Dec 91	Balance c/d	3,550	1 Jan 91	Balance b/d	1,350
			31 Dec 91	Dep'n expense	2,200
		3,550			3,550
			1 Jan 92	Balance b/d	3,550

Depreciation expense

31 Dec 90	Prov Dep'n MV	1,350	31 Dec 90	Profit & loss	2,350
31 Dec 90	Prov Dep'n OE	1,000			
		2,350			2,350
31 Dec 91	Prov Dep'n MV	2,200	31 Dec 91	Profit & loss	3,450
31 Dec 91	Prov Dep'n OE	1,250			
		3,450			3,450

Calculations:

Year ending 31 December 1990		£
Office equipment: 25% of 4,000	=	<u>1,000</u>

Motor vehicles:

Van 1 [(6,000 – 1,000) ÷ 5] × 9/12	=	750
Van 2 [(8,000 – 2,000) ÷ 5] × 6/12	=	<u>600</u>
Total		<u>1,350</u>

Year ending 31 December 1991

Office equipment 25% × (NBV at start £3,000 + £2,000) = £1,250

Motor vehicles £1,000 + £1,200 = £2,200

Activity 13

It might be a bit difficult for a non-accountant to understand. After all, selling an asset for £6,000 which had originally cost £8,000, suggests a loss on sale of £2,000!

Activity 14

1	depreciation expense – charge	500
	profit on sale (£6,000 – £4,500) – credit	<u>1,500</u>
	net credit in profit and loss account	<u>1,000</u>

2	depreciation expense	nil
	profit on sale (£6,000 – £5,000)	£1,000

The effect on net profit under either method is identical; they both result in a net credit to profit of £1,000.

Activity 15

Cost = £36,000 (i.e. £40,000 less £4,000)

Accumulated depreciation £20,977 found as follows:

Accumulated depreciation at 1 January 1990	18,000	
Less: accumulated depreciation on asset sold	<u>2,031</u>	(see *Working 1*)
	15,969	
Add: depreciation for the current year	<u>5,008</u>	(see *Working 2*)
Accumulated depreciation at 31 December 1990	<u>20,977</u>	

Working 1. Depreciation charged in previous accounting periods:

		Total
1 July 1987 Cost	4,000	
Depreciation 1987	<u>500</u>	500
	3,500	
Depreciation 1988	<u>875</u>	875
	2,625	
Depreciation 1989	656	<u>656</u>
		<u>2,031</u>

Working 2. Depreciation for current year:

Cost of assets still owned	36,000
Accumulated depreciation on assets still owned	
(18,000 – 2,031)	<u>15,969</u>
Net book value at beginning of year on assets	
still owned at the end of the year	<u>20,031</u>

Depreciation for the year: 25% of £20,031 = £5,008

Activity 16

Calipers plc should depreciate the asset over three years. This accords with SSAP 12 and the fundamental concept of accruals or matching. The total depreciation charge for the three-year period is £16,800.

Activity 17

Journal entries are as follows:

Journal			**Folio 212**
Date	Account	Debit (£)	Credit (£)
31/7	Accumulated depreciation	2,031.00	
	Disposals – Computer		2,031.00
	Disposals – Computer	4,000.00	
	Fixed assets – Computer		4,000.00
	Bank	1,000.00	
	Disposals – Computer		1,000.00
	Profit and Loss	969.00	
	Disposals – Computer		969.00
	(Being entries raised on		
	disposal of computer		
	showing loss on sale)		
31/12	Depreciation expense	5,008.00	
	Accumulated depreciation		5,008.00
	(Being depreciation for 1990)		
14/2/91	Fixed assets – office machinery	8,000.00	
	Bank		8,000.00
	(Being entries raised on the		
	purchase of office machinery)		

Introduction to Part 2: Financial Accounts

This is the second of two modules on financial accounting. In this part of Accounting in Context, we will be looking at the proper recording and matching of organisational incomes and expenditure within an accounting period – assessing net period earnings or profit and loss. We will also consider valuing organisational assets and liabilities at the end of an accounting period. This provides an assessment of organisational worth in the form of the end-of-period balance sheet.

We will consider the main financial regulations that govern the assessment of profit or loss and balance sheet figures; how we can compile the financial figures in situations in which the financial records of an organisation are incomplete; reconciliations and other adjustments necessary to prepare a full set of financial accounts.

You will also learn how to prepare a full extended trial balance. The extended trial balance shows the nominal ledger balances at the end of a financial period, after all financial transactions have been properly entered into the books of account. The extended trial balance literally extends the set of balances contained in the nominal ledger, making final amendment for any errors that have been discovered and 'end-of-period adjustments' to produce the final figures for the financial statements.

The end-of-period adjustments include depreciation of fixed assets (as covered in Part 1), adjustments for bad and doubtful debts, accruals and prepayments, and business stocks.

This material builds on the fundamental financial understanding and methods that you may have explored at NVQ Level 2/AAT Foundation. The text presumes a good knowledge of the content of Part 1, particularly of double entry principles and the four fundamental accounting concepts.

We introduce technical expressions before asking you to use them in the activities. The terms are used to convey important concepts and you must ensure that you are comfortable with those concepts. The activities have been designed to help you understand and use the terms.

Chapter 1

The fundamental principles of accounting

Introduction

In this chapter, we will look at some of the terminology used in accountancy. We will briefly return to some of the double entry principles considered in Part 1, and look at balance sheets and profit and loss accounts again. Finally, we will consider some of the Statements of Standard Accounting Practice (SSAPs) and Financial Reporting Standards (FRSs) which may be relevant to later chapters.

Objectives

After you have completed this chapter, you should be able to:

■ use the accountant's basic working terminology for entries made to income and expenditure accounts and statements

■ distinguish trading from other incomes

■ differentiate cost of sales expenses from other, general, expenses

■ evaluate gross and net profit figures from given information

■ describe the principles of double-entry book-keeping

■ present balance sheets

■ prepare simple financial statements from specified data

■ recognise the different legal forms of organisation and the impact of profits on owner's investment and capital

■ describe and explain the basic accounting concepts and principles, including the principles in SSAPs 2, 5, 9, and 13.

1 Working terminology

The accountant's working language is a little mysterious at times: some of the words do not mean quite the same thing as in their ordinary English usage, some are specific to accounting, and some seem to have more than one meaning even within the realms of accounting.

Many words used in accounting have restricted meanings. We shall now consider the terms used in relation to income and expenditure statements. For the context of what follows, income may be regarded simply as the amounts that an organisation has earned over a particular financial period. Expenditure may be regarded as the amounts of cost that would be set against income over the same period in the income and expenditure statements to obtain a true and fair assessment of the organisational performance. 'Income and expenditure' statements may, for all practical purposes, be regarded as statements of 'profit and loss'.

Words with restricted meanings

In particular, you will need to understand how the words 'sales', 'purchases', 'matching' and 'expenses' are used.

Sales

Sales figures are the first to appear in profit and loss (or 'income and expenditure') accounts. Sometimes the word 'turnover' is used instead.

The word 'sales' sounds as if it refers to the total sum of money earned over a period of time for everything that was sold during that period. But in accounting, the word 'sales' refers to the sale of trading products – i.e. to the sale of the business goods or services. Sales are recorded when invoices are sent out to customers – not necessarily when cash is received.

Activity 1	Can you think of any incomes that may accrue to an organisation over a financial period other than revenues from the sale of trading products? Remember that you should be considering any amounts that are earned and that therefore add to the financial position of the organisation.

Items such as those suggested in the Key should be reflected in any period statements of income and expenditure. They represent earnings and are therefore truly and fairly part of any profit and loss assessment.

Activity 2	There is one situation where the sale of a delivery van would be classified under the heading of 'sales' in the financial statements of a business. Can you think what it is?

Purchases

This has a restricted meaning in much the same way as 'sales'. It does not refer to everything purchased, but only to the purchase of trading stock which the business intends to sell in the daily course of trade. If, however, the organisation manufactures and sells products, purchases will refer to the raw materials bought for use in the production process.

The term 'purchases' only refers to acquired raw materials to be used in manufacture or goods for resale and will not, therefore, refer to the purchase of fixed assets or any other resource items.

Income and expenditure statements typically refer to the 'cost of goods sold' (usually written as 'cost of sales'). If the business simply buys and sells products, the cost of goods sold will simply equal:

OPENING STOCKS   plus PURCHASES less CLOSING STOCKS

(of the items purchased and sold, all at cost to the organisation)

If the business produces and sells, the cost of goods sold will equal:

OPENING STOCKS plus PRODUCTION COSTS less CLOSING STOCKS

where each of these items is represented by the production cost of the finished items that have been sold by, or remain in, the organisation.

| Activity 3 | Your organisation buys and sells products. It is not involved in production. At the beginning of a particular financial period the organisation had 2000 items of a particular product in stock that cost £2,300; it bought a further 1000 in the period for £1,150. All items were purchased for the same price. At the end of the period, it has sold 2100 items for £2,940. The remaining items are in stock in good condition.

What figure should be regarded as the cost of sales for income and expenditure purposes?

What trading profit or loss do you consider the business has made on this product for the period? |

The accountant's calculation of the cost of sales figure therefore contains an 'adjustment for unsold stock' – i.e. the closing stock figures need to be subtracted from the total of opening stock plus purchases to provide the cost of sales figure.

This is a good example of a working convention called 'matching' – a natural but fundamental principle in accounting. We have already looked at matching in Part 1, but we will quickly review it here.

Matching

When calculating business profits for a period, the trading revenues earned in that period (e.g. from sales) must be matched against the costs of earning that revenue. In the case of purchases, if some of the goods purchased have not been sold by the end of the period, the matching convention involves making an adjustment to exclude the cost of unsold stock when calculating the profit.

Activity 4	Consider the detail of Activity 3. What would be your assessment of profit or loss on trading if the business fails to adopt the principle of matching and simply records sales value and the full cost of all items purchased in its profit and loss calculations?
	Would you consider such an assessment to represent fairly the trading of the business over the period?
	Where might you consider the closing stock balance should be recorded given the definition earlier provided in this chapter?

The matching principle is more correctly called the accruals principle.

Activity 5	Imagine that you have purchased ten watches that you intend to sell for a profit. They cost you £2 each and so you have spent £20 on purchases. During the next month you sold six of them for £5 each giving you total sales of £30.
	Use the matching or accruals principle to set out a calculation of your profit for the month.

You may ask, why has a profit of £18 been reported when your cash position has only improved by £10 (£30 received less £20 spent)? But you do still have four watches that cost £2 each (£8 in total) and these are just as much an asset as cash. You hope to be able to sell them next month.

Expenses

We looked at expenses in Part 1. Expenses are costs or expenditure incurred by the organisation that may justifiably be transferred to the profit and loss account for a particular period.

Expenses are distinguished by accountants from 'assets' – which are items of 'future economic value' – items that will produce benefit in later periods. Assets by definition are recorded in the balance sheet.

Expenses are usually the day-to-day running costs of a business, such as wages, stationery, etc.

Activity 6

By now you should have noticed that calculation of profit is not simply a matter of adding up all the money received in a period and deducting all the money paid out in the same period.

Go back to the first month of your imaginary trading in watches (Activity 5) and assume that the total transactions undertaken in that month were:

Borrowed £10 from a friend to help with the purchase of the watches.
Purchased ten watches at £2 each, £20 in total.
Sold six watches at £5 each, £30 in total.
Paid out £2 in postage for sending watches to customers.
Bought yourself a new pair of shoes for £6.
Paid back £5 to your friend from whom you had borrowed the money.

Set out a calculation of your profit for trading in watches.

Note that:

■ the purchase of a pair of shoes is said to be 'private expenditure' (it has nothing to do with running the business entity)

■ the receipt of borrowed money is not 'sales'. It is an increase in a liability: repaying part of it is reducing a liability.

Gross profit and net profit

Gross profit is simply sales (or turnover) less the cost of sales. It reflects the trading of the organisation. Net profit is the profit remaining after all other adjustments have been made to gross profit, such as the addition of any discounts received, any non-trading incomes and the deduction of general expenses. Non-trading incomes include things like rental incomes from subletting office space and interest and dividends received.

Activity 7

Describe 'gross profit' and state how much it would be for your business in Activity 6.

Describe 'net profit' and state how much it would be for your business in Activity 6.

Depreciation

You should remember depreciation from Part 1. The cost of a fixed asset is just as much a cost of earning profits as is the cost of wages. The main difference is that the benefits derived from buying a fixed asset are used up (consumed) over the years of economic life of the asset within the business. Each year, therefore, a proportion of the original cost is treated as an expense.

Drawings

This refers to the amount withdrawn from the business by the proprietor. It is a bit like the proprietor's wages, except that it is not treated as an expense – it is a withdrawal of part of the proprietor's investment in the business. Note that drawings are only possible where the organisation is a sole trader or a partnership.

Legal forms of business organisation

Sole trader

Businesses can be conducted in various legal forms. The form selected will influence the way that final financial statements are presented. If an individual decides to start trading without the formality of registering the business with the authorities or going into any real legal formality at all, the business is termed a sole trader. The sole trader has to pay tax on the profits earned by the business (they are treated as 'extra personal income' for tax purposes), not on the money withdrawn.

Partnership

Alternatively individuals might 'group together' in some form of common business to make profits, also without any registration with the authorities or real legal formality. The business would then be one of partnership – each individual being taxed on their own proportion of the business profits as an addition to personal income. We are not directly concerned with partnership at NVQ Level 3.

Company

The most common form is a limited company. Limited companies are formed by registration with the authorities at Companies House. Companies are organisations that are legally recognised as entirely separate bodies from their owners. For example, the owners will not have any personal tax liability for the company's profits.

Companies are assessed directly for tax on their profits. Any profits paid out to the business owners are paid as 'dividends' from the after-tax profits. At Companies House, the Companies Registrar keeps copies of company financial statements in a file for each company.

Activity 8	Two similar businesses, A and B, both make profits of £10,000 in a single financial period. Both have been operating as sole traders. The proprietor of A withdraws £2,000 for personal use over the period. The owner of B does not make a withdrawal. Is there any difference in the business profits of these two business organisations? Explain your reasoning.

Profit paid out by a business (in the case of a sole trader, in the form of drawings) is termed an appropriation of profit. Such amounts are not part of the calculation of profit, but are taken to be a form of distribution (or 'sharing-out') of the final profit amounts. Taxation would also be deemed to be an appropriation of profit, as would the setting aside of profits (perhaps in some special accounts to re-invest in the business).

2 Double-entry principles

You may have met the principles and general application of double-entry book-keeping at NVQ Level 2/AAT Foundation.

Double entry recognises that all commercial transactions result in two effects on the organisation. This two-sided effect is reflected in double entry principles and the entries in the books of account.

Sales figures, for example, may result from contracts with clients effected on credit. In such circumstances, the two-sided effect on the business is:

■ creation of an extra asset – reflected by a debit balance in the debtors, or sales ledger control, account

■ creation of a credit in the sales account which, in effect, represents a gross extra amount of income for the business owners.

Activity 9

What is the double entry when an organisation:

■ agrees with a trading partner that is both a supplier and customer that £100 owed to the organisation shall be offset against £300 it owes to the supplier, leaving a net balance of £200 in the supplier's account?

■ repays £14,200 to a creditor – being £14,000 of loan repayment and £200 interest?

■ purchases £400 of stocks on credit?

■ receives fresh owner's capital of £25,000?

Balance sheet entries

Balance sheet presentation should follow the style and content developed in your earlier book-keeping study. A typical balance sheet shows owner's investment and any long-term loans as 'capital' figures.

Double-entry principles ensure that the figures for capital equal the 'net assets' – i.e. the investment of the capital of the business in fixed assets and current assets (those expected to remain in the business for less than one year from the balance sheet date) less current liabilities (those obligations expected to remain with the business for less than one year from the balance sheet date).

Activity 10	Look at the items below and indicate what you think each one is. Choose from a current asset (CA), current liability (CL), fixed asset (FA), loan capital (LC), or owner's capital (OC) :

Stocks outstanding at the year end   **CA   CL   FA   LC   OC**

Retained profits   **CA   CL   FA   LC   OC**

A new five-year loan   **CA   CL   FA   LC   OC**

Sales ledger balances   **CA   CL   FA   LC   OC**

Creditor ledger balances   **CA   CL   FA   LC   OC**

Advance payment of rent   **CA   CL   FA   LC   OC**

Amounts owed to BT on the
latest phone bills   **CA   CL   FA   LC   OC**

Slow-moving stocks not expected
to be sold over the next 18 months   **CA   CL   FA   LC   OC**

Taxes payable on the latest
annual profits   **CA   CL   FA   LC   OC**

Dividends payable on the
latest annual profits   **CA   CL   FA   LC   OC**

£100,000-worth of new assets
provided to the business by the
owners (without extracting direct
payment by the business)   **CA   CL   FA   LC   OC**

We are quickly going to look at balance sheets again, and then we will move on to profit and loss accounts. You should be able to remember how to write up balance sheets from Part 1, but if you can't, you might like to read through the section in Part 1 which is also called Double-entry principles before attempting the next Activity.

Activity 11	From the following information, prepare the balance sheet of Mrs Thakrar, a trader in television sets, at the 1st January 1990:

a) The business owns a delivery van that cost £4,000 and some office equipment that had cost £1,000.
b) There was £2,000 in the bank.
c) Customers owed the business £100 for televisions purchased.
d) The stock of televisions on hand had cost £600.
e) Mrs Thakrar owed her suppliers of television sets £500.
f) There was £800 outstanding on some money which Mrs Thakrar had borrowed from a friend (on a long-term basis) to help finance the business.
g) Mrs Thakrar had introduced £5,000 when setting up the business, but had not introduced any further cash since it had started trading.

BALANCE SHEET

after completing the transactions in Activity 11

Assets	Liabilities
Fixed assets:	**Current liabilities:**
	Long-term liabilities:
Current assets:	
	Capital:

In the key to this activity, we have shown the balance of retained profits as a single figure in the balance sheet. In practice, a single figure for retained profits is not very informative. The proprietor will want to know how the profit for the period has been calculated. We set out the details in a separate statement called the profit and loss account. In the case of a sole trader, the profit and loss account does not include the figure for 'drawings'. The bottom figure in the profit and loss account is the 'net profit' of the business.

Profit and loss accounts

You will get an idea of what information these statements contain by considering the following simplified account.

PROFIT AND LOSS ACCOUNT
year ended 31.12.90

Sales		100,000
Cost of goods sold		40,000
Gross profit		60,000
Expenses:		
Salaries and wages	22,000	
Rent and rates	4,000	
Motor expenses	10,000	
Depreciation	4,000	
		40,000
Net profit		20,000

The profit and loss account attempts to measure the income (net profit) of the business for the year. The balance sheet sets out the financial position at the year end (and at the end of the previous year for comparison purposes) in terms of assets and liabilities.

As regards the proprietor's drawings, there are several ways of presenting this in the financial statements. One is to show it as a separate deduction from profit in the balance sheet. It becomes a little cumbersome to do this after the first year because the figure for retained profit will have to be shown as a balance derived from three components, namely:

1   profits retained at the end of last year
    plus
2   net profit for the current year
    less
3   drawings during the current year.

A more modern approach is to include an additional statement at the foot of the profit and loss account. This statement is usually called an 'appropriation account' because it shows how the profits of the business have been appropriated in terms of drawings and retention.

In the case of Mrs Thakrar in Activity 11, the appropriation account would be as follows:

Retained profits brought forward from previous period	nil
Add: Net profit for the period	1,400
Less: Drawings	nil
Retained profits at the end of the period	1,400

In the case of a company, the amount of cash introduced by shareholders when the shares are first issued must be shown separately from the retained profits in order to comply with the Companies Act.

There is no fundamental difference between the amount invested by shareholders on a share issue and the amount of cash introduced to a business by a single proprietor.

Notice how this explanation refers to 'the amount' of cash invested (or introduced), not to the cash itself. As you know, the actual cash is put into a bank account and after it has been spent loses its separate identity. The next time you look at a balance sheet and see the words 'cash introduced' you will know that it refers to the source of the cash, not the cash itself. There may also be occasions when the proprietors bring assets other than cash into the business as part of their capital.

Now let's consider Mrs Thakrar's financial statements for the first week of January.

Activity 12

During the first week of January 1990, Mrs Thakrar (in Activity 11 above) carried out the following transactions:

a)   Sold one of the television sets on hand for £300. This television had cost £200 to buy. The customer paid cash and the money was banked.
b)   Paid out (by cheque) £10 for some repairs on the delivery van.
c)   Purchased a television set for £100, but did not pay any money because the supplier had agreed that it could be paid for at the end of the month.
d)   Repaid part of the long-term loan by cheque, £100.
e)   Paid herself £50 by cheque.

Draw up a profit and loss account for the week ending 7th January, an appropriation account for that period, and Mrs Thakrar's new balance sheet at the end of the week.

PROFIT AND LOSS ACCOUNT

for week ending 7 January 1990

Sales

Less: cost of sales

Gross profit

Expenses:

   Motor repairs

Net profit

APPROPRIATION ACCOUNT

Retained profits brought forward

Add: net profit for the period

Less: drawings

Retained profits carried forward

BALANCE SHEET
after completing the transactions in Activity 12

Assets	Liabilities
Fixed assets:	**Current liabilities:**
	Long-term liabilities:
Current assets:	
	Capital:

3 Accounting regulation

Financial accounting regulation largely exists to govern the form and content of the financial statements produced in respect of corporations and, most particularly, registered companies.

Sole traders and partnerships are set up without formal registration with the authorities. Such business structures leave the owners with full unlimited liability for the business affairs. This means that if the businesses represented by sole trading or partnership fail to honour their debts and fail to pay creditors, the owners are liable to the creditors to the full extent of their personal assets.

As a consequence, there is no formal regulation of the form and content of their accounts by the authorities, except that the tax authorities (i.e. the Inland Revenue and Customs and Excise) will expect accounts to be produced in line with generally accepted accounting practice in order to record and control tax on business profits and VAT payments.

Company owners (i.e. shareholders) have limited liability in most cases. If creditors are not paid by a company, they typically have the right to repayment only from the capital (and perhaps guarantees) committed to the company by the owners when agreeing to participate in ownership.

Companies are therefore subject to substantial regulation to protect all involved with them – most particularly, present and prospective creditors. The EEC has laid down legislation that is now embodied in the Companies Act 1985, as amended by the Companies Act 1989, that lays down the form and content of company accounts.

All companies must have their accounts audited. The auditors are required under the Companies Acts to consider specifically whether the accounts have been prepared in accordance with all legislation and, in particular, with all relevant SSAPs (Statements of Standard Accounting Practice) and FRSs (Financial Reporting Standards). SSAPs and FRSs are standards for accounting that have been established by the Accounting Standards Board (ASB), and its predecessor the Accounting Standards Committee (ASC), to reflect best generally accepted accounting practice (GAAP).

The report of the auditors must be filed with Companies House and be presented as part of the accounting statements. Departure from the rules is allowable if, but only if, to do so presents a truer and fairer view of the company position – something which very rarely occurs.

In effect the SSAPs and FRSs therefore carry the full force of law and must be adhered to by companies when preparing their accounts. A number of the SSAPs are included within the standards of professional competence for your studies at NVQ Level 3/AAT Intermediate.

SSAP 5 – Accounting for VAT

SSAP 5 is a standard which is very simply applied and which causes no controversy within the accounting profession.

VAT on turnover

The VAT charged on customer invoices and subsequently received in respect of revenues or turnover does not belong to the organisation.

Only the figure earned by the organisation should be reflected in the income and expenditure (profit and loss) account. Profit and loss should therefore show the turnover net of VAT and a liability account should be created to show the amount to be paid to Customs and Excise. We will look more closely at accounting for VAT in Part 5, Preparing VAT Returns.

Activity 13	Your organisation sells a product invoiced at £2,761.25 in one day's trading. The invoice figure includes VAT @ 17.5%.
	Which figure should be credited to the sales or turnover account and how much should be credited to the Customs and Excise creditor account?

If a business is VAT-registered and provides only taxable supplies (i.e. outputs or sales that bear VAT either at standard rate or at zero rate) it will generally be able to recover the VAT on its inputs (i.e. its purchases). In such circumstances the organisation will simply record a net liability or debtor balance on the Customs and Excise account.

Activity 14	A business is registered for VAT and in one month makes zero-rated supplies of £14,250 invoice value, standard rated (17.5% VAT) supplies invoiced at £38,187.50 and purchases inputs of £23,500 inclusive of standard-rate VAT.
	What sales and purchases figures should the business show in its profit and loss account?
	What is the VAT creditor figure on the transactions mentioned?

If an organisation is unable to recover VAT on inputs (either in part or in whole), the input figures must include VAT as part of the cost of the purchases to the business.

Situations in which an organisation may be unable to reclaim VAT either in part or in whole exist where:

■ the organisation is not registered for VAT

■ the organisation provides exempt supplies. Exempt supplies or sales do not have VAT added to them but the organisation cannot recover its related input VAT. If only some of the sales are exempt, it can reclaim a proportion of its input VAT

■ legislation specifies that VAT on certain purchases is not deductible. This situation presently applies, for example, to motor cars purchased for use in the business and business entertainment expenses.

Activity 15	A business is registered for VAT and in one month makes exempt supplies of £14,250 invoice value, standard rated (17.5% VAT) supplies invoiced at £38,187.50 and has purchases inputs with full standard rate VAT of £23,500.
	What sales and purchases figures should the business show in its profit and loss account? The VAT on inputs can be recovered in the proportion that taxable supplies (excluding VAT) form to total supplies.
	What is the VAT creditor figure on the transactions mentioned?

A similar calculation for fixed asset costs to an organisation would apply if the organisation were making exempt supplies.

SSAP 13 - Research and development costs

There is a question of application of two of the fundamental accounting principles, accruals and prudence, if an organisation invests in the future by way of research and development costs.

Accruals would suggest that the costs may be capitalised if there is future benefit to the organisation of the investment in R&D and if there is expectation of future revenues being earned as a result of incurring the R&D cost.

However, prudence would suggest that R&D investment may be 'risky'; at least, future revenues are not guaranteed and therefore it may be prudent to write such expenditure off to profit and loss when it is incurred.

SSAP 13 takes a practical line. It defines:

■ pure research as that which is truly 'scientific' without any specific product aim or application

■ applied research as work with a particular scientific aim, but probably a general form of product in mind for later production

■ development as use of existing technical or scientific knowledge to produce substantially improved materials, devices, products, processes, systems, etc., prior to commencement of commercial production.

SSAP 13 then provides that:

■ any fixed assets created to provide R&D facilities should be treated like any other; they should be capitalised in the balance sheet and depreciated and charged to profit and loss in accord with the provisions of SSAP 12

■ expenditure on pure and applied research (other than on fixed assets) should be written off to profit and loss in the year of expenditure.

Development costs are usually incurred with the reasonable opportunity of commercial success and future earning potential. SSAP 13 suggests that generally prudence should prevail and amounts expended on development should also be written off to profit and loss in the year of expenditure.

However, SSAP 13 will permit capitalisation of development expenditure to the extent to which its recovery can be reasonably assured; SSAP 13 specifies that the circumstances are where:

■ the costs are for a clearly defined project

■ the project is technically feasible and commercially viable considering likely market conditions

■ the aggregate costs deferred or capitalised in the balance sheet can be reasonably expected to be recovered from commercial revenues that will be subsequently earned

■ the organisation has sufficient resources to complete the project.

If development costs are capitalised, they should be charged to the profit and loss account with commencement of the subsequent production process and should be allocated to each accounting period over which the product or process is sold or used.

Activity 16

A cosmetics business spends £14,000 on chemical science in 1992, making tests on the ingredients that may help to create a soap product.

It also spends £18,000 on new production machinery and £12,000 on refining a new product and designing packaging for its launch, which is anticipated in 1994, with regular production and sales of products thereafter anticipated until the end of 1998.

How should it treat the amounts of expenditure in its books?

SSAP 13 further provides that the accounting policy of an organisation investing in R&D should be explained. The total amount of R&D expense charged to the profit and loss account in any period should be disclosed and analysed between present year expenditure and that incurred previously and deferred in the balance sheet.

Movements on any capitalised amounts in the balance sheet should also be disclosed; any figures deferred (and therefore recorded in the balance sheet) being disclosed under intangible assets.

Goodwill

Another example of an intangible asset is goodwill. Goodwill may refer to many aspects of an organisation: a favourable location, a good reputation, the ability and skills of its employees and management, and its long-standing relationships with customers, creditors and suppliers. An organisation may set a price on goodwill, and the price for which an organisation is sold may include an amount for goodwill.

Summary

In this chapter you have been working with many of the underlying principles on which financial statements are based. The main learning points in this chapter are:

- the accountant's basic working terminology can prove ambiguous in use and it is wise, and professional, to question those providing you with information

- expense and asset expenditure is relatively easily distinguished – it is a question of whether resources acquired by expenditure have been fully consumed or used up by the end of a financial period

- trading incomes are reflected in gross profit and represent trading in the organisation's products (goods or services)

- cost of sales figures are simply the buy-in costs of items sold if the organisation is simply a selling agency, or production costs of the items sold if the organisation produces and sells

- net profit figures represent period performance and are calculated as gross profit less general expenses

- balance sheets record owner investment or capital and the way that it is represented in the form of net assets minus organisational liabilities

- all transactions involve commercial exchanges that are of equal value in accounting terms

- different forms of organisation all maintain the same basic forms of accounting system and prepare the same basic financial statements

- accounting statements are generally required to follow the regulation of SSAPs and FRSs and fundamental and other concepts that are designed to produce a 'true and fair view'.

Key to Chapter 1 activities

Activity 1

You may have thought of: money received from the disposal of fixed assets; any income of the business such as rents received from sub-letting part of the premises; other non-trading benefits such as interest received, dividends from investments in other businesses. Discounts received would also be regarded as an income, being a benefit to the business because it pays its debts earlier (similar to investment income).

Activity 2

Maybe this sounds a bit like a trick question. In a way it was but the reason for posing it was not to try and catch you out – it was to emphasise a learning point.

The answer is: when a delivery van forms part of the trading stock of a business, e.g. a motor dealer. Notice how the trading stock of one business can become the fixed asset of another.

Activity 3

The items purchased by the business cost £1.15 each. Cost of sales could be evaluated as:

Opening Stock:	£2,300
Purchases:	£1,150
Less: Closing Stock:	£1,035 (900 items remaining)

This gives a cost of sales of £2,300 + £1,150 - £1,035 = £2,415, and therefore a profit from trading of £2,940 - £2,415 = £525.

Activity 4

Had matching not occurred, the analysis may have been of 'profit' of £2,940 less cash paid – i.e. £2,940 - £3,450. This is a 'loss' of £510 – something which is clearly unrealistic. After all, each unit sold has produced a revenue of £1.40 on average (£2,940/2,100) and cost £1.15 (£3,450/3,000) – a clear profit has been made.

The closing stock of £1,035 is an asset – i.e. it is something that may be used for future benefit by the business. It should therefore be recorded in the balance sheet under the heading current assets.

Activity 5

Your figures should look like this:

Sales	£30
less: Cost of sales	£12
Profit for the month	£18

Activity 6

Your answer could be as follows:

Sales	£30
less: Cost of sales	12
	18
Expenses:	
Postage	2
Profit	16

Activity 7

The gross profit would be the £18 made from trading. General expenses of £2 (postage) would need to be deducted to give a net profit of £16 for the period. Note that if the payment to the friend included any interest on the loan made, that interest would need to be deducted from the £16 also to further reduce net profit.

Activity 8

Profit and loss measures the performance of a business enterprise. The fact is that organisations A and B have performed equally in their trading and the fact that the owners have different withdrawal requirements makes no difference whatsoever to the profit and loss calculation for each. Both have made £10,000 profit.

Activity 9

The double-entry is as follows:

- Debit the supplier account (and purchases ledger control) with £100; credit the customer account (and sales ledger control) with £100.

	Supplier				Customer		
Contra	100	B/d	300	B/d	100	Contra	100
C/d	200				100		100
	300		300				

- Debit the creditor/lenders' account with £14,000; credit £14,200 to the bank/cash account, and debit £200 to an interest expense account.

- Debit purchases with £400; credit £400 to a supplier account.

- Debit £25,000 to the bank/cash account, and credit £25,000 to the owner's capital account.

Activity 10   Here are our answers:

Stocks outstanding at the year-end (provided they are expected to be used in the next year – if not they would be recorded as fixed assets)	**CA**
Retained profits	**OC**
A new five-year loan	**LC**
Sales ledger balances (provided the debtors are expected to pay over the next financial year – if not they would be recorded as fixed assets)	**CA**
Creditor ledger balances (provided the creditors are expected to be paid over the next financial year – if not they would be recorded as long-term liabilities)	**CL**
Advance payment of rent (assuming the benefit of the advance payment will be used over the next year)	**CA**
Amounts owed to BT on the latest phone bills	**CL**
Slow-moving stocks not expected to be sold in the next 18 months (they should be written down to net realisable value)	**CA**
Taxes payable on the latest annual profits (assuming they will be paid over the next year)	**CL**
Dividends payable on the latest annual profits	**CL**
£100,000-worth of new assets provided to the business by the owners (without extracting direct payment by the business) (Capital would be credited to show fresh owner investment and fixed assets would be debited for a similar amount.)	**FA and OC**

Activity 11

BALANCE SHEET

at 1 January 1990

Assets			Liabilities		
Fixed assets:			**Current liabilities:**		
Delivery van	4,000		Trade creditors		500
Office equipment	1,000				
		5,000	**Long-term liabilities:**		
			Loan		800
Current assets:					
Stock	600		**Capital:**		
Debtors	100		Cash introduced	5,000	
Bank	2,000		Retained profits	1,400	
		2,700			6,400
		7,700			7,700

Note: the amount for retained profits has to be found as a balancing figure.

Activity 12

PROFIT AND LOSS ACCOUNT

for week ending 7 January 1990

Sales	300
Less: cost of sales	200
Gross profit	100
Expenses:	
Motor repairs	10
Net profit	90

APPROPRIATION ACCOUNT

Retained profits brought forward	1,400
Add: net profit for the period	90
	1,490
Less: drawings	50
Retained profits carried forward	1,440

BALANCE SHEET

at 7 January 1990

Assets			Liabilities		
Fixed assets:			**Current liabilities:**		
Delivery van		4,000	Trade creditors		600
Office equipment		1,000			
		5,000	**Long-term liabilities:**		
			Loan		700
Current assets:					
Stock	500		**Capital:**		
Debtors	100		Cash introduced	5,000	
Bank	2,140		Retained profits	1,440	
		2,740			6,440
		7,740			7,740

Workings: Bank balance: £2,000 + £300 – £10 – £100 – £50 = £2,140; Stock: £600 – £200 + £100.

Activity 13

The figure of £2,761.25 will be inclusive of VAT and therefore represents 117.5% of the sales revenue earnings of the business. The turnover figure to be credited to sales is 100/117.5 x £2,761.25, or £2,350.00. The VAT liability to Customs and Excise is therefore £2,761.25 - £2,350.00 = £411.25.

Activity 14

The sales figures excluding VAT will be £14,250 and £32,500. The sales figure in the profit and loss account will therefore be £46,750. The purchases figure excluding VAT will be £20,000. The net liability to Customs and Excise will be (£38,187.50 - £32,500) - (£23,500 - £20,000) = £2,187.50.

Activity 15

The sales figures excluding VAT will be £14,250 and £32,500. The sales figure in the profit and loss account will therefore be £46,750. Gross VAT payable to Customs and Excise will be £5,687.50 (17.5% of £32,500).

The purchases figure excluding VAT will be £20,000. The VAT on purchases will be £3,500, of which £3,500 x £32,500/£46,750 is recoverable – i.e. the recoverable figure is £2,433.15. £1,066.85 is not recoverable and must be borne by the business. The business would therefore show purchases valued at £20,000 + £1,066.85; i.e. £21,066.85.

VAT creditor = output tax (£5,687.50) - recoverable input tax (£2,433.15) = £3,254.35

Activity 16

It would appear from the information given that the £14,000 should be written off immediately to profit and loss. The £18,000 expended on fixed assets could be capitalised under the provisions of SSAP 12.

The £12,000 could potentially be capitalised and depreciated over the five-year period. However, there is the question of whether the expenditure involved conforms to the provisions of SSAP 13 to allow capitalisation.

Chapter 2

Accounting for purchases and stocks

Introduction

In this chapter you will be working on the top section of the profit and loss account, where the gross profit is calculated. This section is sometimes called the 'trading account'. You will learn more about some concepts used in accounting, and the regulations contained in SSAP 2 and SSAP 9.

The sections on trading stock take up the largest part of the chapter. This is because there are various practical book-keeping problems to consider, as well as quite a number of concepts and accounting regulations that affect the way stock is dealt with in the financial statements.

Objectives

After you have completed this chapter, you should be able to:

■ record entries for stock and purchases in the books, and calculate cost of sales from the information recorded

■ prepare financial statements that recognise the effect of opening and closing stock, and of credit transactions

■ use and discuss the concepts and regulations included in SSAP 2 and SSAP 9

■ demonstrate the effect on profit measurement of the various methods used in the valuation of closing stock

■ identify the point at which revenues and costs should be recognised in the financial statements.

1 Trading stock – the book-keeping problems

The next time you buy something from a small local shop, try to imagine what accounting records might have been kept as a result of your purchase (a sale of stock by the shop). Forget about double entry for the time being; simply think about the way accounting data might have been captured by the system to enable the double entry to be posted later. Circumstances differ from shop to shop but basically there will be a series of events something like the following:

You take the items (magazine, bar of chocolate, etc.) from the shelf and offer cash to the assistant. The assistant will use the cash till to add up the total price of the goods you are buying, take your money, give you your change and a till receipt. There is probably a register in the till to keep a running total of all sales throughout the day so that the total cash taken can be checked from time to time.

Activity 1	The trader in the above story is likely to have kept a record of the amount paid for purchases during the year. Sales can be determined from the cash takings, but if we were to try and write up a stock account we would probably find a vital item of information has not been recorded. What is this item? (Remember we are trying to find the gross profit.)

It is simply not practical for a small trader to make a note of the cost price of every item in the shop, let alone record these costs at the time of sale. The goods often have a label on them to show the sales price to the customer, but not the cost price to the trader.

At this point, you may be wondering about some of the larger supermarkets with their sophisticated bar codes, computerised cash tills and the like. In some of these cases, it is quite likely that an amount is being recorded for both sales and cost of sales at the same time, but even here there are practical difficulties in using the cost of sales information produced by the system to keep a reliable account for stock in the same way as we do for cash at bank.

You will appreciate how these problems are resolved if you concentrate on the small trader who makes no attempt to keep a continuous record of the cost of sales.

From earlier studies you know that one of the steps in calculating profit is to match the sales revenue for a period with the cost of those sales. You also know that the cost of stock at the end of the period (usually called 'closing stock') is one of the items included under current assets in the balance sheet.

Activity 2

> Think about the cost of closing stock. If, as suggested above, there is no practical way in which we can use the accounting system to produce a reliable figure for the cost of closing stock, how could it be determined?

This procedure is often referred to as the 'annual stock-take'. You can imagine that sometimes it takes quite some time to complete. Maybe there have been times when you have found your favourite store 'closed for annual stock-taking', although it is more usual to do it over a weekend in order to avoid too much disruption of trade.

Any trader, no matter how small, will keep an accounting record of the cost of goods purchased during the period. From the annual stocktake we can calculate the cost of unsold stock. It is not too difficult to put these two things together in your mind to see how cost of sales can be determined. Since sales are recorded, and the cost of sales can be calculated, we can also determine the gross profit.

Activity 3

> Consider the first year of a new business, that is, one with no stock at the beginning of the year. During the year, cost of purchases amounts to £50,000. Total sales for the year are £60,000. The closing stock is counted and valued as follows: at cost price £10,000; at sales price £15,000.
>
> Calculate
>
> 1   Cost of sales
>
> 2   Gross profit

Notice how the sales price of the closing stock (£15,000) is not used in any of the calculations. It was included in the information mainly to force you to think about the relevant figure. We can also use it to bring out a further principle in the next Activity.

If we had used the selling price of closing stock in our calculations, the cost of sales would have been £35,000 (i.e. £50,000 less £15,000) and, therefore, the gross profit would have been calculated as £25,000.

Activity 4

> The trader in this example will eventually make a gross profit of £25,000 on the goods purchased. The goods cost £50,000 to buy, some have already been sold for £60,000, and those still on hand which cost £10,000 can be sold for £15,000. Try to describe what you think is wrong under the fundamental accounting concepts with recognising a gross profit of £25,000 (instead of £20,000) in the accounting period being considered.

This is sometimes referred to as the realisation principle – it is a principle embodied in prudence; profits must only be recognised in the accounting period during which such profits are realised.

You can think of profits as being realised in the period during which the sales price is received in cash or as soon as the ultimate receipt of the sales price becomes reasonably certain; such as where the goods have been sold to a customer on credit, even though actual payment for them is to take place at a later time.

In the case of unsold stock, there is no certainty that the ultimate sales value will be received and so the unrealised profit (£5,000 in Activity 3) must be ignored until the stock is sold. This is conveniently achieved by valuing the closing stock at cost when determining the cost of sales. By taking the cost of stock purchased during the period and deducting the cost of unsold stock at the end of the period, the residual figure represents the cost of stock sold during the period.

There is quite a lot more to learn in relation to stock, but at this stage it will be helpful to think about double-entry book-keeping.

Ledger accounting for stock

We will use the details from Activity 3 for the illustration.

Activity 5	First of all, in order to make a comparison with the double-entry for stock, assume the trader had somehow managed to keep a primary record of cost of sales. In practice, this is unusual. A primary record is one where accounting data is accumulated prior to posting in the ledger. Assume for this example that all new purchases and stock holdings are debited or charged to a single stock account. Assume also that purchases are paid for by cheque on the day of purchase, and that all sales are for cash which is banked immediately.

1 Make a note of the double entry for the relevant transactions:

	Account debited	Account credited
Purchase of goods for resale £50,000		
Sales £60,000		
Cost of sales £40,000		

2 State how the balance on the stock account (£10,000 debit) would have been dealt with at the end of the period. The treatment of closing stock may be thought of as being similar to double entry. The closing of the account results in entries to both sides of the account.

The relevant ledger accounts (prior to the transfers to profit and loss account) would be as follows:

Stock					Sales		
Bank (purchases)	50,000	Cost of sales	40,000			Bank	60,000
		Stock c/d	10,000				
	50,000		50,000				
Stock b/d	10,000						

Cost of sales				Bank			
Stock	40,000			Sales	60,000	Stock	50,000

In this case, the figure for cost of sales was recorded in the primary records and then posted in the ledger by double entry so that the stock account itself revealed the cost of stock on hand at the end of the period.

Now assume, as is often the case, that there is no primary record kept for cost of sales. The annual stocktake is carried out and stock on hand is calculated to be £10,000 at cost price.

Activity 6

We now need to write the cost of closing stock into the books because it is not a balance revealed by entries in the stock account itself. If you assume that purchases have been debited to the stock account (there are other methods, as you will see in a moment) can you think of a way of writing the cost of closing stock into the account by means of double entry? It will help if you recall that closing balances are, in effect, written into the ledger by way of a treatment similar to double entry.

At this stage the ledger accounts will look a bit odd – something like this:

Stock					Sales		
Bank (purchases)	50,000					Bank	60,000
		Stock c/d	10,000				
	50,000						
Stock b/d	10,000						

Cost of sales		Bank	
		Sales 60,000	Stock 50,000

You will often have to use this idea of carrying down a balance on ledger accounts in order to calculate a figure needed for the financial statements. In this case we are using the idea to determine cost of sales. If you look at the stock account you will see that it has a debit balance of £40,000 (£50,000 debit less £10,000 credit) which represents the cost of sales. You can now simply post in the double entry for cost of sales in order to balance off the stock account.

Activity 7	Go back to the above ledger accounts, post in the double entry for cost of sales and balance off the stock account. Then compare the ledger accounts resulting from this activity with those following Activity 5 – what do you notice?

All we have done is alter the sequence of entries in the stock account. By posting cost of sales first (assuming we had a record of the amount) the balance represents the cost of closing stock; by entering the cost of closing stock first, the balancing figure represents cost of sales.

Opening stock

We have been looking at the first year of a new business. There were no balances in the books at the beginning of the year and, in particular, no stock at the beginning of the year.

The closing balances (for various assets and liabilities) at the end of one year will obviously become the opening balances at the start of the next year. In the case of stock, the closing stock at the end of year 1 will become what is known as the 'opening stock' at the start of year 2.

Activity 8	Think about the stock account for the second year of our trader. There will be two types of entry on the debit side of the account – what are they?

At the end of the second year, the trader will count the stock again, calculate the cost of this stock, and then write it into the books in the same way as was done at the end of year 1.

Activity 9	During the second year, our trader (in Activity 6) purchased stock at a cost of £70,000. Sales amounted to £102,000. The stock at the end of the second year was counted and valued at the cost price of £12,000. Calculate:

1   Cost of sales for the second year of trading

2   Gross profit.

Different book-keeping systems for purchases and stock

You need to understand the recording process in order to make sense of the information given in a trial balance.

Unfortunately there is no one method of recording for purchases and stock. There is a basic pattern, and you will have to rely on your ability to visualise this when interpreting information used in the workplace.

In the previous activities, you have been dealing with all the stock entries (opening stock, purchases, cost of sales, closing stock) in one single account called 'stock'. In most simple financial book-keeping the purchases are usually debited to a separate account called 'purchases' and not to the account called 'stock'. The cost of purchases is transferred to the profit and loss account at the end of the year by the double entry:

> debit profit and loss account; credit purchases.

Consequently, the only figure on the stock account throughout the year will be the value of stock brought down from the close of the previous year, and forming the opening stock for the current year. It will stay on that account until it is transferred to the profit and loss account at the end of the current year by the double entry:

> debit profit and loss account; credit stock.

Notice how, at this point, the profit and loss account has been debited with the cost of opening stock, and also debited with the cost of purchases. These are the first two items in the formula for calculating cost of sales. In order to complete the exercise, we need to bring the closing stock (at the end of the current year) into the accounts. This is also done by a double entry, as follows:

> debit stock; credit profit and loss account.

The profit and loss account will now include two debits (the opening stock and the purchases) and one credit (the closing stock). These three items give us the formula for calculating cost of sales, namely: opening stock, plus purchases, less closing stock.

The balance on the stock account will be a debit equal to the cost of closing stock at the end of the current year (opening stock having already been transferred to the profit and loss account). When balancing off the ledger at the end of the year, this balance is simply carried down (credit old period; debit new) to become the opening stock for the following year.

The credit balance on the account for sales is transferred to the profit and loss account (debit sales; credit profit and loss) in the normal way, and so the balance on the profit and loss account at this stage will represent the gross profit.

| Activity 10 | Using the transactions for the second year of the trader in Activity 9, write up the following ledger accounts using the revised system of book-keeping referred to in the above notes. There is no need to balance off the bank account (in any case, we do not know all the entries), but you must deal with all other accounts (stock, purchases, sales, profit and loss) as if balancing off the ledger at the end of the year. Carry down the gross profit on the profit and loss account. |

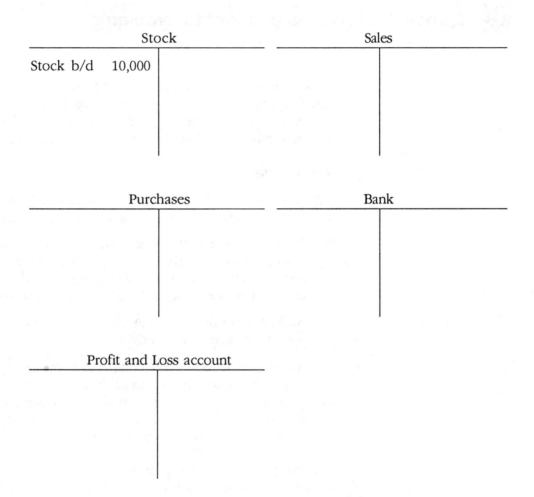

Stock	
Stock b/d 10,000	

Sales	

Purchases	

Bank	

Profit and Loss account	

You will recall from earlier sections that the figures in the ledger account called 'profit and loss' are not presented to the user in the same way as they appear in the account. If you look at the above profit and loss ledger account, you can imagine that figures presented in this format would be almost meaningless unless the user had been trained in double-entry book-keeping. The profit and loss account is presented in the form of a narrative statement so that the key figures can be easily identified by the user.

| Activity 11 | Devise a way of presenting the profit and loss account in Activity 10 in the form of a narrative statement. You have done something similar before, with less detail. Use a separate sheet of paper for your answer. |

The key sets out two formats that are in popular use. At this stage of your studies, it would be preferable to adopt the first of these, that is, the one with full details of how cost of sales has been calculated.

As you are already aware, the top section of the profit and loss account is sometimes called the 'trading account' because it is where the gross profit on trading is calculated. The next section of the statement, where various operating expenses are deducted from the gross profit, is then referred to as the profit and loss account. You may still find some people referring to the complete statement as a 'trading and profit and loss account', but it is becoming more common to drop the word 'trading' and simply call the whole thing a profit and loss account.

2 Trading stock – the conceptual problems

You have been considering the problems of trading stock in so far as they affect the double-entry book-keeping, and the interpretation of accounting information in a trial balance. There are other problems for which practical solutions have to be found based on the accounting concepts involved.

Prudence

Prudence, as you are aware, is a fundamental concept in accounting. It involves a consideration of two aspects in the calculation of profit, namely:

1   Profits are not anticipated, and are only recognised in the period during which they are received, or their ultimate receipt is reasonably certain. Where profits are recognised in advance of their receipt, a conservative view should be taken of the amount to be received.

2   All losses are recognised as soon as they are known to exist, whether they have been realised or not.

One of the problems in accounting is that we have to divide something that is really continuous (the business operating year after year) into artificial slices called the 'accounting period'. In the long term all profits and all losses will be realised, but when calculating profit for any one particular period we need to take a conservative view. Remember that the figure for profit calculated by the accountant is often used to determine how much can be distributed to (or withdrawn by) the proprietors. If profits are overstated, and too much is distributed, it could lead to financial problems in subsequent years.

You must now think about unrealised losses in relation to stock. Suppose a trader had purchased an item of stock at a cost price of £10. He had intended to sell it for £15 but it has become damaged (or maybe the demand for this item has dropped) and can only be sold for £8, which is £2 less than the cost price.

If it is eventually sold for £8 the trader will make a loss of £2, but supposing by the end of the accounting period it has not been sold and forms part of the stock on the shelf; the prudence concept still wants us to recognise the anticipated loss in the current period even though it has not been realised. Prudence is a one-sided, pessimistic concept.

Activity 12	What would be a practical way of making sure that the anticipated loss of £2 is recognised in the current period?

If it had been valued at £10, the trading account would have included the following figures as far as this item is concerned:

Sales   nil

Less cost of sales:

Purchases	10	
Less closing stock	(10)	
		nil
Gross profit		nil

No profit or loss would have been recognised.

If we value the stock item at £8, the trading account may include the following:

Sales   nil

Less cost of sales:

Purchases	10	
Less closing stock	(8)	
		2
Gross loss		(2)

Activity 13	Given that the trading account should reflect gross profit from trading, what would you consider wrong in principle with this form of presentation?

You will appreciate from this simple example that profits will vary according to the principles used for the valuation of closing stock. Because of this, the Accounting Standards Committee (ASC – now superseded by the Accounting Standards Board, ASB) issued an accounting standard on stock (SSAP 9) several years ago.

You will learn quite a lot about SSAP 9 as you work through the course, but for now, the most important requirement in the standard to consider is that stock must be valued at the lower of cost or net realisable value. In the above example, cost was £10, net realisable value was £8, the lower of these being £8.

The wording of SSAP 9 had to be a little more precise than this in order to prevent it from being misinterpreted (deliberately or otherwise). In effect, the wording states that stock must be valued on the basis of:

the total of the lower of cost and net realisable value of the separate items of stock.

Activity 14

See if you can interpret the wording by working on this example. A trader has three items in stock, valued as follows:

		Cost	Net realisable value
Item A		100	200
Item B		200	50
Item C		300	600
	Total	600	850

Calculate the value of the stock to be included in the financial statements, using the principles in SSAP 9.

In fact, company law, as embodied by the Companies Act 1985, insists that companies consider stock items separately when valuing at lower of cost or net realisable value.

SSAP 9 defines cost as being:

'*all expenditure in the normal course of business in bringing stock to its present location and condition*'.

Notice how the definition allows delivery costs incurred (when acquiring the stock) to be included as part of the cost.

Net realisable value is defined as the estimated selling price less the costs of completion and the costs of selling and distribution. Selling and distribution costs relate to things like sales commission and delivery costs; these must be deducted from the estimated selling price when calculating 'net' realisable value.

In the profit and loss account, such costs are not treated as part of the cost of sales in arriving at gross profit – they are usually classified as an expense item called 'selling and distribution costs' and will be deducted from gross profit along with any other running expenses. The calculation of net realisable value for stock valuation purposes is said to be a 'memorandum' exercise, that is, it is calculated to enable a figure to be written into the ledger; it is not a figure generated by the double-entry book-keeping itself.

It may seem a bit odd to talk about the cost of completion in the definition, but remember that some businesses manufacture or construct their trading stock rather than purchase it from someone else. At any particular accounting date these firms may have stock which is still in the process of being made. Such stock is called 'work-in-progress' and it has to be valued at the lower of cost or net realisable value in the same way as any other stock.

This aspect of the definition for net realisable value can also be applied to a trader who simply buys things for resale. Consider the following example:

A trader has purchased an item of stock for £100. It could normally be sold for £150 but it has become damaged in the shop and as it stands it could only be sold for £50. However, the trader can get it repaired at a cost of £20 and if this repair is carried out it is estimated that the item could eventually be sold for £110. The accounting date occurs prior to the repair being carried out.

Activity 15	Try using the definitions and principles from SSAP 9 to calculate what value would be placed on this item of stock in the accounts.

The estimated loss that will be realised when this item is eventually sold is £10, based on an estimated sales price of £110, less the original cost of £100, and the cost of repairing it at £20. By bringing this item of closing stock into the accounts at a value of £90, the estimated eventual loss of £10 is recognised during the current period. You can prove this for yourself in the next activity.

Activity 16	Assuming that the stock item is valued at £90, set out the figures that will appear in the trading and profit and loss account for this item during the current period. Your figures should prove that the estimated loss of £10 will be recognised during the current period.

The calculation of net realisable value is a further example of how estimates have to be used in accounting – you have already seen how depreciation has to be estimated.

3 Credit trading

The final part of this chapter deals mainly with the concepts involved when accounting for the purchase and sale of goods on credit terms. Full details of the book keeping for credit transactions were dealt with at NVQ Level 2/AAT Foundation.

Revenue recognition – accruals concept

The concepts involved are related to the realisation principle referred to earlier in this chapter. We now extend the idea a little further to see how it is related to credit transactions. Consider the following sequence of events:

> On Monday, a motor parts dealer receives a telephone call from a regular customer asking for a clutch slave cylinder for an old Rover 2000. The dealer does not have one in stock but can order it from a supplier, to arrive on Tuesday. The customer agrees to this arrangement. On Tuesday, the part arrives at the dealer's premises. On Wednesday the dealer telephones the customer to say it has arrived and the customer asks for it to be delivered. On Thursday the dealer delivers the part, hands the customer a delivery note but does not collect any cash. On Friday the dealer sends the customer an invoice. The customer pays the invoice two weeks later. The dealer pays the supplier for the part one month later.

If the whole of this trading cycle had occurred within one accounting period we would not be bothered about anything as far as accounting is concerned – there would have been a purchase and a sale within the period, no matter what principles had been applied. But accounting periods have a habit of ending during the course of hundreds of similar cycles, and so we need to apply rules that will determine the point at which profit should be recognised.

In this example, we need to focus our attention on the point at which it would be reasonable to conclude that a sale had been made by the dealer. Between Monday and Wednesday there is very little certainty in the transaction; all kinds of things could have gone wrong that would have allowed either party to escape from the deal. It is quite likely that a lawyer would argue that the sale had actually been made on the Wednesday, because it was at this point that the customer had agreed to accept the article (at whatever price was quoted) and the dealer had put it to one side (appropriated it) for the customer.

For practical accounting purposes, it would be more realistic to conclude that the sale had occurred on the Thursday (when delivered) because at this point there was no doubt that the article had been accepted by the customer. It is quite likely that the invoice made out on the Friday was actually dated for Thursday; this is quite normal in practice.

If you accept that the sale was made on the Thursday, it follows that the purchase must have been made on the Tuesday when it was accepted from the supplier. So for Tuesday and Wednesday this article simply becomes a purchase and an item of stock as far as the dealer's accounts are concerned.

You will notice that in both cases (sale and purchase) the date at which the cash was exchanged is irrelevant. This reflects the 'accruals concept' which recognises the creation of a 'debtor' or 'creditor' as concluding the transaction as far as the profit and loss account is concerned.

Summary

You have covered a lot of ground in this chapter, but the main learning points can be identified as follows:

■ in simple financial book-keeping there is no such thing as a stock account to record the continuous movements of stock received and stock sold

■ the cost of stock received is debited to an account called purchases, the cost of stock sold is not recorded

■ stock on hand at the end of the period has to be counted and valued at the lower of cost or net realisable value for each item of stock

■ once counted and valued, this stock is written into the books by double entry – debit stock; credit trading account

■ cost of sales is a calculation derived from the formula: opening stock plus purchases less closing stock

■ the valuation of closing stock has a significant impact on the figure for cost of sales and, therefore, on the amount of profit reported

■ because of this, there is an accounting standard (SSAP 9) which defines cost and net realisable value, and also sets out the principles to be used for stock valuation

■ profit is recognised on an accruals basis; sales are recognised as soon as they are earned, which may be in advance of the cash receipt in the case of a credit transaction

■ the accruals concept is always tempered by prudence; sales are only recognised if their realisation is reasonably certain, but all losses are recognised as soon as they are known to exist, even if unrealised.

Key to Chapter 2 activities

Activity 1   The cost of sales has probably not been recorded.

Activity 2   You might have suggested something like: physically counting all the items in the shop, listing them on a piece of paper, and then calculating their cost from purchase records, such as the purchase invoices.

Activity 3   The cost of goods sold in the period will be equal to the cost of goods purchased during that period, less the cost of stock still on hand at the end of the period.

1   Cost of sales = £40,000, i.e. cost of purchases £50,000 less cost of closing stock £10,000.

2   Gross profit = £20,000, i.e. sales of £60,000 less cost of sales £40,000.

Activity 4   The additional £5,000 gross profit has not yet been earned. It will only be earned when the goods are eventually sold, presumably during the next accounting period. This treatment is governed by prudence.

Activity 5   1   Purchases £50,000: debit stock; credit bank. Sales £60,000: debit bank; credit sales. Cost of sales £40,000: debit cost of sales (or the trading account); credit stock.

2   The debit balance is carried down to the next period showing £10,000 on the credit side of the account at the end of the old period and £10,000 on the debit side of the account at the beginning of the new.

Activity 6   By carrying down the £10,000 as a closing balance on the stock account, i.e. 'credit the old period' with £10,000 and 'debit the new'.

Activity 7   They are exactly the same.

Activity 8   1   the cost of opening stock (last year's closing stock brought down)

2   the cost of purchases during the second year.

Activity 9   1   Cost of sales is £68,000, calculated as follows:

Cost of opening stock	10,000
Add: cost of purchases	70,000
	80,000
Less: cost of closing stock	12,000
Cost of sales	68,000

2   Gross profit is £34,000, i.e. sales of £102,000 less cost of sales £68,000

Activity 10

	Stock		
Stock b/d	10,000	P & L a/c	10,000
P & L a/c	12,000	Bal c/d	12,000
	22,000		22,000
Stock b/d	12,000		

	Sales		
P & L a/c	102,000	Bank	102,000
	102,000		102,000

	Purchases		
Bank	70,000	P & L a/c	70,000
	70,000		70,000

	Bank		
Sales	102,000	Purchases	70,000

Profit and Loss account

Stock (opening)	10,000	Sales	102,000
Purchases	70,000	Stock (closing)	12,000
Gross profit c/d	34,000		
	114,000		114,000
		Gross profit b/d	34,000

Activity 11

There are two popular formats as follows:

1 A detailed format:

Profit and loss account for year 2

Sales		102,000
Cost of sales:		
Opening stock	10,000	
Purchases	70,000	
	80,000	
Closing stock	(12,000)	
		68,000
Gross profit		34,000

2 An abbreviated format:

Profit and loss account for year 2

Sales	102,000
Cost of sales	68,000
Gross profit	34,000

The second format is normally used in the annual financial statements presented to the shareholders of a company.

Activity 12   By valuing the stock item at its realisable value of £8 instead of its cost price of £10.

Activity 13   The loss in value of the stock item is probably not a loss caused by the trading side of the operation. It is more likely to be a loss caused by simply holding (or 'carrying') the stock items, e.g. through obsolescence or deterioration. To show a true and fair view in the accounts, it may be better to show the figures as:

Sales		nil
Cost of sales:		
Purchases	10	
Less Closing stock	(10)	
		nil
Gross profit/loss		nil
General expenses		
Stock loss		(2)
Net loss		(2)

Activity 14   In total, the cost of £600 is lower, but SSAP 9 requires the lower of cost and net realisable value to be considered for each separate item. Consequently the values to use are: A £100, B £50, and C £300, i.e. a total of £450.

Activity 15   £90. Cost is £100; net realisable value (i.e. eventual selling price of £110, less cost of completion £20) is £90; the lower of these two is £90.

Activity 16

Sales		nil
Less cost of sales:		
Purchases	100	
Less closing stock	(100)	
		nil
Gross profit/loss		nil
Loss on stock items		(10)
Net loss		(10)

Chapter 3
Bad debts, accruals and pre-payments

Introduction

At the end of each financial period, a series of end-of-period adjustments are made into the nominal ledger to enable final presentation of the profit and loss account and the balance sheet.

We have already looked at fixed asset depreciation and stock adjustments. In this chapter we will consider the final two adjustments, bad and doubtful debts and the treatment of pre-payments and accruals. Both are based on simple principles and involve quite simple working.

Objectives

After you have completed this chapter, you should be able to:

■ account fully and properly for bad and doubtful debts

■ account fully and properly for accruals and pre-payments.

1 Bad and doubtful debts

Bad debts written off

If an asset turns out to be worthless, it will have to be 'written off' – that is, the debit balance (representing the asset) is transferred to the profit and loss account and treated as an expense.

This happens with trading debts. If all efforts to recover the amount owing have failed, and the debt is considered to be irrecoverable, the debit balance on the debtor's account is transferred to the profit and loss account and described as 'bad debts written off'.

As mentioned earlier, it is not good practice to write items directly into the profit and loss account, and an expense account called 'bad debts' is normally written up first. This account may include many bad debts written off during the period; the total at the end of the period is then transferred to the profit and loss account.

Activity 1	A trader keeps a debtors' control account as part of the double entry in the ledger. The balance on debtors' control account is £18,765 at 31 December 1990. One of the debtors, Mr Slow, has failed to pay a debt of £450 and the amount is now considered to be irrecoverable. Describe the double entry that will have to be made in relation to this item.

What happens if Mr Slow pays the amount due in a subsequent accounting year? The best way of dealing with this is to treat the cash received as a 'windfall' profit. It will then be credited to the profit and loss account and described as 'bad debts recovered'.

Practices vary as regards the ledger account used to record bad debts recovered before transferring the amount to profit and loss at the end of the year. Sometimes, a separate 'bad debts recovered' account is used; or the bad debts recovered may be credited to the 'bad debts' account so that a net figure (bad debts written off, less bad debts recovered) is transferred to profit and loss. If a separate account is used, the two figures are normally 'netted off' when presenting figures in the profit and loss account.

Provision for doubtful debts

A business can never be absolutely certain which debtors are likely to pay and which are likely to turn out to be bad. But experience may suggest there will certainly be some bad debts. The prudence concept will therefore require the recognition of possible losses through bad debts, even though such losses may not be certain at the accounting date.

This situation is dealt with in the ledger by setting up a 'provision for doubtful debts'. The amount of the provision will be estimated, sometimes by considering the state of specific debtors, sometimes by taking a percentage of debtors outstanding.

In terms of double entry, the initial provision is set up by debiting profit and loss and crediting the provision. Since this is a single end-of-year adjustment, the debit is often made directly to the profit and loss account.

The debit to profit and loss is treated as an expense (often described as doubtful debts expense, or simply debited to bad debts expense, or 'provision for bad debts') and the credit balance on the account called 'provision for doubtful debts' is carried forward in the books. In the balance sheet, this provision will be deducted from debtors.

After setting up the initial provision, it will probably have to be adjusted at the end of each successive year in order to recognise the changing circumstances. It may have to be reduced, or it may have to be increased. This is normally done by carrying forward the revised provision at the end of the year – any difference between the provision brought forward from the previous year and closing provision carried forward at the end of the current year is transferred to the profit and loss account.

This difference will represent an increase, or a decrease, in the provision for doubtful debts and will be described as such in the profit and loss account. See if you can sort out this explanation by working on the following Activity.

Activity 2	A trader commenced business on 1 January 1990. At 31 December 1990, debtors amount to £40,000. At 31 December 1991, the debtors are £52,000. It is a normal practice in this business to recognise that 2% of debtors will never pay, and a provision for doubtful debts is to be set up accordingly.
	Demonstrate how this would be done by writing up the 'provision for doubtful debts' for the two-year period in the account below. Make sure that your entries give the name of any account to which the opposite entry is posted.

Provision for doubtful debts

The debtors in the balance sheet at the end of each year would be:
31 December 1990 (40,000 – 800)	£39,200
31 December 1991 (52,000 – 1,040)	£50,960

It is good book-keeping to keep the bad debts account, and the provision for doubtful debts, as two separate accounts. Sometimes, however, they are mixed up in one account called 'bad and doubtful debts'.

This single account not only contains the debits for bad debts written off, but also the provision for doubtful debts carried forward. In these cases, the final transfer to the profit and loss account is a mixture of bad debts written off (and sometimes bad debts recovered), and the adjustment to the provision. These situations are easy enough to sort out if you have understood the basic principles involved.

2 Accruals and pre-payments

Many expenses, such as electricity, rent and insurance, are only accounted for in the books as they are paid. But expenses charged in the profit and loss account should be the expense incurred for the year and this may not be the same figure as the amount paid for that particular expense.

Some expenses, such as electricity, are paid in arrears; others, such as insurance, are usually paid in advance. Accruals and prepayments are simply ways of making adjustments to the amounts paid so that profit and loss is charged with the amount incurred.

Accruals are a way of recognising any expenses owing at the end of the year; the amounts are often estimated. Prepayments recognise that some payments have been made in advance of the period to which they relate; the amounts are usually calculated on a time-apportionment basis.

The total of all accruals will be included with creditors in the balance sheet; total prepayments are included with debtors.

The easiest way of coping with the double entry for accruals and prepayments is to carry them down on the ledger account for the expense concerned. As mentioned in previous sections, you are making a notional double entry when balances are carried down on a ledger account. For example, when carrying down a credit balance, the notional double entry is effectively: debit the old period, credit the new.

In the context of accruals and prepayments, the effect of the notional double entry is as follows:

Accruals: a debit to the current period, and a credit to the next period

Prepayments: a credit to the current period, and a debit to the next period.

Try to sort this out for yourself by working on the following Activity.

Activity 3

Write up expense accounts for electricity and insurance for year ending 31 December 1990 based on the following data.

A trader sets up business on 1 January 1990. During the year to 31 December 1990, the amount paid for electricity was £820. An invoice for electricity was received in February 1991 (before the accounts for 1990 were finalised) for £300 and it was estimated that two-thirds of this related to 1990. On 1 April 1990, the trader paid £1,200 for insurance which related to the year from 1 April 1990 to 31 March 1991. Blank accounts are set out below.

Electricity

Insurance

_____

The balances are simply left on these accounts and, in effect, provide an automatic adjustment for expenses relating to the earlier stages of the next period. For example, when the electricity bill of £300 is eventually paid it will be debited to the electricity account. Setting this debit against the credit of £200 which has been brought forward from 1990 leaves a net debit of £100, which actually relates to the expense for the first part of 1991 (one-third of £300).

Similarly, the debit of £300 brought down on the insurance account relates to the expense for the period 1 January 1991 to 31 March 1991 which will not actually be paid during 1991 (it was paid in 1990).

We have to repeat the procedure at the end of 1991. Consequently, the expense incurred for any particular year will be based on either:

the amount paid, less accruals brought down, plus accruals carried down,
or
the amount paid, plus prepayments brought down, less prepayments carried down.

Activity 4

What expense will be charged to the profit and loss account for 1990 in the following two cases?

1   The accrual for electricity at 31 December 1989 was £400. Payments for electricity during 1990 were £1,800. The accrual for electricity at 31 December 1990 was £600.

2   Insurance is paid one year in advance on 1 April each year. The premium for 1989 was £1,200. The premium for 1990 was £1,800.

As stated earlier, it is normal practice for the amounts carried down as accruals to be included with the figure for creditors in the balance sheet; the amounts carried down as prepayments are included with debtors. If they are combined in this way, the descriptions in the balance sheet should be changed to:

Debtors and prepayments; and
Creditors and accruals.

At this stage of your studies you should show accruals as a separate item in the balance sheet following the creditors. The figure is simply described as accruals. Similarly, prepayments should be shown as a separate item following the debtors.

Summary

The main learning points in this chapter are:

■ all trading debts considered to be bad must be written off to the profit and loss account as an expense

■ provisions for doubtful debts are set up by debiting profit and loss and carrying the provision forward as a credit balance; after setting up the initial provision, it is only necessary to charge or credit profit and loss with the amounts needed to increase or decrease the provision

■ accruals and prepayments relate to expenses that are accounted for on a cash paid basis; they ensure that expenses charged to profit and loss relate to the expense incurred for the period, as distinct from the amount paid.

Key to Chapter 3 activities

Activity 1

Debit bad debts account £450; Credit sales ledger control account £450. The account for Mr Slow will also have to be written off in the memorandum debtors ledger (a list of how much each individual debtor owes the business) – but this is not part of the double entry. The balance on the bad debts account is transferred to the profit and loss account at the end of the period.

Activity 2

Provision for doubtful debts

1990				1990		
31 Dec	Balance c/d	800		31 Dec	Profit & loss a/c	800
		800				800
1991				1991		
31 Dec	Balance c/d	1,040		1 Jan	Balance b/d	800
				31 Dec	Profit & loss a/c (inc. in provn.)	240
		1,040				1,040

Activity 3

Electricity

1990				1990		
?	Bank	820		31 Dec	Profit & loss a/c	1,020
31 Dec	Accrual c/d	200				
		1,020				1,020
				1991		
				1 Jan	Accrual b/d	200

Insurance

1990				1990		
1 Apr	Bank	1,200		31 Dec	Profit & loss a/c	900
				31 Dec	Prepayment c/d	300
		1,200				1,200
1991						
1 Jan	Prepayment b/d	300				

Activity 4

1   Electricity £2,000 (1,800 – 400 + 600)

2   Insurance £1,650 (1,800 + 300 – 450)

Chapter 4
Incomplete records

Introduction

The techniques covered by this chapter were originally developed to cope with the preparation of financial statements for traders who do not keep double-entry accounting records. You will learn the process in the context of such a business but you must appreciate that the same approach can be applied to any problem where accounting figures have to be derived from incomplete information.

Businesses owned by sole traders tend to be small with few (if any) employees. There is hardly likely to be a trained book-keeper on the staff and the accounting records will most probably be kept by the proprietor. The books are often little more than an analysis of receipts and payments. These accounting records are said to be incomplete simply because the double entry has not been completed. Your task is to learn how financial statements are prepared from such records.

Objectives

After you have completed this chapter, you should be able to:

■ prepare financial statements for a business whose accounting records are not kept on double-entry principles

■ make use of the techniques to find missing figures in many different types of accounting problem.

1 The omitted records

Many small businesses (such as a retail shop) conduct a great deal of their business on a cash basis. The daily cash takings are often used to pay various expenses and the proprietor's drawings prior to banking the balance from time to time. Further payments are then made by cheque, particularly to settle the monthly accounts of credit suppliers.

These businesses usually arrange for a professional accountant to prepare their annual financial statements (mainly as a prelude to agreeing the proprietor's income tax liability). Most professional accountants advise the proprietor to keep two analysed cash books – one to provide an analysis of cash receipts and payments, the other to provide an analysis of bank receipts and payments. The analysis is mainly concerned with determining annual totals for the various types of payment such as purchases, rent and rates, wages, drawings.

Financial statements can then be prepared from these cash books providing there is some memorandum record of outstanding debtors and creditors at the accounting date.

As regards credit transactions, the trader will use various clerical procedures for keeping tabs on the amounts owed to creditors and the amounts owing by debtors. These procedures usually rely on some kind of filing system whereby the paid and unpaid invoices can be separately identified at any particular time.

Activity 1	Compare the accounting records outlined in the foregoing description with those of a business whose records are kept on a double-entry system. Make a list of the main books that are usually omitted in an 'incomplete record' system.

2 Finding the missing figures

To prepare financial statements from incomplete records, we simply apply our accounting knowledge in order to calculate the figures needed.

Opening position

As a starting point, let us think about the opening balance sheet of an existing business. Suppose we were able to determine that the opening assets and liabilities of a business were as follows:

Delivery van – at net book value		6,000
Stock at cost	6,000	
Debtors	4,000	
Cash on hand	200	
Cash at bank	2,800	
	13,000	
Trade creditors	3,000	
Accruals	300	
	3,300	
		9,700
		15,700
Long term loan		5,000
		10,700

Activity 2	From the above detail it is possible to determine another item needed to complete the opening balance sheet. We are so accustomed to seeing it on a balance sheet that it might take you a little while to realise it is missing. Describe the item and state the amount.

In your assessments you may be expected to determine the opening capital from the various items of information given. In practice, the figure would be known from the balance sheet prepared at the end of the previous year.

The amount for capital in this example was simply derived as a balancing figure. This approach of finding a balancing figure lies behind most of the workings on incomplete record problems.

Transactions during the year

At this stage of your studies you will be well aware that the figures for income and expenses in the profit and loss account are not always the same as the corresponding amounts of cash received and cash paid. Profit and loss items are determined on an accruals basis, not on a cash basis. In other words, income relates to the amount earned in the period, and expenditure relates to the amount incurred in that period.

In a double-entry system the accruals concept is automatically applied, for example when a purchase invoice is received, purchases will be debited (through the purchases day book) and a creditor will be credited. In an incomplete record system, the first book-keeping entry will be made when the creditor's account is paid. But it is quite easy to build up the 'accrued' figure from the amount paid.

Activity 3	If you were told that the amount paid for purchases during the first year of a new business amounted to £126,000, and that there was £4,800 owing for purchases at the end of the first year, what amount will be shown as purchases in the trading account for that year?

You probably found this quite easy and are starting to suspect that something more complicated must be involved. Rest assured that the whole process is not much more complicated than this.

You will have to be a little more careful when dealing with the figures of a business that was trading in the previous year. Some of the amounts recorded as payments for purchases during the current year would have been to pay off the creditors at the end of the previous year. These payments relate to the previous year's purchases, not the current year.

Think about this in relation to the trader referred to in Activity 2.

Activity 4	You ascertain that the trader in Activity 2 has recorded the following payments for purchases during the current year:

Purchases paid for by cash   £6,200
Purchases paid for by cheque   £56,300

You also ascertain that the amount owing for purchases at the end of the current year is £4,000. The amount of £3,000 shown in the opening balance sheet for the year as trade creditors relates entirely to purchases.

Calculate the purchases figure for the current year.

This figure was found by a logical calculation. You could have determined the amount as a balancing figure on a 'control account' for purchases. These so-called control accounts are used simply to find missing figures.

If we were to write up a control account for this example we would first write in all the known detail, as follows:

Control account – purchases

Payments	– cash	6,200	Creditors b/d	3,000
	– cheque	56,300		
Creditors c/d		4,000		
		66,500		

The balancing figure on this account represents purchases for the year. The completed account would be as follows:

Control account – purchases

Payments	– cash	6,200	Creditors b/d	3,000
	– cheque	56,300		
Creditors c/d		4,000	Purchases (balance)	63,500
		66,500		66,500

There is no need to worry over the fact that some of the payments would have been for cash purchases rather than credit purchases. We are only constructing the account in order to determine a total for purchases – the distinction between cash and credit purchases is of no significance.

It is up to you to develop your own method of working. If the figures are relatively straightforward, as in the above example, the calculation method is to be preferred. Some students feel more secure when using 'T' accounts for workings but they do take longer to prepare. Furthermore, the calculation approach is better for the development of your mental agility. You may eventually be able to look at the figures in an example like this and quickly see that since the creditors have increased by £1,000 the figure for purchases will be £1,000 more than the amounts paid.

Now see if you can sort out how the figure for sales would be calculated in the following activity. The approach is exactly the same as for purchases.

| **Activity 5** | The trader in Activity 2 has recorded cash takings for the current period as £77,000 (see note below). If you look back at the opening balance sheet, you will notice that debtors at the start of the period were £4,000. You ascertain that debtors at the end of the current period are £4,500.

Calculate the amount for Sales to be included in the trading account for the current period.

Note: the expression 'cash takings' has been used to denote the total amount of money taken from all customers; some of this money will be for cash sales, and some will be the money received from credit customers. Either may be in the form of actual cash or cheques. |

3 Putting it all together

You should now be able to prepare a set of financial statements by using the thought processes you have developed by working through the previous activities.

In the next activity, full details of the cash account have been given. This is a bit of a luxury because it implies that the trader has kept a properly balanced record of all cash transactions. In practice, some of the details for the cash account itself are nearly always missing. We will sort that out after completing the following problem.

Details for Activity 6:

The cash account and bank account for the trader in Activity 2 are now given in summarised form as follows:

Cash account	£	Bank account	£
Balance brought forward	200	Balance brought forward	2,800
Receipts:			
Cash takings	77,000	Bankings	58,700
	77,200		61,500
Payments:		Payments:	
Purchases	6,200	Purchases	56,300
Staff wages	8,000	Electricity	900
Drawings	4,000	Rent and rates	1,500
Cash banked	58,700	Motor expenses	500
		Private expenses	800
Balance carried forward	300	Part repayment of loan	500
	77,200	Balance carried forward	1,000
			61,500

Depreciation of the delivery van is to be based on 20% of the reducing balance. The accrual of £300 in the opening balance sheet relates to electricity; the accrual for electricity at the end of the year is £400. Closing stock at cost amounts to £7,500.

From previous activities you have already determined the figures for: opening capital, purchases and sales.

Activity 6	Prepare the trading and profit and loss account and balance sheet for this trader in the space provided.

Trading and profit and loss account

Balance sheet

4 Incomplete cash information

You will notice how these incomplete record problems require you to think in terms of two different accounts for cash – (1) the actual cash (bank notes and coins), and (2) the cash at the bank.

The bank account does not usually present any problem, although sometimes it may be necessary to make adjustments for unrecorded items such as bank charges.

The information available for the cash account may be complete or incomplete. If you are presented with a neatly balanced cash account, as in Activity 6, there is no additional problem. It is only where the cash information is incomplete that you will have to build up a cash account in order to determine missing information.

In order to cope with problems where the cash information is incomplete, you will have to have a fairly clear image of the cash account itself. The following is an outline of a cash account where one of the items has deliberately not been described:

Cash account

1	Balance b/d	X	3	Cash payments	X
2	Cash takings	X	4	(see Activity 7)	X
			5	Balance c/d	X
		X			X

Activity 7	Look at the above outline and describe what item 4 is likely to be.

The cash banked will appear as a receipt in the bank account (in effect there is a double entry: debit bank and credit cash). If you have to build up a cash account from sketchy information, it is quite likely that the figure for bankings would be taken from details of the bank account.

You will have to be careful if bankings include something other than the balance of cash takings. For example, if the bankings include an amount for capital introduced by the proprietor, the amount involved should be excluded from bankings in the cash account. Alternatively, the capital introduced can be shown as a separate receipt on the debit side of the cash account and the total bankings shown on the credit side. In other words, if you include it in the cash account as part of the bankings you will have to show it as being received into the cash account – even though it never actually passed through the account for cash.

The problem of incomplete information for the cash account really arises where the proprietor has failed to record particular details, or where some of the figures have been incorrectly recorded.

If an item has been completely omitted, it can be found as a balancing figure. For example (referring to the outline in Activity 7), if you were given details of items 1, 3, 4, and 5, you can derive item 2 (the cash takings) as a balancing figure. Similarly, if you were give details of items 1, 2, 3, and 4, you can calculate item 5 (the closing balance).

Where a cash item has been incorrectly recorded, the cash account will not balance and reasonable assumptions have to be made as to the nature of the item needed to make it balance. There are two situations that can arise in this context: either the debits will exceed the credits, or vice versa.

Debits exceed the credits

Imagine that from the data presented, you have been able to build up a cash account as far as the following:

Cash account

Balance b/d	100	Purchases	20,000
Cash takings	160,000	Office expenses	9,000
		Bankings	120,800
		Balance c/d	200

You will notice that the debit side is £160,100 whereas the credit side only adds up to £150,000. Quite clearly there must be another item to enter on the credit side but it has not been given in the details for the problem.

Activity 8	Consider the above situation. Assume that there is nothing wrong with the amounts recorded for purchases, office expenses, or bankings. What item would you assume has been missed on the credit side of this account? Think about the proprietor and the fact that the business provides the proprietor with a source of income.

Credits exceed debits

The reverse of the above situation is more likely to occur in practice. Suppose you have been able to build up a cash account from recorded information as follows:

Cash account

Balance b/d	100	Purchases	20,000
Cash takings	160,000	Office expenses	9,000
		Bankings	120,800
		Drawings	11,100
		Balance c/d	200

You will notice that the debits total £160,100 but the credits total £161,100.

Activity 9

If there is nothing to throw doubt on any of the figures on the credit side, what do you think would account for the difference?

You might be interested to learn that this situation frequently occurs in practice. It is then necessary to ask the client if there is any explanation for the fact that cash outgoings are £1,000 greater than the recorded incomings. The client may respond with something like: 'Oh yes, I remember, I sold the car for £1,000 and paid the cheque into the bank.' But more often than not, the difference relates to unrecorded takings.

Activity 10

A trader has not kept a full record of cash transactions. Build up a cash account from the following: Cash in hand was £500 at the start of the period, and £600 at the end. Takings determined from till rolls amounts to £101,000 for the year. Invoices paid by cash have been analysed and amount to £32,000 for purchases and £4,000 for motor expenses. The trader informs you that drawings are at the rate of £200 per week. No other payments are made by cash. The pay-in slips show a total of £56,000 being banked, including a cheque for £2,000 relating to a legacy received from the estate of a deceased relative. Use the blank outline account that follows this box.

Cash account

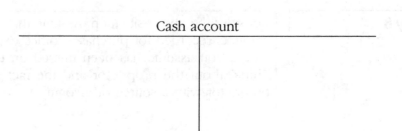

---

5 Information missing from both sides of the cash account

In previous activities you discovered how unrecorded takings, or unrecorded drawings, could be calculated as a balancing figure. This was possible because there was enough detail on receipts and payments to make a reasonable assumption about any difference on the cash account derived from such information.

A more highly contrived situation is one where information is missing from both sides of the cash account. These problems are usually based on the notion that both takings and drawings have not been recorded. Clearly, if both items are missing, neither one of them can be found as a simple balancing figure on the cash account.

These problems require you to find a link between the trading account and the cash account by making use of the gross profit margin (or gross profit mark-up) which is usually expressed as a percentage.

The gross profit margin is the gross profit expressed as a percentage of sales. For the trader in Activity 6 this would be calculated as follows:

$$\frac{\text{Gross profit}}{\text{Sales}} \times 100 \quad \text{i.e.} \quad \frac{15,500}{77,500} \times 100 = 20\%$$

The gross profit mark-up is the amount of gross profit expressed as a percentage of the cost of sales. For the trader in Activity 6 this would be:

$$\frac{\text{Gross profit}}{\text{Cost of sales}} \times 100 \quad \text{i.e.} \quad \frac{15,500}{62,000} \times 100 = 25\%$$

You must be careful over how you interpret information on gross profit percentages. If the percentage is referred to as a mark-up, then it is a percentage of the cost of sales; if it is referred to as a margin, then it is a percentage of sales. It is quite easy to convert one expression to the other. If 25% is added to cost to find the sales, then the amount added must be the same as 25/125 (20%) of the sales. If gross profit margin is 20% of sales then it must be 20/80ths (25%) of the cost of sales.

We now have to think about how this gross profit percentage might be used. If we are dealing with a situation where both takings and drawings have not been recorded, then perhaps we can find one of them by using some of the other information available. If we can find one, the other can be derived as a balancing figure on the cash account.

The best approach will be to estimate cash takings by making use of the normal gross profit percentage earned by the type of business concerned.

It is quite likely that a figure for purchases can be determined from details of payments. Cheque payments for purchases can be ascertained from the bank account and cash purchases can be identified from the purchase invoices. From purchases it is possible to determine cost of sales, providing the cost of opening and closing stock is available.

If we know the gross profit percentage prevailing in the type of business concerned, then sales can be estimated from the cost of sales.

Activity 11	The estimated figure for sales (found from this approach) is not likely to be the amount to be included in the cash account for estimated takings. Make a note of why not.

The following activity provides an opportunity for you to practise the whole approach without having to prepare a complete set of financial statements. The details given are sufficient to enable you to prepare a balanced cash account; a crucial starting point in the preparation of financial statements for the type of situation described.

Activity 12	B Dark is the owner of a small retail shop and has failed to keep any record of cash transactions. An analysis of his bank account includes the following detail:

Bankings	£82,500
Payments:	
Purchases	£68,000

Examination of the invoices received showed that the following cash payments were made:

Purchases	£6,300
Motor expenses	£800

Creditors for purchases at the start of the year were £6,000 and at the end of the year were £6,700. Opening stock at cost was £4,000 and closing stock was £5,500. Opening debtors were £2,000 and closing debtors £2,800. The balance of cash on hand at the end of each day is £100. For the purposes of this Activity, treat all sales receipts as cash rather than cheques or any other form of payment. The gross profit margin earned by B Dark's type of business is 30%. Prepare a balanced cash account for physical cash movements in the space provided. Use a separate piece of paper for the calculations.

Cash account

6 Other types of missing information

Some of the thought processes used to solve the problem in Activity 10 may have to be used to determine other types of unknown information. A fairly common example is to estimate the cost of stock at any particular date. This might be necessary for the annual financial statements (where stock was not counted) or where stock has been destroyed by fire and a claim has to be made on the insurance company.

See if you can find a solution to the problem in the following activity:

Activity 13	The opening stock of a business was £22,000. During the accounting period there was a fire that destroyed most of the trading stock except for some that had cost £2,000. The purchases during the period up to the date of the fire amounted to £139,000. Sales during this period were £172,500. The normal gross profit margin for this type of business is 20%. Estimate the cost of closing stock lost in the fire:

7 Trading goods withdrawn by the proprietor

Most of these incomplete record problems relate to a small business owned by a sole trader. It is usual to find that the proprietor in such a business has used some of the trading stock for personal purposes. For example, the proprietor of a grocery shop may withdraw some of the trading stock for private consumption.

There is hardly likely to be any accounting record of such transfers but it would be quite normal to make an adjustment in the financial statements for any estimated amounts. No cash transactions are involved. The value of amounts withdrawn must be debited to drawings but the other side of the double entry will depend on whether the figure given has been calculated at selling price, or at cost price.

Activity 14	A proprietor withdraws stock which has a cost price of £800 and a selling price of £1,000. Describe the double entry that would be made to reflect this withdrawal in the financial statements if it is recorded at: a) cost price b) selling price

Quite clearly there will be a slight difference in reported profits depending on whether the adjustment is made at cost or selling price. You may be interested to learn that when it comes to determining profits for tax purposes there is a legal case requiring the adjustment to be made at selling price. In other words, the withdrawal has to be dealt with as if the goods had been sold by the business to the proprietor. You will have to make an appropriate adjustment based on whether the value given is at cost price or at selling price.

8 Complete absence of accounting records

In rare circumstances, there may be virtually no accounting records from which a conventional set of financial statements could be prepared. This may happen, for example, where all records had been lost in a fire.

In these circumstances it should still be possible to estimate a single figure of profit for the year. The calculation relies on the balance sheet equation, since we know that profit can be equated to the increase in net assets after taking account of cash withdrawn and cash introduced.

It should be possible to piece together enough information to calculate net assets at the beginning of the period and the net assets at the end. Profit will be equal to the increase in net assets, plus drawings, less any cash introduced. Details of any cash introduced are likely to be known but the figure for drawings will have to be estimated. Clearly, the figure for profit is only an estimate and its reliability is very much related to the reliability of the estimate for drawings.

Activity 15	A small trader's premises were completely destroyed by fire and most accounting records were lost.

It was, however, possible to prepare a statement of assets and liabilities at the date of the fire and these reveal net assets to be £92,000. A copy of the balance sheet at the end of the previous accounting period shows the net assets at that date to be £85,000. Between these two dates, the trader had inherited £5,000 and introduced this into the bank account of the business. An estimate of his drawings during this period (including goods withdrawn) was calculated at £4,000.

Estimate profit for the period.

Summary

The main learning points in this chapter are:

- proprietors of small businesses do not usually keep their accounting records on double-entry principles

- in many cases the proprietor will keep an analysed cash book for both cash and bank transactions

- the preparation of financial statements from cash and bank transactions is simply an application of the accruals concept

- cash amounts can easily be turned into accrued amounts by recognising the effect of the opening and closing creditors and debtors

- where cash transactions are not fully recorded it is necessary to build up a cash account and determine the nature of any balancing figure

- if the recording of both cash receipts and cash payments has been neglected, it is necessary to determine cash takings by the process of using gross profit percentages as a means of calculating estimated sales from the cost of sales – cash takings includes cash from cash sales and cash received from debtors

- goods withdrawn by the proprietor should be debited to drawings; the credit depends on whether the amount is stated at cost price or selling price

- if the value of goods withdrawn is stated at cost price, purchases should be credited; if stated at selling price, sales should be credited

- in cases where no reliable accounting records are available, a single figure of estimated profit for the period can be related to the increase in net assets after making adjustments for drawings and capital introduced.

Key to Chapter 4 activites

Activity 1

The journal, sales day book, purchases day book, creditors ledger, debtors ledger, and the nominal ledger.

Activity 2

Capital account of £10,700. We cannot differentiate between capital introduced and retained profits, but at least we know the total.

Activity 3

£130,800, i.e. the amount paid plus the amount owing.

Activity 4

£63,500. You might have thought this through as follows:

Amount paid during the current year (6,200 + 56,300)	62,500
Less payment of opening creditors	3,000
Paid during the current year for current year's purchases	59,500
Add closing creditors for purchases	4,000
	63,500

Activity 5

77,000 − 4,000 + 4,500 = £77,500 (or cash takings £77,000 plus increase in debtors of £500 equals £77,500).

Activity 6

TRADING AND PROFIT AND LOSS ACCOUNT

Sales		77,500
Less cost of sales:		
Opening stock	6,000	
Purchases	63,500	
	69,500	
Closing stock	7,500	
		62,000
Gross profit		15,500
Expenses:		
Staff wages	8,000	
Electricity (900 + 400 − 300)	1,000	
Rent and rates	1,500	
Motor expenses	500	
Depreciation	1,200	
		12,200
Net profit		3,300

BALANCE SHEET

Fixed assets:

Delivery van – at net book value (6,000 – 1,200)		4,800

Current assets:

Stock		7,500	
Debtors		4,500	
Bank		1,000	
Cash		300	
		13,300	
Current liabilities:			
Creditors	4,000		
Accruals	400		
		4,400	
			8,900
			13,700
Long term loan (5,000 – 500)			4,500
			9,200
Capital account – brought forward		10,700	
Add net profit		3,300	
		14,000	
Less drawings (4,000 + 800)		4,800	
			9,200

Activity 7

Cash banked. It is quite easy to overlook this item when building up a cash account in order to determine missing information.

Activity 8

The missing item (£10,100) will most likely relate to 'drawings'.

Activity 9

It probably relates to unrecorded takings.

Activity 10

Cash account			
Balance b/d	500	Purchases	32,000
Cash takings	101,000	Motor expenses	4,000
Capital introduced	2,000	Stated drawings	10,400
		Unrecorded drawings	
		(balance)	500
		Bankings	56,000
		Balance c/d	600
	103,500		103,500

Capital introduced could be omitted from this account providing the bankings on the credit side are stated at £54,000. The bank account would then include two classifications of bankings, i.e. cash banked £54,000 and capital introduced £2,000.

Activity 11

Because adjustments will have to be made for the opening and closing debtors that are inherent in the determination of sales from cash figures. You also need to keep this type of adjustment in mind when determining purchases from the details of payments.

Activity 12

Workings:
Cost of sales:

Opening stock	4,000
Purchases (68,000 + 6,300 – 6,000 + 6,700)	75,000
	79,000
Closing stock	5,500
	73,500

Sales:

Cost of sales	73,500
Add mark-up (30/70 × 73,500)	31,500
	105,000

Cash takings: 105,000 – 2,800 + 2,000 = £104,200
(note how you have to work in reverse when finding cash takings from accrued sales).

Cash account

Balance b/d	100	Purchases	6,300
Takings	104,200	Motor expenses	800
		Bankings	82,500
		Drawings (bal)	14,600
		Balance c/d	100
	104,300		104,300

Activity 13

Opening stock	22,000
Purchases	139,000
	161,000
Less cost of sales (80% × 172,500)	138,000
Closing stock	23,000
Stock salvages	2,000
Amount claimed as lost	21,000

Activity 14

(a) Debit drawings £800; credit purchases £800.
(b) Debit drawings £1,000; credit sales £1,000.

Activity 15

£92,000 – £85,000 – £5,000 + £4,000 = £6,000.

Chapter 5

Non-trading organisations

Introduction

The skills required in this chapter are simply an adaptation of the incomplete record techniques that you have already learned in the context of a trading organisation.

The name 'non-trading organisations' is used to refer to various associations of members (such as social and sports clubs) whose objective is not to bring a financial gain to the members, but to further the interests and objects of the group and to provide various facilities for their members to enjoy. It can also apply to charitable and religious bodies.

The financial statements of these associations are based on the same concepts as those developed for a commercial entity. Some of the terminology has to be changed in order to reflect the association's non-trading status.

Objectives

After you have completed this chapter, you should be able to:

■   prepare the financial statements for any non-trading organisation

■   examine and critically comment on the financial statements of any club or association of which you are a member.

1 Legal status and constitution

The legal status of a members' association need not concern you, but it is something in which you should take a general interest and will help to broaden your understanding of the subject.

Non-trading organisations can range from small informal (often unincorporated) sports and social clubs to large professional bodies such as the Chartered Association of Certified Accountants, or trade unions such as the National Union of Journalists.

In cases where an association is formed for purposes that can be established as being exclusively charitable, an application can be made to the Charity Commissioners for recognition as a charity. If the registration is accepted, the association will enjoy various taxation advantages.

Most small members' clubs are unincorporated (not registered under any Act) and their constitution consists of a number of rules which its members have agreed to follow as a condition of membership. These rules are often written out on a membership card and sometimes include regulations regarding the financial statements. Unfortunately, most members tend to take very little interest in the financial affairs of their association – until something goes wrong, such as where one of the officers absconds with most of the cash!

An unincorporated association is not a separate legal person, and although this does not usually discourage suppliers (e.g. suppliers of refreshments) from dealing with the association, there is a danger that members could be held responsible for payment of their association's debts.

There are various ways in which an association can be legally constituted as a separate person and the subject can be complex.

You might be interested to learn that the Association of Certified Accountants was originally constituted as a company limited by guarantee. It was granted a Royal Charter in 1974 and then became known as the Chartered Association of Certified Accountants. Companies limited by guarantee do not have a share capital, its members guarantee to contribute a specified sum in the event that their company should become insolvent.

The financial statements of incorporated associations have to comply with the requirements of their legal constitutions. You do not have to worry about this as you will only be dealing with small informal associations. In any event, the financial statements of any non-trading organisation (incorporated or not) are prepared in a similar way.

2 Sources of funds

Non-trading organisations do not have capital in the same way as a trading concern; they raise and accumulate funds by various means, including some activities that resemble trading.

Activity 1	Think about any typical sports or social club, and make a note here of the various means by which it could raise money in order to provide (or improve) facilities for its members. Try to list about four different sources.

Some of the larger sports clubs (particularly tennis and golf clubs) issue debentures in order to raise money for new land, buildings, and equipment. These debentures are similar to those issued by a trading company and will be classified as a liability in the balance sheet. Apart from carrying the right to receive interest, these debentures quite often provide the holders with certain privileges (such as special seating facilities) at sporting events organised by the club.

3 Purpose of the financial statements

A trading concern exists in order to make profits. This profit is determined by preparing a profit and loss account under the accruals convention, and the entity's performance is often assessed by this profit.

In the case of a non-trading concern, the income statement that is analogous to the profit and loss account is called an 'income and expenditure account'. This is also prepared under the accruals convention.

But sports and social clubs do not exist in order to generate profits, they exist to meet an identified objective. Consequently, performance in financial terms is not measured by the surplus of income over expenditure but rather by the way in which the income has been spent. The primary purpose of the financial statements of a non-trading association is to account for the stewardship of the funds entrusted to it by its members. If money is raised for specific purposes, this is reflected in the financial statements by an income and expenditure account for each purpose.

In the case of a small sports or social club, there is usually one general purpose – the provision of facilities for its members. Consequently, there is usually only one income and expenditure account where the excess of income over expenditure each year is determined and then accumulated on a 'general fund'. This general fund is similar to the capital account of a sole trader, and is represented by the association's various assets and liabilities. The balance sheet is similar in appearance to that of a sole trader but with the general fund taking the place of the proprietor's capital account.

Notice how the word 'fund' is used (as it often is in accounting) to refer to an aggregate of various assets and liabilities. The balance on the general fund might represent the amount of cash that has been raised over the years but this cash will be invested in various assets (e.g. pavilions and sports equipment) provided for the benefit of members.

In some cases the association will raise funds for a specified (rather than general) purpose. A separate income and expenditure account is then prepared to determine the net amount raised each year for that purpose. These amounts are accumulated in a separate (named) fund which is then included in the 'capital' section of the balance sheet in addition to the general fund. Sometimes the assets representing these funds are specifically earmarked on the net assets side of the balance sheet, for example by being placed in a separate deposit account at the bank. But more often than not (due to poor financial control) the cash is used for general purposes and loses its separate identity. While associations like this are often called 'non profit making', it must be remembered that, if the associations are to survive, income must exceed expenditure over a period of time.

4 Format of the financial statements

Some small associations are quite content to account for their activities by presenting members with a 'receipts and payments' account. This account is nothing more than a summarised version of the cash book. In your assessments you will be required to prepare a full set of financial statements from information that includes the receipts and payments account. The financial statements required will consist of an income and expenditure account (prepared under the accruals and matching conventions) and a balance sheet.

The 'income' in the income and expenditure account is not likely to be the same as cash received in the cash book, and 'expenditure' is not likely to be the same as cash paid because of the 'accruals' adjustments.

Activity 2	Make a note of as many points as you can that explain why income might differ from receipts, and why expenditure might differ from payments. List them under the following headings:
	income/receipts expenditure/payments

The difference between total income and total expenditure is not referred to as a profit (or a loss) but as the 'excess of income over expenditure' (or the excess of expenditure over income). We could determine this excess by simply listing all the different items of income and all the different items of expenditure. But this is not likely to tell the members very much.

The club might have generated funds from various functions, such as the summer fair, the autumn bring and buy sale, and the Christmas raffle. Each one of these will have generated its own surplus or loss. There is no need to prepare a separate income and expenditure account for each function since they are all contributing to the general fund, but it is quite helpful to the membership if the income and expenses of each function are matched within the format of a single income and expenditure account. This is normally done before adding on any general items of income (such as subscriptions) and deducting general expenses such as repairs to premises.

The remaining activities in this chapter are based on the financial information provided for the Barnwood Orchard Club. This information is set out below.

The purpose of the Barnwood Orchard Club is to provide social and keep-fit facilities for its members.

The receipts and payments account for the year ending 31 December 1990 was as follows:

Receipts	£	Payments	£
Opening balance	305	Bar purchases	7,590
Bar sales	13,500	Barman's salary	2,600
Subscriptions	3,500	New bar furniture	1,095
Keep-fit course fees	4,580	New keep-fit equipment	800
		Loan repayment	200
		Loan interest	50
		General expenses	3,230
		Keep-fit tutor's salary	4,500
		Donations to charities	1,480
		Repairs to premises	110
		Closing balance	230
	21,885		21,885

The assets and liabilities of the club were as follows:

	1 Jan 1990 £	31 Dec 1990 £
Bar stock	290	410
Subscriptions in arrears	160	230
Subscriptions received in advance	35	20
Bar furniture at net book value	675	?
Keep-fit equipment at net book value	200	?
Creditors for bar stock	340	460
Loan payable	500	300
Premises	15,000	14,500

Bar furniture and keep-fit equipment should be depreciated at the rate of 10% on net book value, with a full year's depreciation in the year of purchase.

| Activity 3 | Review the information given for Barnwood Orchard Club to see if you find any separate functions for which it should be possible to match the relevant income with related expenses in order determine the gain (or loss) arising from the function. Make a note here of the ones you notice. |

The surplus arising on bar sales is determined in a separate statement and only the net income is brought into the income and expenditure account. This separate statement is drawn up on similar lines to a trading and profit and loss account and should include a calculation of the gross profit (which can be called gross income in order to avoid the word 'profit') before any expenses are deducted. The gross profit is quite important; keeping an eye on the gross profit percentage from bar sales is one of the financial controls that a small association can adopt. It should be possible to estimate the percentage expected and any marked variation between this and the actual percentage achieved should be investigated.

| Activity 4 | Make a note of the types of expense (not the amount) that will be deducted from gross income in order to determine the net income (or loss) from bar sales in the case of Barnwood Orchard Club. |

The gain or loss on 'keep-fit courses' could be shown within the income and expenditure account itself. This could be done by insetting the calculation of income and related expenses, the net result being shown in the main income column.

| Activity 5 | Make a note of the types of expense that will be deducted from the keep-fit course fees in the case of Barnwood Orchard Club. |

5 Finding the missing figures

In order to calculate figures for the financial statements you must approach the problem in the same way as you did for a trading organisation. In order to encourage you to develop a methodical approach (and deal with any problems peculiar to clubs) you should work through the following Activities and check each one with the Key before proceeding to the next.

| **Activity 6** | The opening balance on the general fund will be equal to the club's assets minus liabilities at the beginning of the year. Calculate this figure now and make a note of it here. |

There are two other workings that are worth doing before you start to draft out the statements.

| **Activity 7** | Calculate the amount to include in the bar trading account for purchases. |

| **Activity 8** | Calculate the amount to be included in the income and expenditure account for subscriptions. Take care with this one – subscriptions is an income item, not an expense. |

| **Activity 9** | Subscriptions for the year is another figure over which the members can keep a watchful eye. It is usually possible to predict what the amount for subscriptions should be in the financial statements. Make a note of how this could be done. |

| **Activity 10** | You can do the remaining workings as you draft the financial statements. You should do these now, using your own paper. Deal with the separate income statement for the bar first. This is given various names but you should call it 'Income from bar sales'. It is not really a bar trading account since the club is not trading in the usual sense of the word. |

Summary

The main learning points in this chapter are:

- the financial statements of a non-trading organisation are based on the same principles as a trading concern

- the purpose of the financial statements is to show the income received and the way this income has been spent

- income is raised by various means and the excess of income over expenditure (or of expenditure over income) for each year is accumulated in a general fund

- the general fund is similar to a sole trader's capital account

- if the association raises funds for a specific purpose, a separate income and expenditure account is prepared and the net income is accumulated in a separate fund account

- most clubs raise funds by various activities and the net gain or loss on each activity is presented in the income and expenditure account by matching income from that activity with its related expenditure

- in cases where funds are raised by activities that are similar to trading (such as running a bar or a dining room) the net income from such activities should be calculated on a separate statement; the net income is then shown as a single figure in the income and expenditure account.

Key to Chapter 5 activities

Activity 1

There is no one definitive answer to this question. The most obvious sources include: (1) members' subscriptions; (2) profits from bar sales; (3) surpluses from activities such as fairs, gate entrance fees and raffles; (4) donations from various sources; (5) legacies.

Activity 2

The learning point of this activity will have been made if you came up with lists similar to the following:

Income/receipts	Expenditure/payments
1 subscriptions owing or prepaid 2 receipts include sale of assets 3 receipts include loans received	1 expenditure recognises creditors, accruals, prepayments, and stocks 2 payments include purchase of fixed assets 3 expenditure includes depreciation 4 payments include repayment of loans

Activity 3

There are only two: (1) bar sales and (2) keep-fit courses.

Activity 4

There are two: (1) barman's salary and (2) depreciation on bar furniture.

Activity 5

There are two: (1) the keep-fit tutor's salary and (2) depreciation on keep fit equipment.

Activity 6

The answer is £15,755. If you did not come up with this figure you may have forgotten the opening bank balance (it isn't in the list of balances). Hopefully you will have recognised that subscriptions in arrears are debtors and subscriptions in advance are creditors.

Activity 7

The amount is £7,710 (i.e. 7,590 + 460 – 340).

Activity 8

The amount is £3,585. Subscriptions very nearly always involve making adjustments for income due and income prepaid. If you find this awkward to handle, set out a 'T' account as follows:

Subscriptions

Subs in arrears b/d	160	Subs in advance b/d	35
Subs in advance c/d	20	Subs in arrears c/d	230
Income from subs	3,585	Bank account	3,500
(balance)	3,765		3,765

Activity 9

From the number of members times the annual subscription.

Activity 10

Barnwood Orchard Club.

Income from bar sales
for year ended 31 December 1990

Sales		13,500
Less cost of sales:		
Opening bar stock	290	
Purchases	7,710	
	8,000	
Closing bar stock	410	
		7,590
Gross income		5,910
Bar expenses:		
Barman's salary	2,600	
Depreciation of furniture	177	
		2,777
Net income		3,133

Income and expenditure account
for year ended 31 December 1990

Net income from bar sales			3,133
Loss on keep-fit courses:			
Fees received		4,580	
Tutor's salary	4,500		
Depreciation of equipment	100	4,600	
			(20)
Income from subscriptions			3,585
Total income			6,698
Expenditure:			
Loan interest		50	
General expenses		3,230	
Donations to charities		1,480	
Repairs to premises		110	
Depreciation of premises		500	
			5,370
Excess of income over expenditure			1,328

Balance sheet
at 31 December 1990

Fixed assets:

Premises at net book value		14,500
Bar furniture at net book value		1,593
Keep fit equipment at net book value		900
		16,993

Current assets:

Bar stock	410	
Subscriptions in arrears	230	
Bank balance	230	
	870	

Current liabilities:

Creditors for bar stock	460	
Subscriptions in advance	20	
	480	
		390
Total assets less current liabilities		17,383
Loan payable		300
		17,083

General fund:

Accumulated balance at 1 January 1990		15,755
Excess of income over expenditure		1,328
Accumulated balance at 31 December 1990		17,083

Guidance note:

The depreciation of £500 on the premises was a little sneaky (see schedule under the receipts and payments account) and you should not be too cross with yourself if you missed it – but it does emphasise the importance of reading very carefully all the information you are given.

Chapter 6
The extended trial balance

Introduction

The extended trial balance is a tool used by accountants to bring together the accounting balances extracted from the nominal ledger. This follows the routine entry of transactions over an accounting period and the end-of-period adjustments – i.e. adjustments for stocks, depreciation, bad and doubtful debts and accruals and pre-payments.

The extended trial balance is designed to incorporate any corrections necessary for errors in the period entries to the nominal ledger, to incorporate the adjustment necessary to complete the accounts and to provide for final presentation of a set of figures for the period profit and loss as well as figures to represent the balance sheet of the organisation.

Objectives

After you have completed this chapter, you should be able to:

- list and total nominal ledger balances at the end of a financial period in a basic trial balance

- create appropriate suspense accounts to reflect any differences found in the basic trial balance

- clear any trial balance suspense accounts by making appropriate trial balance extension entries to the suspense accounts and other accounts listed in the trial balance

- enter any end-of-period adjustments for stocks, depreciation, bad and doubtful debts, accruals and pre-payments into an extension of the trial balance

- extract income and expenditure (profit and loss) figures from the extended trial balance figures you have prepared, thus leaving balance sheet items in the remaining extended trial balance figures

- present final balance sheet figures in the end columns of the extended trial balance.

1 Producing a basic trial balance

The entries made over a financial period into the nominal ledger will reflect all transactions recorded in the organisation's daybooks over the period.

Entries will be made from the sales, purchases, sales returns and purchases returns daybooks, the receipts and payments cashbooks and petty cash daybook. The entries made over a period into the nominal ledger should result in a set of accounts with total debits equal to total credits. A listing can then be produced with the names of the nominal ledger accounts alongside their respective balances. If the balances are listed in columns, with separate columns for debits and credits, the total of the debit column should equal the total of the credit column – providing some degree of cross-check for, and confidence in, the entries from the day-books to the nominal ledger.

Activity 1	A listing of account balances as taken from a set of business accounts following day-book entry appears below. Total the debits and credits and check they agree.
	If they do not agree, suggest why they do not.

Trial Balance as at 31st Dec. 1993:

NL	Account	£	£
1	Acc. dep'n – fixed assets		16,100
2	Capital		28,000
3	Cash at bank	1,420	
4	Depreciation expense		
5	Bad debts expense		
6	Fixed assets	54,820	
7	Inland Revenue		1,780
8	Loan		22,000
9	Office & general exp.	9,800	
10	Petty cash	240	
11	Profit and loss (retained)		13,000
12	Purchases	16,280	
13	Purchases ledger control		4,160
14	Purchase returns		520
15	Provision for bad debts		
16	Sales		42,200
17	Sales ledger control	17,110	
18	Sales returns	210	
19	Staff salaries	2,320	
20	Stocks	17,360	
21			
22	VAT		4,200

It is usual to investigate immediately if any differences occur in the trial balance. Before doing so, however, it is usual to make the trial balance balance, with total debits equalling total credits by entering a figure into the trial balance which is listed as a suspense account balance.

Activity 2

Enter an appropriate balance into the listings recorded above to make the total of debits and credits agree.

Note the difference as a suspense account balance and appropriately record the balance in the correct column – i.e. either as a debit or credit. An appropriate space has been left to record the entry (NL 21).

The possible areas of error that have given rise to the suspense account would now be carefully investigated. The idea would be to locate the errors and correct for them by extending the basic trial balance.

2 Adjustments for error in the basic trial balance

The following activities are based on the details given in Activities 1 and 2.

Activity 3

Investigation has now taken place into the suspense account balance that has been registered in your trial balance. The errors that have been located are listed below.

Make a note beside each error of the correction entries that should be made, carefully noting which accounts should be debited and which should be credited.

Each correction should result in an entry to the suspense account. Provided all errors have been located the suspense account should be cleared by your correcting entries.

Error located	Debit Account	Credit Account
1. Total invoiced sales figure overstated in sales daybook by £2,200		
2. Purchases net of VAT understated by £3,000 in the purchases daybook		
3. Fixed assets were transcribed incorrectly into the trial balance and should be £64,820		
4. Accumulated depreciation is incorrectly recorded and should be £14,500		

Your investigation should clear the suspense account. The net debit or credit to the suspense account from your adjustments should therefore clear the suspense balance you calculated in Activity 2.

Activity 4

Total the debits and credits made to the suspense account and check that they will indeed clear your suspense balance. Show the suspense account.

These adjustments will now be entered into the extended trial balance.

The Extended Trial Balance - 31st December 1993

NL		Dr.	Cr.	Adjustments Dr.	Cr.	Accruals/PPMTs Dr.	Cr.	Profit & Loss Dr.	Cr.	Balance Sheet Dr.	Cr.
1	Acc. Depreciation		16,100								
2	Capital		28,000								
3	Cash at Bank	1,420									
4	Depreciation Exp.										
5	Bad debts exp.										
6	Fixed assets	54,820									
7	Inland revenue		1,780								
8	Loan		22,000								
9	Office & gen. exp.	9,800									
10	Petty cash	240									
11	Profit and loss		13,000								
12	Purchases	16,280									
13	Purchases Ledger Control		4,160								
14	Purchases returns		520								
15	Prov. for bad debts										
16	Sales		42,200								
17	Sales Ledger Control	17,110									
18	Sales returns	210									
19	Staff salaries	2,320									
20	Stocks	17,350									
21	Suspense	12,400									
22	VAT		4,200								
	TOTALS	131,960	131,960								

Activity 5	Using the columns marked 'Adjustments', write in the correcting debits and credits to the nominal account balances in the extended trial balance. Simply show the adjustment figure as a debit or credit in the 'Adjustment' column. We will work revised figures for the nominal ledger balances later, by combining the original balances with the adjustments. Do not work revised totals at this stage or total your adjustment columns.

3 End-of-period adjustments

We will now make adjustments in the extended trial balance for the traditional end-of-period adjustments. It is important that you understand the logic of the entries that follow and how they finally help to produce correct statement balances for profit and loss and the balance sheet. Firstly we shall deal with depreciation.

Activity 6	The business has to provide for depreciation. Its policy is to provide 12% depreciation on a reducing balance basis. Compute the period depreciation figure (accounts are being produced for the full year to 31st December 1993). Work to the nearest £ only. The fixed assets balance is £64,820, the accumulated depreciation figure is £14,500. What is the figure to which the depreciation percentage is to be applied? Note the accounts to be debited and credited below: Depreciation Amount: Debit Credit

The depreciation for the period will need to be charged ultimately to profit and loss but will first be recorded in an expense account.

Activity 7

The business has to deal with bad and doubtful debts. Its specific bad debts are £2,200. In addition, its policy is to set aside a 5% provision on the balance of the sales ledger control account after specific bad debts. The sales ledger control account balance in the trial balance before adjustment is £17,110.

What is the figure from which the figure for the provision of doubtful debts is to be calculated?

Compute the bad and doubtful debts figures for the period. Work to the nearest £ only.

Note the accounts to be debited and credited below:

Amounts: Debit   Credit

We will now enter the figures for depreciation and bad and doubtful debts in the extended trial balance as adjustment figures.

Activity 8

Enter the depreciation and bad and doubtful debts figures into the extended trial balance as adjustment figures in the adjustment columns.

Now total the adjustment columns to ensure they cross-check – i.e. that total debits equal total credits.

We will now make adjustments for accruals and pre-payments.

Activity 9

General office expenses for the business is prepaid by £3,200; staff salaries are to be accrued by £400. Use the accruals and pre-payments (PPMTS) column in the extended trial balance to make adjustments to the expense figures in the expense accounts – to provide for entry into profit and loss.

Enter the accruals and pre-payments figures in accruals and pre-payments (PPMTS) column in the extended trial balance.

These are the only accruals and pre-payments. Enter the totals at the bottom of the accruals and PPMTS columns.

The accrual made for staff salaries must show as a liability figure in the balance sheet. Similarly, the general office expense pre-payment must show as an asset. This is why arrows are shown on the extended trial balance – to remind you to include these items in the balance sheet.

Note that the arrows imply that you must take the total of each of the columns into the balance sheet. This is because we have only one accrual and one pre-payment. Therefore the total of the accruals column equals the single accrual, and the total of the pre-payment column equals the single pre-payment. Obviously, if we had many accruals and pre-payments, we could not transfer the column totals – we would have to transfer each single item to the appropriate place in the balance sheet.

| Activity 10 | Enter the accruals and pre-payments figures into the balance sheet columns of the extended trial balance in accordance with the arrows.

Check that you agree with the nature of the balances in the balance sheet. |
|---|---|

Finally, we will make adjustments for the stocks; in particular, the closing stock balance. Note that the closing stock will result in an asset being recorded in the balance sheet (i.e. a debit) and a credit appearing in the profit and loss account, to be offset, as usual, against the costs of opening stocks and purchases.

Activity 11	The closing stock for the business is £18,000. Make appropriate entries for this figure into the profit and loss and balance sheet columns.

Now that we have made all the adjustments, we just have to total the figures in each row in the extended trial balance and record them appropriately in the profit and loss and balance sheet columns.

| Activity 12 | Review the extended trial balance and decide which rows need to be transferred into profit and loss. You must identify income and expenditure of the period. Transfer the balance of each of these rows into the profit and loss columns.

If a profit or loss is made, the profit and loss debit and credit columns will not balance. In this case the credits will total more than the debits. A profit has been, made so enter a DEBIT in the profit and loss row (11) in the profit and loss columns to make the two columns agree.

Where does that net balance need to be transferred to? |
|---|---|

As the profit figure belongs to the business owners it must be appropriately adjusted into the balance sheet. Making a profit causes retained profits to increase.

| Activity 13 | Enter a figure for retained profits into the profit and loss row in the balance sheet.

The retained profits figure should be the figure brought forward in the trial balance plus the new profit figure for the latest period. |
|---|---|

We can now complete the balance sheet columns by carrying the remaining balances in each row that represents a balance sheet item into the final two columns. The nature of accounting means that all balances now remaining (assets, liabilities and capital) must be shown on the balance sheet.

| Activity 14 | Enter figures into the balance sheet columns of the extended trial balance for all rows that contain a balance sheet figure.

This should mean including a figure for every row that was not taken across into the profit and loss columns.

Total up the balance sheet columns – they should now agree. |
|---|---|

If your balance sheet columns agree then your extended trial balance is correct and complete.

If you have been successful, you should write out your profit and loss account and balance sheet into vertical statements.

| Activity 15 | Use the proforma given below to enter the profit and loss statement directly from the figures in your extended trial balance. |

Profit and loss account for the year ended 31 December 1993

	£	£
Sales		
Less: Sales returns		_____
Opening stock		
Purchases		
Less: Purchase returns	_____	
Less: Closing stock	_____	
Cost of sales		_____
Gross profit		
General expenses:		
Depreciation		
Bad debts		
General office expense		
Staff salaries	_____	
		_____
Net profit		=====

| Activity 16 | Finally, use the proforma given below to produce the balance sheet directly from the figures in your extended trial balance. |

Balance Sheet as at 31st December 1993:

	£	£

Fixed Assets
Current Assets:
    Stock
    Debtors
    Less: Provision for bad debts
    Pre-payments
    Bank
    Cash   ————

Current Liabilities:
    Creditors
    Inland revenue
    VAT
    Accruals   ————

Net Current Assets: ————

Total assets less current liabilities: ————

Financed by:
Capital:
    Brought forward
    Profits   ————

Creditors due after one year
Long term loan   ————
          ————

Summary

Having worked through this chapter, you should be able to prepare a fully extended trial balance, and from this prepare a profit and loss account and a balance sheet.

Notice that there is nothing new in the content of the extended trial balance (ETB); it simply summarises the book-keeping and accounting you have been using in earlier chapters to enable you to prepare a profit and loss account and a balance sheet that balances.

Key to Chapter 6 activities

Activity 1

The total figure for debits is £119,560.
The total figure for credits is 131,960.

The difference must be attributed to either incorrect entries or totalling of figures in the daybooks, incorrect transfer for figures into the nominal ledger, incorrect balancing of accounts in the nominal ledger or incorrect transfer of amounts from the nominal ledger to the listings.

Activity 2

The amended trial balance should appear as follows:

Trial Balance as at 31st Dec. 1993:

NL	Account	£	£
1	Acc. dep'n – fixed assets		16,100
2	Capital		28,000
3	Cash at bank	1,420	
4	Depreciation expense		
5	Bad debts expense		
6	Fixed assets	54,820	
7	Inland Revenue		1,780
8	Loan		22,000
9	Office & general exp.	9,800	
10	Petty cash	240	
11	Profit and loss (retained)		13,000
12	Purchases	16,280	
13	Purchases ledger control		4,160
14	Purchase returns		520
15	Provision for bad debts		
16	Sales		42,200
17	Sales ledger control	17,110	
18	Sales returns	210	
19	Staff salaries	2,320	
20	Stocks	17,360	
21	**Suspense**	**12,400**	
22	VAT		4,200
		131,960	131,960

Activity 3

The correcting entries should be as follows:

Error located		Debit Account	Credit Account
1.	Total invoiced sales figure overstated in sales daybook by £2,200	Suspense	Sales ledger
2.	Purchases net of VAT understated by £3,000 in the purchases daybook	Purchases ledger	Suspense
3.	Fixed assets were transcribed incorrectly into the trial balance and should be £64,820	Fixed assets	Suspense
4.	Accumulated depreciation is incorrectly recorded and should be £14,500	Accumulated depreciation	Suspense

Activity 4

The balance in the suspense account was £12,400 debit. The adjustments from Activity 3 give a debit to suspense of £2,200 and credits totalling £14,600; thus giving a net £12,400 and therefore a balance that will clear the suspense account.

Suspense

Balance	12,400	Purchases	3,000
Sales Ledger Control	2,200	Fixed Assets	10,000
		Acc. Depreciation	1,600
	14,600		14,600

Activity 5

The extended trial balance is shown on the next page.

Activity 6

The figure on which depreciation is to be calculated is £64,820 - £14,500 = £50,320. The depreciation amount is 0.12 x £50,320 = £6,038.

Depreciation Amount:	Debit	Credit
£6,038	Depreciation expense	Accumulated depreciation

Activity 7

The figure from which the provision for bad debts is to be calculated is £17,110 - £2,200 = £14,910.

Amounts:	Debit	Credit
£2,946	Bad debts expense	
£2,200		Sales ledger control
£746		Provision for bad debts

The method being used here is one in which actual bad debts and creating/increasing doubtful debts provision are all entered in a 'bad debts expense' account.

Activity 5

The Extended Trial Balance – 31st December 1993

NL		Dr.	Cr.	Adjustments Dr.	Adjustments Cr.	Accruals/PPMTs Dr.	Accruals/PPMTs Cr.	Profit & Loss Dr.	Profit & Loss Cr.	Balance Sheet Dr.	Balance Sheet Cr.
1	Acc. Depreciation		16,100	1,600							
2	Capital		28,000								
3	Cash at Bank	1,420									
4	Depreciation Exp.										
5	Bad debts exp.										
6	Fixed assets	54,820		10,000							
7	Inland revenue		1,780								
8	Loan		22,000								
9	Office & gen. exp.	9,800									
10	Petty cash	240									
11	Profit and loss		13,000								
12	Purchases	16,280		3,000							
13	Purchases Ledger Control		4,160								
14	Purchases returns		520								
15	Prov. for bad debts										
16	Sales		42,200		2,200						
17	Sales Ledger Control	17,110									
18	Sales returns	210									
19	Staff salaries	2,320									
20	Stocks	17,360									
21	Suspense	12,400			12,400						
22	VAT		4,200								
	TOTALS	131,960	131,960								

Activity 8

The Extended Trial Balance – 31st December 1993

NL		Dr.	Cr.	Adjustments Dr.	Adjustments Cr.	Accruals/PPMTs Dr.	Accruals/PPMTs Cr.	Profit & Loss Dr.	Profit & Loss Cr.	Balance Sheet Dr.	Balance Sheet Cr.
1	Acc. Depreciation		16,100	1,600	6,038						
2	Capital		28,000								
3	Cash at Bank	1,420									
4	Depreciation Exp.			6,038							
5	Bad debts exp.			2,946							
6	Fixed assets	54,820		10,000							
7	Inland revenue		1,780								
8	Loan		22,000								
9	Office & gen. exp.	9,800									
10	Petty cash	240									
11	Profit and loss		13,000								
12	Purchases	16,280		3,000							
13	Purchases Ledger Control		4,160								
14	Purchases returns		520								
15	Prov. for bad debts				746						
16	Sales		42,200								
17	Sales Ledger Control	17,110			2x2,200						
18	Sales returns	210									
19	Staff salaries	2,320									
20	Stocks	17,360									
21	Suspense	12,400			12,400						
22	VAT		4,200								
	TOTALS	131,960	131,960	23,584	23,584						

Activity 9

The Extended Trial Balance – 31st December 1993

NL		Dr.	Cr.	Adjustments Dr.	Adjustments Cr.	Accruals/PPMTs Dr.	Accruals/PPMTs Cr.	Profit & Loss Dr.	Profit & Loss Cr.	Balance Sheet Dr.	Balance Sheet Cr.
1	Acc. Depreciation		16,100	1,600	6,038						
2	Capital		28,000								
3	Cash at Bank	1,420									
4	Depreciation Exp.			6,038							
5	Bad debts exp.			2,946							
6	Fixed assets	54,820		10,000							
7	Inland revenue		1,780								
8	Loan		22,000								
9	Office & gen. exp.	9,800					3,200				
10	Petty cash	240									
11	Profit and loss		13,000	3,000							
12	Purchases	16,280									
13	Purchases Ledger Control		4,160								
14	Purchases returns		520								
15	Prov. for bad debts				746						
16	Sales		42,200								
17	Sales Ledger Control	17,110			2x2,200						
18	Sales returns	210									
19	Staff salaries	2,320				400					
20	Stocks	17,360									
21	Suspense	12,400			12,400						
22	VAT		4,200								
	TOTALS	131,960	131,960	23,584	23,584	400	3,200				

Activity 10

The Extended Trial Balance – 31st December 1993

NL		Dr.	Cr.	Adjustments Dr.	Adjustments Cr.	Accruals/PPMTs Dr.	Accruals/PPMTs Cr.	Profit & Loss Dr.	Profit & Loss Cr.	Balance Sheet Dr.	Balance Sheet Cr.
1	Acc. Depreciation		16,100	1,600	6,038						
2	Capital		28,000								
3	Cash at Bank	1,420									
4	Depreciation Exp.			6,038							
5	Bad debts exp.			2,946							
6	Fixed assets	54,820		10,000							
7	Inland revenue		1,780								
8	Loan		22,000								
9	Office & gen. exp.	9,800					3,200			3,200	
10	Petty cash	240									
11	Profit and loss		13,000								
12	Purchases	16,280		3,000							
13	Purchases Ledger Control		4,160								
14	Purchases returns		520								
15	Prov. for bad debts				746						
16	Sales		42,200								
17	Sales Ledger Control	17,110			2x2,200						
18	Sales returns	210									
19	Staff salaries	2,320				400					400
20	Stocks	17,360									
21	Suspense	12,400			12,400						
22	VAT		4,200								
	TOTALS	131,960	131,960	23,584	23,584	400	3,200				

3,200

400

Activity 11

The Extended Trial Balance – 31st December 1993

NL		Dr.	Cr.	Adjustments Dr.	Adjustments Cr.	Accruals/PPMTs Dr.	Accruals/PPMTs Cr.	Profit & Loss Dr.	Profit & Loss Cr.	Balance Sheet Dr.	Balance Sheet Cr.
1	Acc. Depreciation		16,100	1,600	6,038						
2	Capital		28,000								
3	Cash at Bank	1,420									
4	Depreciation Exp.			6,038							
5	Bad debts exp.			2,946							
6	Fixed assets	54,820		10,000							
7	Inland revenue		1,780								
8	Loan		22,000								
9	Office & gen. exp.	9,800					3,200			3,200	
10	Petty cash	240									
11	Profit and loss										
12	Purchases	16,280	13,000	3,000							
13	Purchases Ledger Control		4,160								
14	Purchases returns		520								
15	Prov. for bad debts				746						
16	Sales		42,200								
17	Sales Ledger Control	17,110			2x2,200						
18	Sales returns	210									
19	Staff salaries	2,320				400					400
20	Stocks	17,360						18,000	18,000	18,000	
21	Suspense	12,400			12,400						
22	VAT		4,200								
	TOTALS	131,960	131,960	23,584	23,584	400	3,200				

Activity 12

The Extended Trial Balance – 31st December 1993

NL		Dr.	Cr.	Adjustments Dr.	Adjustments Cr.	Accruals/PPMTs Dr.	Accruals/PPMTs Cr.	Profit & Loss Dr.	Profit & Loss Cr.	Balance Sheet Dr.	Balance Sheet Cr.
1	Acc. Depreciation		16,100	1,600	6,038						
2	Capital		28,000								
3	Cash at Bank	1,420									
4	Depreciation Exp.			6,038				6,038			
5	Bad debts exp.			2,946				2,946			
6	Fixed assets	54,820		10,000							
7	Inland revenue		1,780								
8	Loan		22,000								
9	Office & gen. exp.	9,800					3,200	6,600		3,200	
10	Petty cash	240									
11	Profit and loss		13,000					5,566			
12	Purchases	16,280		3,000				19,280			
13	Purchases Ledger Control		4,160								
14	Purchases returns		520						520		
15	Prov. for bad debts				746						
16	Sales		42,200						42,200		
17	Sales Ledger Control	17,110			2x2,200						
18	Sales returns	210						210			
19	Staff salaries	2,320				400		2,720			400
20	Stocks	17,360						17,360	18,000	18,000	
21	Suspense	12,400			12,400						
22	VAT		4,200								
	TOTALS	131,960	131,960	23,584	23,584	400	3,200	60,720	60,720		

Activity 13

The Extended Trial Balance – 31st December 1993

NL		Dr.	Cr.	Adjustments Dr.	Adjustments Cr.	Accruals/PPMTs Dr.	Accruals/PPMTs Cr.	Profit & Loss Dr.	Profit & Loss Cr.	Balance Sheet Dr.	Balance Sheet Cr.
1	Acc. Depreciation		16,100	1,600	6,038						
2	Capital		28,000								
3	Cash at Bank	1,420									
4	Depreciation Exp.			6,038				6,038			
5	Bad debts exp.			2,946				2,946			
6	Fixed assets	54,820		10,000							
7	Inland revenue		1,780								
8	Loan		22,000								
9	Office & gen. exp.	9,800					3,200	6,600		3,200	
10	Petty cash	240									
11	Profit and loss		13,000					5,566			18,566
12	Purchases	16,280		3,000				19,280			
13	Purchases Ledger Control		4,160								
14	Purchases returns		520						520		
15	Prov. for bad debts				746						
16	Sales		42,200						42,200		
17	Sales Ledger Control	17,110			2x2,200						
18	Sales returns	210						210			
19	Staff salaries	2,320				400		2,720			400
20	Stocks	17,360						17,360	18,000	18,000	
21	Suspense	12,400			12,400						
22	VAT		4,200								
	TOTALS	131,960	131,960	23,584	23,584	400	3,200	60,720	60,720		

Activity 14

The Extended Trial Balance – 31st December 1993

NL		Dr.	Cr.	Adjustments Dr.	Adjustments Cr.	Accruals/PPMTs Dr.	Accruals/PPMTs Cr.	Profit & Loss Dr.	Profit & Loss Cr.	Balance Sheet Dr.	Balance Sheet Cr.
1	Acc. Depreciation		16,100	1,600	6,038						20,538
2	Capital		28,000								28,000
3	Cash at Bank	1,420								1,420	
4	Depreciation Exp.			6,038				6,038			
5	Bad debts exp.			2,946				2,946			
6	Fixed assets	54,820		10,000						64,820	
7	Inland revenue		1,780								1,780
8	Loan		22,000								22,000
9	Office & gen. exp.	9,800					3,200	6,600		3,200	
10	Petty cash	240								240	
11	Profit and loss		13,000					5,566			18,566
12	Purchases	16,280		3,000				19,280			
13	Purchases Ledger Control		4,160								4,160
14	Purchases returns		520						520		
15	Prov. for bad debts				746						746
16	Sales		42,200						42,200		
17	Sales Ledger Control	17,110			2x2,200					12,710	
18	Sales returns	210						210			
19	Staff salaries	2,320				400		2,720			400
20	Stocks	17,360						17,360	18,000	18,000	
21	Suspense	12,400			12,400						
22	VAT		4,200								4,200
	TOTALS	131,960	131,960	23,584	23,584	400	3,200	60,720	60,720	100,390	100,390

Activity 15

Profit and loss account for the year ended 31 December 1993

	£	£
Sales		42,200
Less: Sales returns		210
		41,990
Opening stock	17,360	
Purchases	19,280	
Less: Purchase returns	(520)	
	36,120	
Less: Closing stock	18,000	
Cost of sales		18,120
Gross profit		23,870
General expenses:		
Depreciation	6,038	
Bad debts	2,946	
General office expense	6,600	
Staff salaries	2,720	
		18,304
Net profit		5,566

Activity 16

Balance Sheet as at 31st December 1993:

	£	£
Fixed Assets		44,282
Current Assets:		
Stock	18,000	
Debtors	12,710	
Less: Provision for bad debts	(746)	
Pre-payments	3,200	
Bank	1,420	
Cash	240	
	34,824	
Current Liabilities:		
Creditors	4,160	
Inland revenue	1,780	
VAT	4,200	
Accruals	400	
	10,540	
Net Current Assets:		24,284
Total assets less current liabilities:		68,566
Financed by:		
Capital:		
Brought forward	28,000	
Retained profits	18,566	
		46,566
Long term loan		22,000
		68,566

Introduction to Part 3: Cost Accounting

The learning material in this part of the book has been written on the assumption that it will be used as a sequel to the two financial accounting parts of the book. Although the subject of cost and management accounting is usually separated from financial accounting, it is an integral part of an overall information system, designed to assist management with their stewardship responsibilities. The managers of an enterprise have many responsibilities but we can identify three that are supported by the accounting function, namely:

- ensuring that business operations provide an adequate profit on the funds entrusted to them by the shareholders
- safeguarding the company's assets accumulated through trade
- reporting the results of business activities to the shareholders.

All three are regarded as a part of the directors' stewardship function. Directors are held responsible by the shareholders for the profitable use of resources in a large and complex business unit. Their task would be impossible without an adequate information system.

The system for recording transactions as they occur, and then reporting to the shareholders on the results of trading for a past period, are covered in other parts of this book. That particular part of the information system is usually called financial accounting. The book-keeping aspects covered by the financial accounting course can be applied to almost any business but will not be adequate to cope with the information needs of most manufacturing companies.

All organisations require an additional sub-system to determine the cost of individual products (goods or services). This information is needed for both financial accounting purposes (profit measurement and stock valuation) and management accounting purposes (to monitor profit margins). The sub-system used in this process is called 'cost accounting'. Cost accounting is an integral part of a double-entry book-keeping system.

The essential purpose of the costing system is to find the costs of whatever goods or services are produced by an organisation. In the UK, many organisations produce services rather than goods.

Throughout most of this course we will be taking our examples from manufacturing firms for convenience. However, cost accounting is relevant to all types of organisation. Airlines will want to know the cost per passenger mile on all of their operating routes, hospitals will want to know the cost per day of keeping a patient in hospital, and so on.

For costing purposes, there are two classes of business and five different costing methods.

Specific order businesses

Here orders are received by the customer before production commences. Specific order businesses will choose from three types of costing method, depending on their actual business:

- contract costing is used by businesses such as ship-builders and large buildings contractors, where the contract is long-term and the product units are large

- job costing is used by plumbers, electricians and suppliers of small items of furniture, where the job is smaller in scale and will take less time to complete

- batch costing is similar to job costing, but implies that the customer requires more than one unit of the same product – perhaps 50 reams of letterhead paper, or 200 football shirts for a professional football team.

Operation businesses

Here production is followed by sale to the customer. Operation businesses will choose from two types of costing, depending on whether their products are goods and/or services:

- process costing, or continuous operation costing, is used when costing the majority of items found in our shops, such as books and hi-fi units

- service costing is used by hospitals, bus companies, banks and other service industries. The major point about service costing is that it is often difficult to identify a product or cost unit.

The role of management accounting includes the provision of information from the cost accounting system, but it goes well beyond the task of preparing a detailed analysis of past results. The directors have the responsibility of making the most profitable use of funds entrusted to them by the shareholders and so they will need accounting information to help with the following:

- making business decisions
- planning and controlling business operations.

In these two areas, the accounting information is based on forward-looking projections and forecasts. Information for decision making is usually provided on an *ad hoc* basis and does not form part of any regular system of reporting to management. On the other hand, planning and controlling relies on a system of budgeting, and the comparison of actual results with the budget on a regular basis (usually monthly). Differences between budgeted and actual results are analysed in such a way as to help management to take remedial action where operations are not proceeding according to plan.

Chapter 1

The accounts of a manufacturer

Introduction

Parts 1 and 2 dealt with the basic system for recording transactions and reporting the results of business activity in the form of financial statements. The concepts and mechanics of that system form a bedrock upon which financial accounting studies are based.

Most of your remaining studies in financial accounting will be concerned with the specific accounting problems presented by the type of business entity. Some of these problems stem from the different forms of ownership, and some from the different forms of economic activity.

In this chapter you will learn how the basic system has to be modified in order to deal with the problems specific to a manufacturing business.

Objectives

After you have completed this chapter, you should be able to:

■   outline the role of cost accounting in management information systems.

1 The accounting problem

In previous chapters, business activity was confined to buying goods for resale. This made it relatively easy to determine the cost of sales for any particular period.

The main difference between a retailer/wholesaler and a manufacturer as far as cost of sales is concerned is that a retailer simply incurs the cost of purchasing goods for resale whereas a manufacturer will incur the cost of making them. The main problem that we need to address, therefore, is how the financial accounting system could be used to determine the cost of making the finished goods during the period.

Before studying that particular point, however, it would be helpful if you focused your attention on the trading account. At the trading account level, there are broad similarities between the figures for a retailer and the figures for a manufacturer. The cost of making the finished goods will simply take the place of the cost of purchases when determining cost of sales.

Activity 1	In the case of a retailer, cost of sales is determined from the basic equation: *opening stock + purchases – closing stock*. Set out the basic equation which would apply to a manufacturer.

Note that the stock being referred to in Activity 1 is the stock of finished goods. This description identifies an important concept because a manufacturer will have various kinds of stock at any particular accounting date, but it is only the stock of finished goods (those ready for sale) that is used in this form of the cost of sales calculation. This finished goods stock is brought into the books at cost, although determining the cost is somewhat more of a problem than in the case of a retailer.

Activity 2	See if you can describe another class of closing stock that a manufacturer could be holding at the accounting date, other than finished goods:

There will often be another class of stock known as 'work-in-progress'. These are goods which are in the process of manufacture but are not yet completed. This will happen where the manufacturing process is spread over a number of days, weeks or months.

Both the stock of raw materials and the stock of work-in-progress (if any) will be taken into account when determining the cost of finished goods manufactured during the period.

In financial accounting, the cost of making finished goods during the period is determined by preparing an additional statement known as a 'manufacturing account'. This statement precedes the trading account and so the full set of statements from which net profit is determined could be referred to as: manufacturing, trading, and profit and loss account.

2 Manufacturing costs

Given that the purpose of the manufacturing account is to determine the cost of all finished goods manufactured during the period, the first step in trying to make sense of this account is to consider the way in which such costs might be classified.

Activity 3	Think about an imaginary factory (or perhaps one that you know about) and make a list of some of the costs that are likely to be incurred in the manufacture of finished goods.

The costs referred to in this answer (and probably in your own) have been described by what is known as their natural classification. We have described them according to the nature of the cost.

It is more usual to group costs under 'functional' headings. Each type of cost can be included under one of four main functional headings, namely:

    Direct materials
    Direct labour
    Direct expenses
    Indirect costs (or overheads).

Direct materials are those materials that can be conveniently identified and recorded as a constituent part of the cost of a finished product. Think about a table. There could be a wooden top screwed to a steel frame and legs. It would be relatively easy to keep a record of the timber and steel used to make such a table and these would be classified as direct materials.

Some of the materials used to make this imaginary table cannot be easily measured as forming a part of its direct cost and will have to be classified as indirect materials or overheads.

Activity 4	List some of the materials that might have been used which cannot be directly identified and recorded as a constituent part of the final product.

The same consideration applies to labour costs. The expression 'direct labour' refers to the employees who are actually involved in putting the finished product together.

<table>
<tr><td></td><td>There will be many other employees in the factory, other than those who are directly involved in making the finished product. Make a list of some of these employees.</td></tr>
</table>

The cost of wages paid to these members of staff is referred to as 'indirect labour' and, as with indirect materials, the cost forms part of the total of manufacturing overheads. Clearly, there are many other manufacturing overheads apart from indirect materials and indirect labour, for example electricity, depreciation of manufacturing plant, and so on.

Direct expenses are any costs, other than those of material issued from stores and labour costs recorded in the payroll, that can be specifically identified with product units. These include items such as patents, royalties, copyrights and payments to sub-contractors where those payments can be linked to product units.

As you study cost accounting, and the cost of individual products, you will find that the main difference between direct and indirect costs is that a basis has to be found for spreading indirect costs over all the products made – whereas direct costs are specifically attributed to particular products. A good part of your cost accounting study is directed towards learning the various ways in which overheads are attributed to the cost of finished goods.

The total of direct costs (i.e. direct materials, labour and expenses) is called 'prime cost'. The relationship between the different types of cost for a particular product can be set out as follows:

Direct materials	X
Direct labour	X
Direct expense (such as royalties)	X
Prime cost	X
Manufacturing overheads	X
Total factory cost	X

Prime cost is closely linked to a concept of cost known as *variable (or marginal)* cost because the total amount expended on prime cost in any period will vary with the number of units made. By contrast, most manufacturing overheads will be classified as *fixed costs* because the total amount expended is not influenced by the number of units made.

3 Materials

The material costs to be included as part of the cost of making finished goods for a particular period will be the cost of materials consumed (or used) during that period. This will not be the same figure as the cost of materials purchased, since there will undoubtedly be some material stocks to take into account.

When calculating the cost of goods sold for a retailer we added the cost of opening stock to the cost of goods purchased, and deducted the cost of closing stock. The cost of materials consumed (used up) can be found by using the same approach.

Activity 6	The cost of materials in store at the start of an accounting period was £4,500. The cost of materials purchased from suppliers during the period was £102,800. The cost of materials in store at the end of the period was £5,300. Calculate the cost of materials consumed in manufacturing finished goods during the period.

In a manufacturing business of any size there will be a control account for material stocks that forms part of the sub-system of cost accounting. This account records all movements (i.e. receipts from suppliers and issues to production) from which the balance of material stocks can be ascertained. In such a system, the cost of materials issued to production equates to the cost of materials consumed. In financial accounting an assumption is made that material purchases are recorded in the 'material purchases' account and that materials consumed is derived by making adjustments for opening and closing stock.

4 Cost and net realisable value

All three categories of stock are subject to the valuation principles contained in SSAP 9. (SSAPs regulate financial reporting – they do not necessarily influence cost accounting.) This means that each item of stock, whether it is an item of raw material, work-in-progress or finished product, must be brought into the books at the lower of cost or net realisable value.

Cost

Whilst the cost of closing stocks of raw materials is often determined quite easily from purchase invoices, a cost accounting system is needed to determine the cost of work-in-progress and the cost of finished goods. As mentioned earlier, these cost accounting records are usually integrated with the financial accounting records.

Such systems generally determine the number of units in stock assuming that no units were lost. In this case the calculation is based on: opening quantity, plus quantity made, less quantity sold.

When it comes to calculating the cost of each unit for the closing stock valuation, there are two bases that could be used, namely marginal cost or absorbed cost.

Marginal cost per unit can be found by dividing total variable costs (direct materials, direct labour, and any variable overheads) by the number of units made. Variable cost is often treated as being the same as prime cost, although strictly speaking these are two separate concepts of cost.

Absorbed cost per unit is found by taking the marginal cost per unit and adding an amount for fixed production overheads per unit. Strictly speaking the amount of fixed production overheads per unit should be found (according to SSAP 9) by dividing the total fixed production overheads by the normal quantity that could be produced, not the actual quantity produced. However, in some assessments the normal production levels may not be given and you have to use the actual production levels.

It should be obvious to you that the absorbed cost of finished goods stock is higher than marginal cost and that reported profits will vary according to the basis used for valuing closing stocks. SSAP 9, which governs the valuation principle for limited companies, requires manufactured stock to be valued on the basis of absorbed cost.

| **Activity 7** | A sole trader has set up business to manufacture a single product. Manufacturing costs during the first period were as follows: |

Raw materials consumed	£42,000
Direct labour	£38,000
Prime cost	£80,000
Fixed production overheads	£20,000
Total production costs	£100,000

40,000 units were manufactured and there was no work-in-progress at the end of the period. 38,000 units were sold for a total sales value of £140,000. Prepare two trading accounts, using (a) marginal cost, and (b) absorbed cost, as the basis for valuing finished goods stock, using the space below.

(a) **Trading account**

Closing stock at marginal cost

(b) **Trading account**

Closing stock at absorbed cost

Note that the absorption costing profit is higher than that for marginal costing simply because some of the fixed overhead costs for the period (£1,000) end up being charged into the value of closing stock. This figure is then registered in the balance sheet rather than simply being charged to profit and loss as it is under marginal costing.

Net realisable value

As regards net realisable value, there are no new aspects to consider except in the case of work-in-progress. Net realisable value is defined as sales value less any costs of selling.

Activity 8	At the accounting date of 31 December 1990, a manufacturer had a partly manufactured item of stock on hand. The cost accounting records show that costs incurred on this item up to 31 December 1990 amount to £6,800. In its partly completed state it could be sold for scrap at a price of £2,000 but when it is finished it can be sold for £9,000. Estimated costs to complete the item during the next period amount to £1,200. State the value at which this item of work-in-progress should be included in the accounts at 31 December 1990.

Summary

The main learning points in this chapter are:

■   the trading account of a manufacturer is similar to a retailer except that cost of sales is based on the manufactured cost of finished goods instead of the purchase cost

■   the manufactured cost of finished goods stock could be based on marginal cost or absorbed cost (marginal cost plus a proportion of fixed production overheads)

■   SSAP 9 requires the cost of finished goods stock to be based on absorbed cost – with overheads per unit determined on the basis of the normal levels of production

■   a manufacturing entity may have a sub-system of cost accounting in order to determine cost of sales for the financial accounts. However, it may for convenience be a separate stand-alone system. Cost and management accountants will often want different methods of issue pricing from financial accountants, for example, they may prefer to use LIFO which gives more up-to-date unit costings. Cost and management accountants will want to include notional charges to get the full unit costs, and will want to use different depreciation methods from financial accountants. They will prefer to use usage depreciation methods to even out the assessment of unit costs. It may be better, therefore, to have separate (or 'interlocking') accounts.

■   manufacturing costs include materials consumed which is found by taking the cost of materials purchased and making adjustments for opening and closing stocks of materials

■   the balance sheet of a manufacturer usually includes three categories of stock: raw materials, work-in-progress, finished goods.

Key to Chapter 1 activities

Activity 1

Opening stock of finished goods + manufacturing costs of items finished in the latest period – closing stock of finished goods.

Activity 2

You may have thought of raw materials, bought-in components, or work-in-progress (partly completed units).

Activity 3

There are literally dozens of different types of cost. You may have included things like: raw materials, wages of those working in the factory, electricity, rent, rates and insurance of the factory, depreciation of any plant and machinery used in the factory, packing costs, running costs of fork-lift trucks, oil and lubricants.

Activity 4

You may have thought of things like: machine oils and lubricants, spare parts for machines and cleaning materials.

Materials such as these are referred to as 'indirect materials' and form part of the total of manufacturing overheads.

Activity 5

You may have included employees such as: supervisors and foremen, security staff, cleaners, maintenance engineers, fork-lift drivers and store keepers and the production management and directors.

Activity 6

£4,500 + £102,800 – £5,300 = £102,000

Activity 7

(a) **Trading account**
Closing stock at marginal cost

Sales		140,000
Less cost of sales:		
Manufacturing costs	80,000	
Less closing stock		
(2,000 × £2)	4,000	
		76,000
Gross profit		64,000

(b) **Trading account**
Closing stock at absorbed cost

Sales		140,000
Less cost of sales:		
Manufacturing costs	100,000	
Less closing stock		
(2,000 × £2.50)	5,000	
		95,000
Gross profit		45,000

In marginal costing the fixed production overhead is then charged as a period cost (of £20,000) to give a profit of £44,000.

Activity 8

At cost of £6,800. Note that net realisable value is not the scrap value of £2,000. Net realisable value is the ultimate selling price of £9,000 less the costs of completion £1,200. This amounts to £7,800 and is greater than cost.

Chapter 2
Basic principles

Introduction

This chapter provides a foundation for your studies of cost and management accounting. It is an essential chapter because it encapsulates the overall framework of a cost and management accounting system.

Objectives

After you have completed this chapter, you should be able to:

■ contrast the objectives of financial accounting with the objectives of cost and management accounting

■ identify cost units and cost centres appropriate to a particular business

■ classify the elements of cost and interpret various coding systems.

1 Objectives of the cost accounting system

Cost accounting is a separate but integrated part of the overall accounting information system. This system includes various clerical procedures, and also requires a record of past transactions to be kept in the ledger by means of double entry. A prime objective of cost accounting is to identify the costs associated with product units and segments of the business, and to plan for and control these costs.

Activity 1	An accounting system for determining the cost of goods manufactured is clearly vital for a manufacturing entity of any size. There are two main reasons why management needs information regarding the cost of manufactured products. See if you can think what they are, and make a note of them here: 1 2

If you look more closely at the explanation for item 1 in the Key, you will notice that it does not specifically refer to 'determining' the selling price. If the business operates in a competitive market, prices are more likely to be influenced or set by market forces than by the business itself. In this case, management needs to know the cost for control purposes. If management considers the profit margin inadequate but selling prices cannot be increased, management will have to take remedial action such as reducing costs or withdrawing the product.

The cost accounting system may provide the information for making a single business decision and, since each decision is a unique event, the necessary information may be extracted from the system on an *ad hoc* basis. It will almost certainly provide for full annual planning and the setting of budgets for all business functions. This gives a platform for full control of all aspects of the business – i.e. the matching of actual costs and revenues with budgets to highlight differences and provide for management action and control.

2 Relevant data – a change of viewpoint

A decision taken today will change what happens in the future. To shape the future and get the best use of resources, business must plan ahead. The information contained in routine accounting reports has limited use because it relates to past events. The past cannot be altered. Similarly, costs already committed are referred to as 'sunk' costs and nothing to be decided now can alter the amount previously spent.

Looking at the future rather than at the past is one of the most important changes you have to make when producing figures for management instead of the owners. This change of direction in the way that you look at business events can sometimes seem a little strange until you become accustomed to the idea. See how you get on with the following activity.

Activity 2	A company holds an item of damaged stock which originally cost £900. The company has a choice of either selling the item for £800, or repairing it at a cost of £20 and selling it for £850. Despite the fact that the best option is obvious, you are required to prepare a statement for management to help them with the decision. You must observe the following two constraints: 1 You are not allowed to simply inform management what they should do; you must prepare a statement analysing the figures. 2 Your analysis must not include data which is irrelevant to the decision. Set out your analysis in the space beneath this activity box.

You will note that both presentations in the Key ignore the original cost of £900 because it is not relevant to the decision. It is a sunk cost.

The original cost is relevant to the measurement of profit or loss, but profit measurement is a part of the process of reporting to the owners rather than to management. The profit and loss account figures for this item of stock will show a loss of £100 if it is sold damaged, and a loss of £70 if repaired and sold. Our statement to management shows that there will be an improvement to future profits of £30 if the item is repaired and sold.

This is not to suggest that past costs are always irrelevant in decision making problems. In the first place, past results might precipitate the need to make a decision, such as where the results of a branch or a product reveal inadequate profits or a loss. Past costs can also be used to predict how costs might behave if certain conditions are changed in the future.

In order to conclude this introduction to relevant data, try working on one more activity.

Activity 3	A company has the opportunity to scrap an existing machine and replace it with a new one costing £30,000. Available data on the old machine:

Original cost (five years ago)   £10,000
Annual depreciation charge   1,000
Net book value   5,000
Present scrap value   3,000
Annual running costs   6,000

The production director is trying to decide whether the estimated benefits from installing the new machine will justify the cost of £30,000. Try to identify data relating to the old machine that is likely to be relevant to this decision, and justify your answer.

3 Basic analysis of cost

We have said that costs can be included under one of four headings:

Direct materials
Direct labour
Direct expenses
Indirect costs (or overheads).

The three elements of cost are materials, labour and expenses, and these three elements can be classified as direct or indirect costs. The indirect costs are also called overheads.

The division of materials (M), labour (L) and expenses (E) between direct and indirect costs looks something like this, where the unshaded area shows the proportion of direct costs, and the shaded area shows the proportion of indirect costs:

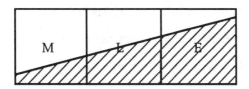

The sum of the indirect costs gives a figure for the overhead costs, and the sum of the direct costs gives the prime cost. The overhead costs can also be sub-divided into manufacturing overheads, administrative overheads, marketing overheads, and so on.

Cost accounting principles dictate that all costs consumed in the manufacturing process will eventually form a part of the cost of products. Initially these costs are charged to either:

- a *cost unit* – defined as a quantitative unit of product (goods or service) for which costs are ascertained, or

- a production or factory *cost centre* – defined as a location or function for which costs are ascertained before relating them to cost units.

You will need a mental image of the two terms (cost unit and cost centre) in order to appreciate the way costs are routed through the system. Try using your imagination in the following activity:

Activity 4	Refer to the definition of a cost unit again, and make a note of what you think might be used as the basis for a cost unit in the following cases.

Possible cost unit

Coal mining
Car manufacture
Beer manufacture

You can suggest anything that seems appropriate; we cannot know for sure what measurements these business use, without asking them.

Cost units in the service industry are a little more difficult to imagine. We might have cost units such as: kilowatt hours for electricity production, passenger miles for a bus company, and so on.

As regards cost centres, we are only concerned with those that are part of the factory. The administration department might be treated as a cost centre, but it is outside our present definition because the costs of administration do not enter into the calculation of the cost of a manufactured product.

In order to appreciate the idea of a cost centre, try to imagine a business that makes desks and chairs. There could be three distinct stages in the whole process, such as:

1   cutting (timber cut to size)

2   assembly (of the cut materials)

3   finishing (sanding and varnishing).

Each process takes place in a separate cost centre, as illustrated below:

Cutting   Assembly   Finishing

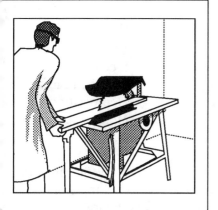

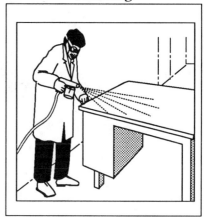

These three departments are known as production cost centres; they are the locations where the actual business of making a product take place. There are also service cost centres. They are not involved in actually making the products but they provide service to the production cost centres.

Activity 5	Make a note of any departments (in the factory, not in the office) that provide services to production cost centres.

4 Classification and coding systems

Classification is a process of arranging items (usually costs) into groups according to some common characteristic. Items are usually grouped on the basis of two classifications, namely:

1   Their function. This relates to the purpose of the cost in terms of providing departmental facilities such as: production, marketing, distribution, administration, research and development.

2   Their nature. This means the particular type of item – for costs this may be materials, rent and rates, wages, stationery, and so on.

The system of functional and natural classification produces a total cost for each department (or function), and an analysis of this total according to the type of expense.

Sometimes a third element in the classification is needed, such as location. We could, for example, have a system under which expenditure is analysed under headings shown in the following example:

Location	Function	Nature
London	Production	Wages
Leeds	Research and development	Electricity
Glasgow	Marketing	Rent and rates
	Distribution	Depreciation
	Administration	Motor expenses

In some cases, expenditure can be allocated directly to a specific heading, such as admin. salaries. In others, the expenditure has to be apportioned to various departments, such as rent and rates for the whole building.

A coding system allocates code numbers to each item in these groups. This will facilitate the process of analysis, collation, and entry in the books. Coding is particularly relevant to the processing of data by a computer.

Most coding systems allocate a block of code numbers to each group. These blocks must have a sufficient range to allow for additions to the group. For example, the above company has three branches and so the code numbers for location might range from 01 to 10 (or higher if the company considers that it might ultimately have more than 10 branches).

You will see how these systems work by going back to the above tabulation and allocating code numbers to each item according to the instructions in the following activity.

Activity 6	Allocate code numbers to each cost in the above tabulation by writing the code number to the left of each item on the following basis:
	Location: The block of numbers allocated to this group is 01 to 10. Number each branch in sequence, starting with London as number 01.
	Function: The block of numbers allocated to this group is 11 to 20. Number each function in sequence, starting with production as number 11.
	Nature: The block of numbers allocated to this group is 100 to 200. Number each type of expense in sequence, starting with wages as number 100.

You should just check with the Key (in case the instructions were not clear) to make sure that your code number allocation is correct, and then deal with the following activity.

Activity 7	If the code number for the motor expenses of a salesman at the Glasgow branch is 03 13 104, determine code numbers for the following expenses:

1   depreciation of plant and machinery in the London factory
2   motor expenses of the chief accountant at the Leeds branch
3   wages of employees in Glasgow's research laboratory.

The proliferation of computer systems has resulted in almost everything (and every person) being identified by a code number. There are endless systems that can be used; you will see examples everywhere, on library books, the bar codes in a supermarket, your bank account, and so on.

Summary

The main learning points in this chapter are:

- cost accounting provides management with an information system that enables them to control the business, and with information (cost of goods manufactured) for the annual financial statements

- information provided to help management make decisions is usually forward looking and often ignores past events

- all production costs are treated as unexpired until such time as the goods have been sold – they are then treated as an expense to be matched with sales income

- the elements of cost are materials, labour and expenses

- material, labour and expenses costs can also be classified as either direct or indirect

- the costs of direct materials and direct labour can be identified with specific cost units

- indirect costs are charged to production cost centres and absorbed into cost units on some pre-determined basis

- the total cost of a manufactured product will include many costs derived from the exercise of judgement and the application of accounting policies.

Key to Chapter 2 activities

Activity 1

1 To ensure that selling prices of each item are adequate and provide for an adequate profit margin over cost.
2 To value unsold stock at the end of financial periods for financial accounting purposes.

Activity 2

Two ways of setting out the analysis could be:

	Choice		Incremental gain if repaired and sold
	Sell damaged	Repair and sell	
Sale proceeds	£800	£850	£50
Future costs	nil	20	(20)
	Additional profit if repaired and sold		30

Or

Choice	Sale proceeds	Future costs	Net inflow
Sell damaged	£800	nil	£800
Repair and sell	850	20	830
	Gain through repairing and selling		30

Activity 3

Original cost is not relevant; it is a sunk cost. Annual depreciation is not relevant; depreciation is an accounting device for allocating original cost to accounting periods. The annual running costs are relevant for comparison purposes; they will not be incurred in the future if the machine is scrapped. The scrap value is also relevant because it represents cash that will be received if a decision is taken to scrap the old machine.

Activity 4

The following cost units could have been suggested:

Coal mining – a ton of coal (or some metric measure)
Car manufacture – a car (or batch of similar cars)
Beer manufacture – a barrel (or litre) of beer

Activity 5

There were several that you might have thought of such as maintenance departments, staff canteens, stores departments and boiler houses.

Activity 6

	Location		Function		Nature
01	London	11	Production	100	Wages
02	Leeds	12	Research and	101	Electricity
03	Glasgow		development	102	Rent and rates
		13	Marketing	103	Depreciation
		14	Distributing	104	Motor expenses
		15	Administration		

Activity 7

1   01 11 103   2   02 15 104   3   03 12 100

Chapter 3
Material and labour costs

Introduction

The cost of raw materials purchased is debited to a stores control account. When materials are issued to production the cost is debited to work-in-progress and credited to stores control account. At the end of the period, the balance on the stores control account shows the cost of raw materials stocks that should be in the store, thus providing an accounting control over the actual physical stock.

In this chapter we will look more closely at the ways in which the cost of raw materials issued to production are determined when the purchase prices have been changing throughout the period. You will also learn some of the financial controls used to ensure that stock levels are neither too high, nor too low, for the budgeted level of production activity. These control levels are really a part of the budgeting process but it is easier for you to see how they work whilst the idea of movements on the stock account are fresh in your mind.

The sections dealing with certain aspects of accounting for labour costs are mainly concerned with payroll calculations, and the analysis between direct and indirect labour costs.

Objectives

After you have completed this chapter, you should be able to:

■ write up perpetual inventory records using various methods for pricing issues

■ calculate optimum stock levels

■ discuss various remuneration schemes and calculate remuneration under any of the schemes described

■ differentiate between direct and indirect labour costs

■ write up a payroll control account.

1 Perpetual inventory

The Chartered Institute of Management Accountants (CIMA) defines perpetual inventory as 'the recording as they occur of receipts, issues, and the resulting balances of individual items of stock in either quantity, or quantity and value'. The perpetual inventory record is, therefore, similar in appearance to a bank statement where a balance is shown after each transaction. The main difference is that the columns for bankings and payments are replaced by columns for receipts and issues.

The word 'inventory' is simply another word for stocks. In this chapter we are dealing with the stock records for raw materials, but the same concepts are equally applicable to finished goods.

You will note that the definition refers to the record being kept in either quantity, or quantity and value. Most businesses today use computers in order to maintain their stock records and since these are quite often a part of the double-entry system, the record is kept in quantity and value.

Where records are written up manually, it is quite common to find two forms of stock record kept on an in/out balance basis. One is called a 'bin card' and the other a stores ledger account.

The bin card is a memorandum record of quantities for each item of stock. It is located close to the storage area and is written up by the storekeeper. The storekeeper has several responsibilities – one of them is to requisition the purchase of further stores when quantities on hand have fallen to their pre-determined re-order level. The bin card provides a clerical record to assist the storekeeper with this responsibility.

The stores ledger account is kept by the accounts department and forms a part of the double-entry book-keeping system.

The bin card and the stores ledger account are both written up from copies of the same source documents. When materials are received from a supplier, the receiving department creates an internal document called a 'goods received note' (or GRN). The GRN includes several duplicate copies that are distributed to various departments within the company. These departments include the purchase ledger department, where the GRN is used to substantiate the purchase invoice, and the cost accounting department where it is used for writing up the stores ledger account.

When the production department requires raw materials to be issued from store, a document called a material requisition (or stores requisition) is written up and approved by a production supervisor. The approved requisition acts as an authority for the storekeeper to issue the materials, and a copy of this requisition (usually called a material issue note – MIN) is used to initiate entries in the stores records.

Both GRNs and MINs are often pre-printed with a serial number so that an internal control (based on checking the sequence of numbers) can be built into the system to ensure that all documents are processed.

The accounts in the ledger usually consist of a single control account and many individual accounts for each type of stock. The concept is the same as where control accounts are kept for debtors or creditors; postings to the control account are for total value of receipts and issues, postings to the individual stores account are for the receipts and issues of that particular material. At the end of the period, the total of the balances on individual stores accounts should agree with the total value on the control account.

2 Pricing the issues

The cost of raw materials issued is debited to either work-in-progress account or to overhead control accounts. Direct materials are debited to work-in-progress and indirect materials to production, administration or sales and distribution overheads. The corresponding credit is to the stores account for the particular type of material issued.

Identifying the cost of materials issued is simple enough if purchase prices are stable, but this is not usually the case. The company must, therefore, adopt an accounting policy for determining the purchase cost of the materials issued. The main choices of policy available to management are as follows:

- First in, First out (FIFO)
- Last in, First out (LIFO)
- Average cost (AVCO)

The company does not have this problem if standard costing is used because the issues will be priced at a pre-determined standard cost. You will be learning about this in Chapter 5.

SSAP 9 recommends FIFO as it truly and fairly reflects physical practice. LIFO is not specifically banned by SSAP 9, but companies are discouraged from using it for stock valuation purposes because it results in amounts that bear little relationship to recent cost levels. LIFO will, however, ensure that the charges to production for materials consumed are based on recent costs and to this extent it can be justified as being a more realistic basis.

The details for the first two activities are as follows:

The purchase prices and stock movements for a certain type of material are as follows:

			Qty.	Unit price
1	January	opening balance	500	£0.80
31	January	purchased	1,000	£0.90
14	February	issued	700	
31	March	purchased	800	£1.00
28	April	issued	900	

Activity 1	You are required to write up a perpetual inventory record (using the format provided below this box) on the basis that materials issued to production are priced on a FIFO basis.

			Qty.	Unit price £	Receipts £	Issues £	Balance £
1	January	opening balance	500	0.80			400
31	January	purchased	1,000	0.90			
		balance	1,500				
14	February	issued	(700)				
		balance	800				
31	March	purchased	800	1.00			
		balance	1,600				
28	April	issued	(900)				
30	April	closing balance					

Activity 2	Write up the perpetual inventory record (below) again, using LIFO for pricing the issues.

			Qty.	Unit price £	Receipts £	Issues £	Balance £
1	January	opening balance	500	0.80			400
31	January	purchased	1,000	0.90			
		balance	1,500				
14	February	issued	(700)				
		balance	800				
31	March	purchased	800	1.00			
		balance	1,600				
28	April	issued	(900)				
30	April	closing balance					

If you now compare your two perpetual inventory records, you will notice that FIFO produces a stock valuation based on more up-to-date cost levels but charges production with costs incurred at an earlier time. Under LIFO the position is reversed – production has been charged with recent costs but the stock is being valued on the basis of older prices.

Bearing in mind that the cost of materials issued to production is eventually debited to cost of sales, we can see that inflation causes a conflict between the two methods. FIFO produces a more realistic stock value but an unrealistic cost of sales figure (i.e. one which does not reflect up-to-date costs), whereas LIFO produces a more realistic cost of sales figure but a less realistic stock value.

Average cost (AVCO) methods provide issue prices that are based on the average costs of items purchased. One AVCO method in particular is based on what is known as the 'weighted average price'. This is defined by CIMA as 'a method of pricing material issues using a price which is calculated by dividing the total cost of material in stock by the total quantity in stock at the time of issue'. If you reflect on this definition for a moment you will appreciate that a new average price has to be calculated every time there is a purchase of materials. This tends to make it an unpopular method in practice except where computers are used. Try using the definition by working on the following activity.

Activity 3	Write up the perpetual inventory record for the situation dealt with in the previous two activities by using AVCO. A format is provided below this box. You will find it helpful to enter the weighted average price in the price column. This is easily found by dividing the debit balance on the account by the new balance of quantities after each purchase. You will have to work to three decimals of £1 for these prices in order to get reasonably accurate figures. Work to the nearest £1 for the cost of issues and the balance.

			Qty.	Unit price £	receipts £	issues £	balance £
1	January	opening balance	500	0.80			400
31	January	purchased	1,000	0.90			
		balance	1,500				
14	February	issued	(700)				
		balance	800				
31	March	purchased	800	1.00			
		balance	1,600				
28	April	issued	(900)				
30	April	closing balance					

You will notice how the use of averages provides a compromise for the conflict between FIFO and LIFO mentioned earlier. Beyond this one positive point there is little to justify the method.

3 Optimum stock levels

There is always a conflict when attempting to determine the levels of stock that should be held for a particular type of raw material.

The production department would like the company to carry as much stock as possible so as to avoid the likelihood of running short of materials during a production run.

The purchasing department would like to place large orders as infrequently as possible so as to take advantage of bulk discounts and lower ordering costs (fewer orders means less work and lower departmental costs).

The financial controller would like to carry as little stock as possible in order to reduce the cost of carrying stocks. All funds invested in the company have a cost (finance is not provided free) and by reducing the amount of funds invested in stocks, the company's financing costs are reduced. Apart from these finance charges, the cost of carrying stock will include storage charges which can be reduced if smaller quantities are held.

These conflicts have to be solved through the planning and budgeting process. When a production plan has been agreed for the year, it will be possible to determine optimum stock levels. These levels take account of information such as the time it takes for suppliers to deliver the goods after placing an order (known as the supply 'lead time'), and the likely rate of consumption by the production department.

Three levels are normally calculated for each type of material, namely:

- re-order level
- minimum stock level
- maximum stock level.

The three stock levels referred to above can be calculated from given data by the use of formulae, but this is not a very good way of learning the subject. If you can sort out what each formula is trying to do, you will have no problem in remembering how to do the calculations.

In the activities, you will working on the following data for one particular type of material:

Maximum consumption per week	400 units
Minimum consumption per week	200 units
Supply lead time	4 to 6 weeks

Notice the following: consumption of the material can vary from 200 units to 400 units per week (an average of, say, 300 units per week); suppliers might take from four to six weeks (an average of five weeks) to deliver the goods after receiving the order.

The re-order level

This is a point at which a definite action is required, that is, an order must be placed for new supplies.

Keep in mind that the production department will continue to use the material after the order has been placed and that there will be a delay before the new materials arrive. We wish to avoid the likelihood of running out of materials before the new order arrives. We must, therefore, place an order when stocks have reached a level that should be enough to keep the production department running until the new order arrives. In order to be on the safe side we will have to assume that the most adverse of circumstances will occur after the order has been placed.

Activity 4	In the context of the above discussion, see if you can identify what would be the most adverse of circumstances after placing the order. Make a note of the point here:

It should now be possible for you to turn the objective into a formula (or the basis of a formula) and calculate the re-order level for the situation described in our example.

Activity 5	State the formula for calculating the re-order level, and carry out the calculations for the above example in the space below.

Formula and calculation:

The minimum stock level

This is a warning level that requires a follow-up action after the order has been placed.

Try to imagine a situation where the stocks fell to their re-order level of 2,400 units, then a new order (for 2,000 units) was placed, but this order has not yet arrived. In the meantime, the production department has continued to use up the existing stocks. We will reach a point where we ought to chase up the outstanding order since there is a danger of running out of materials. This is called the minimum stock level.

Activity 6	See if you can turn the explanation into a formula (using the average basis) and calculate minimum stock level for our example.

Formula and calculation:

The maximum stock level

This is also a warning level where further action might be needed. If stocks exceed this level then either something unexpected has happened, or a mistake has been made in the ordering process.

It is the level that will be reached if the new order happens to arrive at the end of the minimum lead time and only the minimum quantities had been consumed during that lead time.

Activity 7	See if you can turn the explanation into a formula, and do the calculation of maximum stock level for our example. Don't forget that when the new order arrives it will be added to the current stock level.

Formula and calculation:

If stocks exceed this maximum stock level an investigation is needed to try and find out why it has occurred.

Activity 8	State (by deleting yes or no) whether the following circumstances might be the cause of a particular stock item exceeding its maximum level:

	Event	Could event cause stocks to exceed maximum level?
1	An error in quantity delivered.	Yes/No
2	A reduction in usage of the item.	Yes/No
3	An error in the quantity ordered.	Yes/No
4	An increase in the supply lead time.	Yes/No

Notice how the calculations for these optimum stock levels have to commence with the re-order level. The other two levels (minimum and maximum) are both anchored to the re-order level.

4 Labour costs

The subject of labour costs can usually be divided into three headings:

- payroll calculations
- analysis of labour costs between direct and indirect
- payroll book-keeping

These are all fairly short topics and will not be very demanding on your study time. Payroll calculations usually involve the interpretation of various kinds of bonus incentive schemes. The analysis between direct and indirect labour costs is not simply a matter of identifying whether the employee is directly involved in making goods or not; some of the payroll costs of direct workers have to be treated as indirect. Payroll book-keeping is mainly concerned with accounting for deductions such as income taxes under the PAYE system.

5 Payroll calculations

There are three basic methods of remunerating production employees:

- a time rate
- a piece-work rate
- a bonus incentive scheme.

The first two are usually so well known that they do not really call for any explanation. A time rate is simply a rate per hour, and a piece-work rate is simply an amount for each quantifiable unit produced. You may be asked to compare the two methods in terms of advantages and disadvantages.

Piece-work rates are usually offered to motivate employees into producing a greater quantity of units. This usually results in an increase in the total payroll cost but a reduction in the labour cost per unit.

Activity 9

A production worker was previously paid £5 an hour and produced (on average) 10 units per hour. A piece-work scheme was introduced whereby the worker was paid 45 pence per unit, and resulted in 14 units per hour being produced. Calculate and compare the following labour costs:

	Cost per hour	Cost per unit
Time rate basis		
Piece-work basis		

The benefits of producing a larger volume of units are not simply related to the labour costs per unit; there is a beneficial effect in relation to fixed overheads, i.e. a better spreading of fixed costs. If overheads are fixed, then the total amount spent in any period is not affected by the volume of activity. In a simple situation we can find the fixed overhead cost per unit by dividing the fixed overheads for a period by the number of units produced in that period.

Activity 10	Assume that the person in Activity 9 is the only production worker in the business and works a 40-hour week. The total fixed production overheads are £700 per week. Calculate the fixed overhead cost per unit under the two different schemes of remuneration. Overhead cost per unit Time rate basis Piece-work basis

It should be fairly clear from the above analysis that for the situation described, the employer could offer a piece-work rate substantially in excess of 45 pence per unit and still be able to reduce costs per unit by comparison to what they were under the old time rate basis.

Despite the obvious advantages of piece-work rates, it has to be accepted that there are several situations where this method of remuneration is not really suitable for production staff.

Activity 11	Make a note of the situations where it would be inappropriate to remunerate production staff by a piece-work rate. Aim at finding four: 1 2 3 4

In some cases a guaranteed minimum wage is offered as a part of the piece-work arrangement. The guaranteed minimum is often based on a percentage of what the pay would be if it were calculated on an hourly basis, and simply represents an amount that will be paid if the piece-work earnings are less.

You will be able to see how these arrangements work by carrying out some pay calculations in the following activity.

Activity 12	A company previously remunerated its factory workers on a time basis. It has now introduced a piece-work scheme with a guaranteed minimum wage. The details for two employees are as follows: <table><tr><td></td><td>Mr Caldicott</td><td>Mr Kennett</td></tr><tr><td>Hours worked</td><td>45</td><td>40</td></tr><tr><td>Hourly rate of pay</td><td>£5</td><td>£5</td></tr><tr><td>Units produced</td><td>500</td><td>300</td></tr></table> The piece-work rate is 50 pence per unit produced, with earnings guaranteed at 80% of pay calculated on a time basis. Calculate the pay for each employee in the space provided below this box.

Pay calculations	Mr Caldicott	Mr Kennett

There are a number of schemes for providing incentives to production workers other than by way of a piece-work rate. They are generally referred to as bonus incentive schemes.

The bonus incentive scheme may be applied to an individual worker, or to a group of workers operating collectively in some way. Most incentive schemes are based on a similar idea. The workers receive their normal hourly rate plus bonus pay calculated on the amount of time saved for the production achieved.

In order to calculate the amount of time saved, a standard time is agreed for the length of time that it should take to produce one unit. A record is kept of the number of units produced and the standard time allowed for these is compared to the actual time taken.

The bonus is calculated at an hourly rate on a percentage of the time saved.

Activity 13	A company has introduced a bonus incentive scheme whereby a bonus (based on 50% of the time saved) is added to pay calculated on an hourly basis. The details for one employee are as follows: Hours worked 40 Hourly rate of pay £5 Units produced 560 The standard time for producing one unit is six minutes. Calculate the pay for this employee in the space provided below this box.

Pay calculations:

As with any scheme designed to increase the volume of output, the benefits to the company must be seen in the light of the fixed overhead costs per unit. As volume increases, so the fixed overhead cost per unit will fall.

6 Analysis of production labour costs

Labour costs are analysed between direct and indirect labour. Direct labour costs are debited to work-in-progress; indirect labour costs are debited to production overheads.

It is fairly clear that the entire amount of remuneration paid to indirect workers will be classified as an indirect labour cost. The accounting problem relates to certain amounts that might be paid to the direct workers which will have to be classified as an indirect cost and charged to production overheads.

In the normal course of events, the following two items paid to direct workers are classified as indirect costs:

- overtime premiums and shift premiums
- cost of idle time.

An overtime premium is not the actual pay for the overtime hours worked, but the additional amount paid (over the normal rate) for working during a period beyond the contracted hours. For example, someone paid £5 per hour during normal time might be paid an overtime rate of 'time and a half' and so will receive a rate of pay during the overtime period of £7.50 per hour. The extra £2.50 is the overtime premium. The same concept applies to shift working where the premium is an additional amount paid to compensate staff for having to work during unsocial hours such as on a night shift.

Activity 14	We have said that overtime premiums and shift premiums paid to direct workers will not be treated as a direct labour cost, but will be treated as indirect and charged to production overheads. Can you think of any reason to justify this practice? This is not an easy question; it might help if you recall that by treating costs as indirect they are spread over all units made during the period, whereas direct costs are charged to specific units. If you can think of a reason make a note of it here and then check your idea with the Key:

There is one exception to this treatment. If the overtime (or extra shift) is being worked at the specific request of a customer who has agreed to reimburse the additional costs (e.g. by paying an increased price), then the premium should be treated as a direct cost of the job concerned.

Note that productivity-related bonuses are classified as direct costs.

'Idle time' is a technical expression; it is not meant to be an insult. It is defined by CIMA as 'the period of time for which a work station is available for production but is not utilised due to shortage of tooling, material, operators, etc.'

It is clearly wrong to treat the wages paid to direct workers for avoidable idle time as a specific cost of any units produced within the same period. Avoidable idle time is normally the result of poor production scheduling (or lack of orders). Avoidable costs are charged to profit and loss to avoid overcosting of the units produced around the idle time.

Apart from idle time, there are other times when a direct worker is paid a wage but is not actually working on production, such as holidays. These are unavoidable costs. The cost of holiday pay is a direct cost and can be dealt with by calculating an inflated 'charge-out' rate for each hour of productive employee time over the entire financial period. The inflated charge-out rate is used to calculate the debit to work-in-progress for direct labour hours. More typically, unavoidable costs are treated as overheads, so that they can be spread over the total production for the period.

Charge-out rates have to be determined at the beginning of the period and are calculated by dividing the direct labour cost of an employee for the period by the number of hours the employee is expected to be available for productive work in that period. In a simple case, the available hours is the number of contractual hours for the period, less any expected absences.

Activity 15	During a four-week period, an employee's contracted hours are 160. Expected absences during this period are as follows:

Annual holiday   40 hours
Bank holiday   8 hours

The employee is paid at the rate of £5.60 per hour. Calculate the available hours and the charge-out rate per hour.

Available hours:

Charge-out rate:

In cases like this, all normal idle time should be catered for in the charge-out rate – i.e. idle time that is unavoidable and could be treated as a direct cost by inflating the charge-out rate. This would involve including an allowance for all normal idle time (holidays, bank holidays, tea-breaks, sickness) when calculating the number of hours that an employee is likely to be available for productive work over a full financial period.

Note that this activity is just an example of how a charge-out rate might be calculated. A grossed up charge-out rate must be worked over a full financial period – if you are considering annual holiday, then the period is one year.

However, in practice the cost of unavoidable idle time is treated as production overheads. The following activity is based on a past AAT cost accounting question:

| **Activity 16** | The following information gives details of the gross pay calculated for a production worker. |

Basic pay for normal hours worked: 40 hours at £5 per hour   £200.00
Overtime: five hours at time and a half   37.50
Group bonus payment   4.00
Gross wages for the week   241.50

Although paid for 40 hours in normal time, the worker was in fact unable to work for six hours because of machine breakdowns. Analyse the total of £241.50 into direct and indirect costs.

7 Payroll book-keeping

The first entry on payment of wages is to debit the amount paid to a payroll control or wages clearing account. The costs are then transferred out of this account and charged to various cost centres, direct labour costs being charged to work-in-progress, indirect labour to production overheads, and administration salaries to administration expenses.

This is an oversimplification because the amounts actually paid are the net wages after deduction of various items such as PAYE and national insurance contributions. These deductions will have to be paid to the Inland Revenue and so the true cost to the employer is the gross wage. The employer must also make a contribution towards the employee's national insurance. Total employment costs are, therefore, gross wages plus the employer's contribution towards the employees' national insurance.

The payroll control account is used to build up the total employment costs on the debit side of the account, prior to charging out this total to the various cost centres. The first double entry is for the net wages paid. This is simply credit bank, debit payroll control account. At this point we have a debit on the payroll control account for the net wages paid, and so we will have to debit the deductions to this account in order to increase the debit to the gross wages.

| **Activity 17** | If the only deductions are for PAYE and national insurance, the total amount deducted will have to be paid to the Inland Revenue. It is not payable immediately but at the point when the amounts are deducted, there is a liability to account for these deductions to the Inland Revenue. Describe the double entry for the these deductions. |

Debit:

Credit:

The employer will also, as stated previously, have to make a contribution to the employees' national insurance scheme. This amount must be treated as a part of the employment costs, and is also due to the Inland Revenue at the time when the wages are paid.

Activity 18	Describe what the double entry will be for the employer's share of national insurance contributions at the time the wages are paid.
	Debit:
	Credit:

It should now be fairly clear that when the PAYE and national insurance are paid to the Inland Revenue, the double entry will be: debit Inland Revenue; credit bank. The debit side of the payroll control account has been built up with the total employment costs. This will then be charged out to the various cost centres according to an analysis. The resulting balance on the payroll control account should be nil.

You should now practise the complete procedure with a simple example.

Activity 19	Write the following into some suitably named ledger accounts.

Gross salaries and wages	£20,000
National insurance and PAYE deductions	4,000
Net wages paid	16,000
Employer's national insurance contribution	1,000

The analysis of total employment costs was as follows:

Direct labour	£10,000
Indirect production labour	2,000
Administration	9,000
	21,000

You should use your own paper and file your work at the end of this text.

The employer's share of national insurance is included in the charge-out rate for the direct workers concerned. You should note that some companies do not bother to calculate inflated charge-out rates to take account of holiday pay and national insurance. Instead, these costs are treated as overheads when they are paid.

Summary

The main learning points in this chapter are:

- a perpetual inventory is written up on an in/out balance basis as each movement of stock occurs

- the perpetual inventory is written up from controlled source documents

- the issues may be priced on a FIFO, LIFO, or AVCO basis

- FIFO prices issues at the oldest prices and values stock at the latest prices; LIFO prices issues at latest prices but values stock at the oldest prices; AVCO is a compromise between the two

- financial control of stocks includes determining various optimum stock levels (re-order, maximum, minimum)

- production workers are often remunerated by various incentive schemes designed to increase output

- the company benefits from increased output by lower unit costs

- certain payments to direct production workers are treated as an indirect cost; these include overtime and shift premiums, and idle time

- holiday pay for direct workers can be included in direct labour cost by calculating an inflated charge-out rate

- the payroll control account is used to build up gross employment costs prior to the allocation of this cost to various cost centres.

Key to Chapter 3 activities

Activity 1

			Qty.	price	receipts £	issues £	balance £
1	January	opening balance	500	£0.80			400.00
31	January	purchased	1,000	£0.90	900		
		balance	1,500				1,300.00
14	February	issued	(700)			580	
		balance	800				720.00
31	March	purchased	800	£1.00	800		
		balance	1,600				1,520.00
28	April	issued	(900)			820	
30	April	closing balance	700				700.00

Activity 2

			Qty.	price	receipts £	issues £	balance £
1	January	opening balance	500	£0.80			400.00
31	January	purchased	1,000	£0.90	900		
		balance	1,500				1,300.00
14	February	issued	(700)			630	
		balance	800				670.00
31	March	purchased	800	£1.00	800		
		balance	1,600				1,470.00
28	April	issued	(900)			890	
30	April	closing balance	700				580.00

Activity 3

			Qty.	price	receipts £	issues £	balance £
1	January	opening balance	500	£0.80			400.00
31	January	purchased	1,000	£0.90	900		
		balance	1,500	£0.867			1,300.00
14	February	issued	(700)	£0.867		607	
		balance	800	£0.867			693.00
31	March	purchased	800	£1.00	800		
		balance	1,600	£0.933			1,493.00
28	April	issued	(900)	£0.933		840	
30	April	closing balance	700	£0.933			653.00

Activity 4

It would be that the goods take six weeks to arrive and in the meantime the production department is using 400 units a week.

Activity 5

Formula: maximum usage during maximum lead time. Using appropriate operands it could be stated as: maximum lead time × maximum usage. Calculation: 6 × 400 = 2,400 units

Activity 6   Formula: re-order level less the average usage during the average lead time
                      Calculation: $2,400 - (5 \times 300) = 900$ units

Activity 7   Formula: re-order level, less minimum usage in minimum lead time, plus
                      the re-order quantity.
                      Calculation: $2,400 - (4 \times 200) + 2,000 = 3,600$ units

Activity 8   1 Yes   2 Yes   3 Yes   4 No

Activity 9

	Cost per hour	Cost per unit
Time rate basis	£5.00	50 pence
Piece-work basis	£6.30	45 pence

Activity 10   Under the time rate basis (40×10) 400 units per week are produced;
                      under the piece-work basis (40×14) 560 units per week are produced.

		Overhead cost per unit
Time rate basis	(£700 ÷ 400)	£1.75
Piece-work basis	(£700 ÷ 560)	£1.25

Activity 11   You might have thought of various instances such as:

1 where quality is more important than quantity
2 where no quantifiable unit is produced by a single person (such as
   assembly workers operating part of a mass production line)
3 where the employee is a trainee learning the craft
4 where there are definite upper limits on the number of particular
   products required by the business (e.g. where the market size is
   limited) and the business could not justify overproduction.

Activity 12

Pay calculations		Mr Caldicott		Mr Kennett
Piece-work earnings	(500 × £0.50)	£250	(300 × £0.50)	£150
Guaranteed minimum	(80% × £225)	£180	(80% × £200)	£160
Remuneration paid		£250		£160

Activity 13

Pay calculations:			
Time taken		40	hours
Time allowed	(560 x 6 ÷ 60)	56	hours
Time saved		16	hours
Bonus hours	(50%)	8	hours
Basic pay	(40 × £5)	£200	
Bonus pay	(8 × £5)	40	
Total pay		£240	

Activity 14

If the premiums were treated as a direct cost, units made during the overtime (or night shift) would be shown to cost more than those made during normal time. Yet the overtime and shift hours are being worked to increase the total volume of units produced over a full financial period. Extra costs of such hours should therefore be spread over all units produced in the financial period by charging them to overheads.

Activity 15

Available hours: 160 – 48 = 112 hours
Charge out rate: £896 ÷ 112 = £8 (the £896 was found by 160 × £5.60).

Activity 16

	Direct	Indirect	
Normal hours	£170.00	£30.00	(six hours idle time charged to profit and loss)
Overtime	25.00	12.50	(overtime premium charged to production overheads)
Bonus	4.00		
Totals	199.00	42.50	

Activity 17

Debit payroll control account; Credit Inland Revenue (note that the account with the Inland Revenue is a personal account, not an expense).

Activity 18

Debit payroll control account; Credit Inland Revenue.

Activity 19

Payroll control account

Bank	16,000	W.I.P.	10,000
Inl Rev	4,000	Prod o'hds	2,000
Inl Rev	1,000	Admin.	9,000
	21,000		21,000

Inland Revenue

Bal c/d	5,000	Payroll	4,000
		Payroll	1,000
	5,000		5,000
		Bal b/d	5,000

Work-in-progress

Payroll	10,000	

Production overheads

Payroll	2,000	

Administration expenses

Payroll	9,000	

Chapter 4
Absorption costing

Introduction

In this chapter you will learn how to deal with production overhead costs and how to allot such costs to units of product.

Objectives

After you have completed this chapter, you should be able to:

■ prepare a work-sheet for allocating and apportioning factory overheads to production cost centres

■ identify the most appropriate measurements of activity and calculate an appropriate absorption rate

■ post the appropriate double entries in the ledger for overheads

■ discuss the principles of SSAP 9 in respect of production overheads, and demonstrate the effect of these principles on profit measurement

■ separate mixed overheads into fixed and variable.

1 The basic absorption process

As you read this chapter you will be surrounded by manufactured products such as your clothes, a desk, a chair, the lamp, and so on. If you look at any one of these you can now imagine how the manufacturer would have been able to keep an accounting record of the costs of the main materials used. You can also imagine how the payroll records will enable the manufacturer to determine the labour cost for each item.

But overheads are a different matter; when you look at the article there is nothing for the mind to focus on in order to see how the manufacturer would have been able to add on an amount for production overheads.

Activity 1	Consider your desk or table and make a note of any resources you feel will have been utilised in its construction that are likely to have been treated as an overhead.

These types of cost do not manifest themselves in anything that can be measured as having been directly consumed in the manufacture of an individual article.

You will recall from Chapter 2 that the overhead rate per unit is a budgeted or estimated rate. You will get a basic idea of how these rates are calculated and dealt with in the books by imagining a factory that produces one specific type of article and nothing else. This is clearly unrealistic because most companies produce many different products. Even if a company made nothing other than (say) desks, it is likely to produce different types and sizes of desk. But the idea of a single-product firm gives us a starting point.

From past accounting records, the company should be able to estimate what its total production overheads are likely to be for the next accounting period. It will also be able to estimate how many units it could produce in that period. Calculating an overhead rate per unit is then simple arithmetic.

Activity 2	A company estimates that production overheads during the next accounting period will be £100,000 and that it should be able to produce 200,000 units. Calculate the budgeted overhead absorption rate.

Despite its simplicity, the calculation in the above activity forms the basis of the formula used for determining budgeted overhead absorption rates (BOAR) irrespective of the basis used. This formula is as follows:

$$\text{BOAR} = \frac{\text{Estimated (or budgeted) overheads}}{\text{Estimated (or budgeted) activity}}$$

BOARs are also known as 'recovery rates'.

In Activity 2 the estimated activity was the number of units to be produced. Later on you will be using different activity measurements such as machine hours or direct labour costs, but the basic formula remains the same.

During the accounting period for which the estimates were made, the company will be incurring actual overhead costs that are different to the estimated figures, and will produce quantities that are likely to be different to the original estimate. But irrespective of the actual overhead costs incurred, or how many units are actually made, the company in Activity 2 will treat each completed unit as having 'absorbed' an overhead cost of 50 pence. For all accounting purposes the overhead cost per unit is 50 pence.

The actual overhead costs incurred are debited to a production overheads account (the contra entries being credits to bank or to creditors). As each unit is completed, an amount of 50 pence is credited to production overheads and charged to the cost of the unit through the work-in-progress control account.

Activity 3	During the next accounting period of the company in Activity 2, production overheads amounted to £102,960 and 198,000 units were produced. Write up the production overheads account in the outline format provided.

Production overheads account

As can be seen, the company has incurred overhead costs of £102,960 but has only included costs of £99,000 in the cost of products. This difference is described as overheads under-absorbed (or overheads under-recovered) and must be treated as an expense for the period, i.e. must be transferred to profit and loss at period-end.

Activity 4	Go back to the production overhead account for Activity 3 and demonstrate how this would be balanced off at the end of the period by making the appropriate entry.

Notice how the overheads under-absorbed can be identified as resulting from two variances between estimated and actual results, namely:

- an expenditure variance of (£100,000 – £102,960)   £2,960
- an activity variance of (2,000 × £0.50)   £1,000
                                                                                              £3,960

The situation dealt with above was unrealistic for two reasons. First, a company is likely to produce more than one type of product. Even if it only produced two types of article such as clocks and watches, there is no unique quantity of similar units that can be divided into estimated overheads in order to calculate a rate per unit.

Secondly, production may be divided into a number of successive stages where the output from one process becomes the input to the next. If you look back at Chapter 2, you will see an illustration of a manufacturer dividing the process of making desks and chairs into three distinct stages, each stage taking place in a separate production cost centre. In these cases, overhead costs will differ in each cost centre, as will the type of production activity taking place in that cost centre. In order to determine the total overhead cost of each product, an absorption basis will have to be devised for each cost centre. In order to control the costs of each cost centre a production overhead control account will be maintained for each.

There are two components in the formula for BOAR: the overheads of each cost centre, and the measurement of activity for that cost centre. We will look at the budgeted overheads first.

2 Overheads of production cost centres

The factory will be made up of several departments. Some will be involved in actually making the products; others (such as the stores department) will be providing services to production. As you know from Chapter 2, these are called *production cost centres* and *service cost centres* respectively.

If you can recall your lessons from Chapter 2 you will remember that one of the objectives in accounting for production overheads is to ensure that they are all ultimately treated as the costs of production cost centres, even though some might initially have been incurred by the service cost centres.

There are three distinct stages in the process of attributing total factory overheads to the production cost centres. The first two stages relate to both types of cost centre (production and service) and recognise that some factory overheads can be specifically identified as the cost of a particular cost centre, whereas others are common costs relating to the whole factory and must be spread across the cost centres. The first two stages require application of the following procedures:

1   Cost allocation: this involves charging discrete identifiable items of cost to the cost centres to which they specifically relate.

2   Cost apportionment: this involves dividing up common costs amongst a number of cost centres in proportion to the estimated benefit received.

Activity 5	See if you can distinguish between factory overheads that could be allocated specifically to a particular cost centre, and overheads that will have to be apportioned amongst several cost centres. Make a note of two types of cost that might be treated under each of the following headings: 1 Cost allocation: 2 Cost apportionment:

On completing the first two stages of cost allocation and cost apportionment, the total factory overheads have been attributed to production cost centres and to service cost centres. The third and final stage is then as follows:

3   Apportion the total overheads of each service cost centre to production cost centres.

Notice that there are two stages at which factory overheads are apportioned: (1) apportioning non-specific costs (such as rent and rates) to all cost centres, including service cost centres, and (2) re-apportioning overheads of service cost centres to the production cost centres.

The process is quite logical – it simply involves using some kind of basis to measure the estimated benefits that each cost centre has received from the expenditure.

Activity 6	See if you can suggest a suitable basis for apportioning the following factory costs to cost centres:

1   Rent and rates of the whole building

2   Insurance of plant and machinery

3   The costs of a staff canteen

4   The costs of running the stores department

You must now practise using these first concepts by working through an example in stages. Most of the activities on overheads in this chapter are based on the details and requirements of one particular company, as set out in Appendix 1 of this chapter. This appendix is followed by working sheets that you will be using to build up solutions to the complete problem.

You will notice that there is quite a lot of detail in the problem, a great deal of which you do not need for the current stage of the exercise. Furthermore, most of the requirements will seem strange at the moment, unless you have studied this topic previously. Don't let this put you off – you will soon be able to solve the entire problem.

The Key provides a stepped solution after each activity.

Activity 7	Using the working sheet provided, deal with the first two stages of the overhead allocation and apportionment as follows:

1   Write in the allocated overheads (this simply involves copying data from the question).

2   Deal with the apportionments of rent etc., and insurance. Make a note of the basis used (they are both fairly obvious) and make sure that the total of the apportioned costs agrees with the total given in the question.

The third stage is to sub-total the service cost centres and apportion their totals to the production cost centres. You will note that one of the service cost centres (the canteen) provides services to another service cost centre – the maintenance section.

In this situation, it saves a little time if the costs of the department that provides services to another service cost centre are apportioned first. If you do not follow this rule in this example, you will find yourself having to apportion the costs of the maintenance section twice. But whatever the sequence of reapportionment of service costs, the final (total) production cost centre costs will be the same.

Activity 8	Sub-total the overheads for the service cost centres and apportion these totals as appropriate. Deal with the canteen first. You can indicate that the overheads for each service cost centre have been apportioned to the other centres by including the total amount apportioned in brackets below the relative sub-total.

You have now shuffled everything into the production cost centres. It is a good idea in these problems to check that the total overheads attributed to production cost centres agrees with the total overheads given in the problem. If you do this with this example you will find that the total attributed is (£84,320 + £48,060) £132,380, which agrees with the total overheads given in the question.

The next stage is to calculate an absorption rate for each production cost centre, but you need to learn the principles of activity bases first. We can return to Bookdon plc after you have made sense of these basic principles.

3 Activity bases and absorption rates

In Section 1 of this chapter we used the estimated number of units to be produced as an activity measurement. We were able to do that because the company was producing one homogeneous type of article. Multi-product firms have to adopt one of several other bases.

The most plausible bases are those that are related to a time measurement. If one type of product takes two hours to make, and another type takes one hour to make, then it seems reasonable to treat the product taking two hours as having absorbed twice as much overhead as the one taking one hour.

Activity 9	Can you think of any convincing argument for the statement made in the previous paragraph? Think about the actual factory overheads themselves, or at least the largest share of these overheads. Make a note of any points that occur to you, and then check with the Key.

There are two time measurements that can be used in practice: machine hours and direct labour hours.

| **Activity 10** | In practice it is usually a little more convenient to use direct labour hours rather than machine hours. Can you think why this might be? Think about the records that are likely to be available to the cost accountant. |

However, many modern items of plant and equipment include metering devices that can produce information on the number of hours used.

| **Activity 11** | See if you can think of the factors that will influence a choice between machine hours and direct labour hours. Think about the different methods of production.

Machine hours when:

Direct labour hours when: |

Calculating absorption rates based on machine hours or labour hours is simply a matter of using the basic formula (see Section 1 of this chapter) and dividing the budgeted overheads for the cost centre concerned by the budgeted hours for that cost centre.

The total number of hours might not be given directly and will have to be calculated from related data. The resulting absorption rate is referred to as a machine hour rate, or direct labour hour rate, depending on the activity base being used.

| **Activity 12** | Return to details on Bookdon plc and you will see that part (a) of the problem requires a machine hour rate to be calculated for the machine shop. Do this now. You will have to calculate the total number of machine hours first; don't forget there are three products passing through the machine shop. There is a space at the foot of the working sheet for your calculations. Ignore the fitting section for the time being. Write the results of your calculations in Sections 4 and 5 of the working sheet. |

You might have noticed that the absorption rate to be calculated for the fitting section is referred to as a percentage rate; in this particular case a percentage of the direct labour cost. The formula is the same as before except that the result of the fraction is expressed as a percentage, rather than a rate per hour. Before doing the calculations for Bookdon, we should consider the principle of using costs as a measure of activity in more general terms.

Production activity can be measured in terms of either units produced, hours taken, or costs incurred. There are three cost measurements that can be used in this context: direct materials, direct labour, and prime cost.

If direct material costs are to be used as a measure of production activity, the approach can be explained by the following example:

$$\frac{\text{Budgeted production overheads}}{\text{Budgeted direct materials to be consumed}} = \frac{£100,000}{£50,000}$$

The fraction is the same as in the basic formula except that the result is expressed as a percentage. As can be seen in the above example, the percentage is 200%. Consequently, we would talk about an absorption rate of 200% of direct material costs. If the direct material cost of a unit was £100, then the overhead to be added to the cost of that unit would be £200.

Activity 13	There is a serious flaw in correlating the overhead cost per unit with the direct material cost per unit. Can you think what it is? Think about the point that we discovered earlier regarding the nature of most overheads.

An absorption rate based on a percentage of prime cost simply compounds this particular problem.

There is some correlation between direct labour cost and time taken and this makes it an expedient basis to use in practice. From the payroll analysis, the cost accounting clerk will charge out the direct labour costs to the cost of production; it is then a simple matter to charge a pre-determined percentage of this labour cost for overheads.

Although the correlation between time taken and direct labour cost is quite strong, there can be a slight flaw when the workforce is made up of different types of labour. Consider the following example:

An article can be made by either a skilled worker or an apprentice. The time taken and rates of pay are as follows:

1   The skilled worker takes one hour and is paid £6 per hour
2   The apprentice takes two hours and is paid £3 per hour

As can be seen, the direct labour cost is the same but the time taken by the apprentice is twice that of the skilled worker. However, this was an extreme example, and such differences tend to be smoothed out in an average workforce.

Activity 14	Return to the problem of Bookdon plc and calculate the absorption rate based on a percentage of direct labour cost. You will have to calculate the total direct labour cost in the fitting section first, and then express this as a percentage of the overheads for the fitting section.

You now need to see what use is made of all these calculations, and how the figures are dealt with in the books, by working the following activities.

Activity 15

The first thing to do is answer part (b) of the problem. You are required to calculate the total cost of a unit of product X. The total cost is made up of direct materials, direct labour, and production overheads. Don't forget that the product goes through two production cost centres. There is a place on the working sheet for you to set out an answer.

Although the question does not ask you to deal with the relative book-keeping aspects, writing up the ledger accounts is the best way of providing an answer to part (c) of the question (overheads under- or over-absorbed). In this case, there will be two production overhead accounts, one for the machine shop and one for the fitting section.

Activity 16

Using the blank accounts provided in the work-sheet, write up the production overhead accounts for both production cost centres. Remember that the actual overheads incurred are debited, and overheads absorbed (at the BOAR on actual activity) are credited. Show how any differences will be dealt with.

The final part of the exercise is to deal with requirement (d). There is no need to write out a complete answer in essay form but you must identify the key points. The request by the production director seems quite reasonable on the surface, but there are two aspects in his suggestion where you will have to respond: (1) the use of units as a measurement of activity, and (2) the use of actual overheads for the month instead of budgeted overheads.

Activity 17

Consider the request by the production director in part (d) of the problem and make a summary of the key points you would include in a written answer. There is a place at the end of the work-sheet for making your notes on this.

One further point to make about absorption rates is that the labour hour or machine hour is only a realistic base when product X, which spends six machine hours in a particular cost production centre, really does incur twice the overhead costs incurred by product Y, which only spends three hours there. For example, perhaps product Y is the sole user of a particularly expensive piece of machinery whose depreciation is included in the department's overhead cost calculations, and in fact accounts for 70% of the overhead. Product Y should obviously be allotted a greater overhead as it costs the business far more than is implied by the machine hour absorption rate.

Activity-based costing (ABC) states that in order to properly cost products, we must attribute overheads with full regards to the resources used in the production of the products. It also suggests that businesses critically look for cost drivers – the activity elements that incur costs and that should be used to attribute costs to products. In the case of products X and Y, time spent on the expensive piece of machinery would be called a cost driver.

4 Product costs and profit measurement

The principles used to determine the cost of products will determine how much of the current period's costs will be carried forward as an asset in the form of finished goods stock. It also has a bearing on the usefulness of information provided to management for decision making.

You will know from several previous lessons that there are two principles that can be applied in arriving at the cost of finished goods, namely:

- absorbed cost
- marginal cost.

You have now seen from your work in this chapter how absorbed cost attributes all production overheads to the cost of finished goods, including those that are fixed, such as rent, rates and insurance.

This is required for financial accounting purposes in order to comply with SSAP 9. This SSAP requires that the cost of converting raw materials into finished goods should include all production overheads, even if fixed. This is because stock should be valued at the total cost to the enterprise.

SSAPs are concerned with matters of principle, not the practical difficulties of applying those principles. Consequently, SSAP 9 contains no regulations on how the company should attribute overheads to production cost centres, nor on specific bases to be applied for absorbing these overheads. There is, however, one principle in SSAP 9 regarding absorption that the company must recognise in its accounting procedures – fixed production overheads must be absorbed on the basis of normal capacity, not actual production.

This is quite an important principle in the context of profit measurement because its effect is to exclude from finished goods stock any costs arising through the inefficient use of resources during the current period. You will see this for yourself by working the following activity.

Activity 18	After taking account of the stoppages and breakdowns that occur in the normal course of business, a company considers that it has the technical capacity to produce 10,000 units in a period. During the current period it suffered a loss in output due to an industrial dispute and was only able to produce 4,000 units. Its fixed production overheads for the period were £10,000. Determine the amount of fixed production overhead that should be included in each unit of finished goods stock at the end of the period.

Note that if the actual production quantities had been used, the overhead cost per unit would be £2.50. This does not create any problem if all the goods produced are sold; the fixed overhead cost of £10,000 will be matched with sales income through the cost of sales expense.

But this is not likely to happen and by including £2.50 for fixed overheads in each unit of closing stock, instead of £1 per unit based on normal capacity, the company would be carrying forward a higher proportion of costs for no reason other than the fact that output had fallen during the current period.

According to SSAP 9, the costs to be included in closing stock are those that arise in the normal course of trade. The extra cost of £1.50 per unit is not a cost in the normal course of trade and should therefore be treated as an expense in the current period. This is achieved by absorbing fixed overheads on the basis of normal capacity. Fixed overheads of (4,000 × £1) £4,000 are then absorbed into finished goods, leaving £6,000 to be written off to cost of sales.

As you know from previous lessons, marginal cost (the cost that can be avoided if the unit is not made) excludes fixed production overheads from product costs under cost and management terminology. Marginal cost is usually considered to consist of the following:

- direct materials
- direct labour
- direct expense
- variable overheads.

You will learn about the techniques that can be used in order to identify the amounts for variable overheads in the next section.

One of the reasons why SSAP 9 was introduced was that some companies at the time were valuing their finished goods stock on the basis of marginal cost, whilst others were using absorbed cost. This made it difficult to compare the results of different companies.

Since stock valuations based on absorbed cost are different to those based on marginal cost, there will be a difference in reported profits. There are a number of different ways in which the figures in these statements can be presented; some are more confusing than others. The best approach is to think about the problem on the following lines:

- the actual expenditure incurred in manufacturing will not differ simply because a different basis is used for valuing finished goods stock, the costs incurred will be the same under either method

- cost of sales is based on the opening stock of finished goods plus the expenditure incurred in manufacturing the goods less the closing stock of finished goods

- the only differences are in the stock valuation.

If you approach the problem like this you will avoid the need to determine overheads under- or over-absorbed. It also emphasises that the differences in profit measurement are simply the result of different stock valuations.

5 A closer look at variable costs

In analysing the relationship between cost, volume, and profit it is necessary to make an assumption that all costs can be classed as either variable costs or as fixed costs for the period.

In many cases the distinction between fixed and variable is not difficult. Expenses such as rent, rates, insurance, administration, and so on, are likely to be fixed, at least in the short term, and will remain at the same level irrespective of any changes in the volume of activity.

Variable cost is sometimes called marginal cost but it is misleading in the context of cost, volume, profit analysis to treat these two terms as meaning the same thing. The term marginal cost refers to the cost of a product (the cost that can be avoided if the unit is not made, or purchased) and although the marginal cost of a product will include its variable cost it is not the only cost to be included.

Some variable costs are quite easy to identify. The cost of raw materials consumed in the case of a manufactured product, and the purchase cost of a product in the case of a retailer, are clearly variable costs. Direct labour costs are also treated as variable. In reality, direct labour costs are often fixed over a narrow range of output, but in order to achieve greater volumes of output it will be necessary to increase the direct labour force and so the direct labour cost will increase as the level of output is increased. Over a sufficiently wide range of output the direct labour cost can be assumed to vary in a straight line, even though in reality this line is likely to be a series of narrow steps.

Activity 19	There is really only one method of remuneration that will result in the direct labour cost being truly variable. See if you can think what this method is and make a note of it here.

However, you must always treat direct labour costs as variable except where you are dealing with a situation where this is clearly not the case, such as estimating costs within a narrow range of output.

The difficulty with many manufacturing costs, and with distribution costs such as the cost of running a fleet of delivery vans, is that the amounts recorded in the ledger are a mixture of fixed and variable costs. Delivery expenses are a good example because the total cost is made up of running expenses (such as fuel, tyres, repairs, etc.) which are likely to be variable, and standing costs (such as road tax, insurance, and depreciation) which are fixed.

Cost, volume, profit analysis rests on the assumption that all costs can be identified as being either fixed or variable; yet here we see examples of costs that are a mixture of the two. The company could attempt to analyse costs between fixed and variable as they are incurred, but we will assume that this has not been done. We now need a technique to separate the fixed from the variable without going back through all the entries in the ledger account and analysing each item again.

Various techniques are used, but we will be looking at a fairly simple technique known as the 'high/low' method. It works by observing changes in total costs between two levels of activity. The correlation between the increase in costs and the increase in activity enables an estimate to be made of the variable cost. Fixed costs are derived as a balance. The explanation sounds more complicated than the actual technique, as you will see by working on the following example:

A company is attempting to analyse its delivery costs between fixed and variable. From past records it is able to determine the following data:

Period	Miles run	Delivery costs
1	2,000	£4,000
2	4,000	£6,050
3	8,000	£10,000

The variable cost is to be expressed as an amount per mile. There have been no changes in price levels over the three periods concerned.

The high/low technique will make observations of costs at the lowest activity level of 2,000 miles, and at the highest activity level of 8,000 miles. The first step is to set out a tabulation of the miles run, and the associated costs, at each of these two levels. A third column is included for recording the increases in miles and costs.

Activity 20

Use this outline tabulation for the above example. Complete this by entering the relevant figures, including the increase in both costs and miles run.

Activity levels

	Low	High	Increase
Activity measure (miles run)			
Total delivery costs (£s)			

If your figures agree with the Key you can move to the next activity.

Activity 21

It is the 'increase' column that tells us something. We can draw a reasonable conclusion from the figures in that column. Make a note of what this is.

Fixed costs can now be determined by deducting variable costs from the total costs. It is a good idea to deduct the variable costs from total costs at both levels of activity. This acts as a check on the arithmetic because the amount for fixed costs should be the same at both levels if the calculations are correct. This does not prove the truth of the figure for fixed costs – it is only a check on the arithmetic. Figures produced by the high/low method are estimates, but they are good enough for most accounting purposes.

Activity 22	Determine fixed costs for the example, using the following tabulation:

	2,000 miles	8,000 miles
Total costs		
Less variable costs		
Fixed cost (balance)		

In the above example we used miles run as an activity measurement but there could be many others such as hours worked, units produced, units sold, sales value in £s, and so on.

Variable production overheads might include items such as consumable stores (sprays, paints, lubricants) and power costs for running the plant. As you know, these costs are charged to production overheads because it is impossible to measure how much has been consumed by each unit.

If the company wishes to separate variable production overheads from fixed production overheads, the costs should be classified between fixed and variable at source so that they can be charged to separate overheads accounts. If this is not done, variable overheads become mixed with fixed overheads in a single overheads account. Consider the following example:

A company charges all indirect costs to a single production overheads account. It now needs to ascertain a variable overhead cost per machine hour so that it can determine a variable overhead cost per unit. The following information has been extracted from past records:

Year	Machine hours	Total overheads
1990	110,000	£330,000
1989	100,000	£305,000
1988	90,000	£280,000
1987	87,000	£272,500
1986	105,000	£317,500
1985	80,000	£255,000

Activity 23	Use the high/low technique to determine a variable overhead cost per machine hour.

The high/low technique is used in many situations when a prediction of costs for different levels of activity is required. It is also a useful for learners to experiment with the technique because it focuses on the way costs behave in response to changes in the level of activity. Try using it again on the next problem.

The following example is contrived in the sense that some of the information that would be available in real life has been omitted:

The historic data of a company is as follows:

	Period 1	Period 2
Sales	£28,000	£41,000
Net profit/(loss)	(990)	3,300

It is a single-product company and the sales price is £4 per unit. There were no changes in price levels over the two periods. The company wishes to determine how many units it must sell in order to earn a profit of £6,600.

You might think that this problem cannot be solved, at least until you hit on the idea of using logical assumptions and the high/low technique. Admittedly the costs for each period have not been given, but you know enough about accounting to realise that net profit (or loss) is derived from sales income less total costs. You also know that total costs are comprised of fixed and variable costs.

Try solving the problem in two stages by working through the following two activities.

Activity 24	The first step is to determine the variable cost per unit, and the fixed cost for the period, by using the high/low technique. Use the number of units sold as the activity measure.

We now know that the variable cost per unit is £2.68 and so we can calculate the contribution per unit. The contribution is the difference between sales income and direct costs, and it contributes towards the organisation's overheads. The extra units produce an extra sales revenue of £4 per unit and incur extra variable costs of £2.68 per unit. So the extra units contribute an extra £4 - £2.68 = £1.32 per unit to profit. In order to cover the fixed costs of £10,230 and leave a profit of £6,600, the company will have to sell enough units to bring in a total contribution of (£10,230 + £6,600) £16,830.

Activity 25	If the total contribution needed is £16,830, and the contribution per unit is £1.32, it is a matter of simple arithmetic to determine how many units must be sold to earn a contribution of £16,830. Calculate this number, and set out a profit statement.

Problems that initially look difficult quite often turn out to be relatively easy providing we can find the right approach and an appropriate tool.

Summary

The main learning points in this chapter are:

- budgeted overhead absorption rates are found by dividing the budgeted overheads for each production cost centre by the budgeted activity for that cost centre

- budgeted overheads for each production cost centre are calculated through a three-stage process of cost allocation, cost apportionment, and the re-apportionment of service department costs to production cost centres

- activity bases can either be time-related such as machine hours or direct labour hours; or cost-related such as a percentage of direct labour cost

- overheads incurred are debited to a production overhead account for each production cost centre; overheads absorbed (BOAR on actual activity) are credited to these accounts and debited to work-in-progress

- differences between overheads incurred and overheads absorbed are written off to profit and loss

- SSAP 9 requires fixed production overheads to be absorbed on the basis of normal capacity, not actual production

- the difference between the selling price and variable cost of a unit is known as the contribution

- contribution theory relies on the assumption that all costs can be identified as either a variable cost per unit or a fixed cost for the period

- if costs are a mixture of fixed and variable, techniques such as the high/low method are used to give an approximate analysis between the two types of cost.

Appendix 1

Details for the activities starting with Activity 7

Bookdon plc manufactures three products in two production departments, a machine shop and a fitting section; it also has two service departments, a canteen and a machine maintenance section. Shown below are next year's budgeted production data and manufacturing costs for the company.

Product	X	Y	Z
Production	4,200 units	6,900 units	1,700 units
Prime cost:			
Direct materials	£11 per unit	£14 per unit	£17 per unit
Direct labour:			
Machine shop	£6 per unit	£4 per unit	£2 per unit
Fitting section	£12 per unit	£3 per unit	£21 per unit
Machine hours, per unit	6 hours	3 hours	4 hours

Budgeted overheads	Machine shop	Fitting section	Canteen	Maintenance	Total
Allocated overheads	£27,660	£19,470	£16,600	£26,650	£90,380
Rent, rates, heat and light					£17,000
Insurance of equipment					£25,000
Additional data:					
Book value of equipment	£150,000	£75,000	£30,000	£45,000	
Number of employees	18	14	4	4	
Floor space (square metres)	3,600	1,400	1,000	800	

It has been estimated that approximately 70% of the machine maintenance section's costs are incurred in servicing the machine shop; the remainder relates to the fitting section.

Requirements:

a) Calculate the following budgeted overhead absorption rates:

a machine hour rate for the machine shop
a rate expressed as a percentage of direct wages for the fitting section.

b) Calculate the total production cost of one unit of product X.

c) After the year end, it was ascertained that the actual figures for this year were as follows:

i)   Overheads incurred: machine shop £86,000; fitting section £50,000
ii) Activity measurements: machine shop 50,000 machine hours; fitting section incurred direct wages cost of £105,000.

Determine the amount of overhead under- or over-absorbed in each cost centre.

d) The production director of Bookdon plc has suggested that 'as the actual overheads incurred and units produced are usually different from that budgeted and profits are distorted by over/under absorbed overheads, it would be more accurate to calculate the actual overhead cost per unit each month end by dividing the total number of units actually produced during the month into the actual overheads incurred'. Critically examine this suggestion.

Note: the foregoing details are based on a past ACCA Level 1 cost accounting exam question. The details and requirements in part (c) were not included in the original question.

Working sheet for activities on Bookdon plc

		Machine shop	Fitting section	Canteen	Maintenance	Total
		£	£	£	£	£
1	Allocated costs					
2	Apportioned costs:	Basis				
	Rent, rates, heat and light	Floor area				
	Insurance	Eqpt value				
	Sub-total of service cost centres					
3	Apportion service centre costs					
	a) Canteen	Employees				
	b) Maintenance	% given				
	Totals					

Activity bases	machine hours	d/labour cost (£)

4 Activity measurements
    (calculations below)

5 Absorption rate
    (calculations below)

Calculations

Total machine hours   Total direct labour cost
for the machine shop   for the fitting section

Absorption rate for machine shop   Absorption rate for the fitting section

Total production cost of 1 unit of product X

Ledger accounts:

Production overheads account – machine shop

Production overheads account – fitting section

d) Points regarding production director's suggestion:

1 Use of units as the activity measure

2 Using actual costs per month instead of budgeted figures

Key to Chapter 4 activities

Activity 1   You might have thought of things like wages of the maintenance engineers, supervisors' salaries, rent, rates and insurance of the building, depreciation of the plant, electricity costs and so on.

Activity 2   £100,000 ÷ 200,000 = £0.50 per unit

Activity 3

Production overheads account

Bank/creditors	£102,960	Work-in-progress (198,000 × £0.50)	£99,000

Activity 4

Production overheads account

Bank/creditors	£102,960	Work-in-progress (198,000 × £0.50)	£99,000
		P&L (o'hds under-absorbed)	3,960
	102,960		102,960

Activity 5   Notes: It was easier to identify costs that might have to be apportioned. The allocation of specific costs often depends on whether a record is kept of the specific location incurring the cost. Don't forget that we are dealing with overheads and so it would be wrong to mention costs such as direct materials and direct labour. The following gives an indication of how you might have been able to differentiate between the two types of cost:

Cost allocation: wages of staff working in particular service cost centres (the wages of most employees working in production cost centres are direct labour costs, not overheads); consumable stores (such as paints, sprays, and lubricants) used by a specific cost centre; depreciation of plant in a specific cost centre.

Cost apportionment: occupancy costs common to cost centres such as rent rates and insurance; repairs to buildings; electricity costs; overall production manager's salary.

Activity 6   Possible apportionment bases:

1   relative floor area of each cost centre
2   book value of plant used in each cost centre
3   number of employees in each production cost centre
4   cost of materials used in each production cost centre

Notice that items 1 and 2 can apply to either production cost centres or service cost centres; items 3 and 4 relate to the apportionment of service cost centre overheads to production cost centres.

Activity 7   At this stage your working sheet should look like this:

		Machine shop	Fitting section	Canteen	Maintenance	Total
		£	£	£	£	£
1	Allocated costs		27,660	19,470	16,600	26,650	90,380
2	Apportioned costs:	Basis					
	Rent, rates, heat and light	Floor area	9,000	3,500	2,500	2,000	17,000
	Insurance	Eqpt value	12,500	6,250	2,500	3,750	25,000

Activity 8   Your working sheet should now be as follows:

		Machine shop	Fitting section	Canteen	Maintenance	Total
		£	£	£	£	£
1	Allocated costs		27,660	19,470	16,600	26,650	90,380
2	Apportioned costs:	Basis					
	Rent, rates, heat and light	Floor area	9,000	3,500	2,500	2,000	17,000
	Insurance	Eqpt value	12,500	6,250	2,500	3,750	25,000
	Sub-total of service cost centres				21,600	32,400	
3	Apportion service centre costs						
	a) Canteen	Employees	10,800	8,400	(21,600)	2,400	0
	b) Maintenance	% given	24,360	10,440		(34,800)	0
	Totals		84,320	48,060	0	0	132,380

Note that the total number of employees for the canteen cost allocation is based on the number of employees in cost centres other than the canteen.

Activity 9   It might have occurred to you that most factory overheads are time-related. Costs such as rent, rates, insurance, depreciation, are all related to the passage of time. Even costs such as electricity are strongly time-related.

Activity 10   Because there will be an accounting record (the time-sheets) of the number of hours spent on production. Machine hours will require an additional record to be kept of how long each machine is used.

Activity 11   Machine hours when production is machine intensive; labour hours when production is labour intensive.

Activity 12   Total machine hours $(4,200 \times 6) + (6,900 \times 3) + (1,700 \times 4) = 52,700$
Machine hour rate $(\pounds84,320 \div 52,700) = \pounds1.60$ per machine hour

Activity 13   Most overheads accrue on a time basis. There is usually no relationship between the amount spent on materials and the length of time taken to produce the article, or the likely level of overheads expended on the product in a production cost centre.

Activity 14   The direct labour cost in the fitting section is: $(4,200 \times \pounds12) + (6,900 \times \pounds3) + (1,700 \times \pounds21) = \pounds106,800$

The absorption rate is: $\dfrac{\pounds48,060}{\pounds106,800} = 45\%$ of the direct labour cost

Activity 15
Total cost of a unit of product X		
Direct materials		£11.00
Direct labour: machine shop	£6.00	
fitting section	£12.00	
		£18.00
Prime cost		£29.00
Production overheads:		
machine shop (6 × £1.60)	£9.60	
fitting section (45% × £12)	£5.40	
		£15.00
Total production cost		£44.00

Activity 16
Production overheads account – machine shop

Bank/creditors	86,000	Work-in-progress	80,000
		(50,000 × £1.60)	
		Work-in-progress	6,000
		(under-absorbed)	
	86,000		86,000

Production overheads account – fitting section

Bank/creditors	50,000	Work-in-progress (45% × £105.000)	47,250
		Cost of sales (under-absorbed)	2,750
	50,000		50,000

Activity 17

1   Use of units:
Products are not homogeneous in terms of their use of production facilities; for example, product X takes twice as long to process in the machine shop than product Y.

2   Use of actual costs:
There are three essential points, although you may only have thought of one of these from the chapter.

    1)   It will be quite some time after the end of the month before all actual costs are known.

    2)   Some costs are cyclical in nature; for example, heating costs are higher in the winter than in the summer; repairs are high in some months and low in others. If actual costs were used, overhead costs per unit would fluctuate depending on the costs in the month when the units were made. By using budgeted figures for the whole year, these fluctuations are smoothed.

    3)   Should actual expenditure be higher than expected (and perhaps higher than reasonable) due to poor business control, using actual prices will overprice the product. Lower costs than usual (unusually low cost of materials, for example) may lead to underpricing. Over- or underpricing of products may lead to wrong decisions being taken, e.g. setting the selling price at an unrealistic level.

Activity 18

£10,000 ÷10,000 = £1 per unit

Activity 19

Piece-work rates with no guaranteed minimum.

Activity 20

	Activity levels		
	Low	High	Increase
Activity measure	2,000 miles	8,000 miles	6,000 miles
Total delivery costs	£4,000	£10,000	£6,000

Activity 21

We can assume that variable costs are £1 per mile (an increase in 6,000 miles has caused costs to increase by £6,000).

Activity 22

	2,000 miles	8,000 miles
Total costs	£4,000	£10,000
Less variable costs	£2,000	£8,000
Fixed cost (balance)	£2,000	£2,000

Activity 23

	Low	High	Increase
Hours worked	80,000	110,000	30,000 hours
Total costs	£255,000	£330,000	£75,000

Variable costs can be estimated at (£75,000 ÷ 30,000) £2.50 per hour

Activity 24

	Low	High	Increase
Units sold	7,000	10,250	3,250 }
Total costs	£28,990	£37,700	£8,710 }

∴ variable costs per unit =
£8,710 ÷ 3,250 = £2.68

	Low	High
Less variable costs	18,760	27,470
Fixed cost (derived)	10,230	10,230

Activity 25

Number of units is £16,830 ÷ £1.32 = 12,750 and so the profit statement is:

Sales (12,750 × £4)	£51,000
Variable costs (12,750 × £2.68)	34,170
Contribution	16,830
Fixed costs	10,230
Net profit	6,600

Chapter 5

Using standard costs

Introduction

In this chapter you will learn how the cost of products can be based on a pre-determined cost called the standard cost. Standard costs are calculated in advance of the accounting period and are based on assessment of the material prices, labour rates, and various operating conditions that are expected to apply during the next period. Standard costs are often determined as a part of the budgeting process.

Use of standard costs enables the cost accountant to reflect differences from budgeted activity in the cost accounting system by way of variances – i.e. by way of the effects of those differences on the business profit and loss. This process is known as variance accounting. It provides management with an excellent tool for control purposes.

Objectives

After you have completed this chapter, you should be able to:

■   discuss the concept of standard cost and its relevance to product costs

■   demonstrate the basic approach in standard cost book-keeping

■   prepare a basic analysis of production cost variances.

1 Objectives and basis of the system

According to the CIMA definitions, standard costing provides management with two (sometimes three) facilities, namely:

■ a basis for control through variance accounting

■ a basis for the valuation of stocks and work in progress

■ a basis, in some cases, for assessing selling prices.

For NVQ Level 3, the subject is mainly concerned with control by means of variance analysis, i.e. measuring differences between planned and actual activity by way of effects on profit and loss.

The assessment of standard costs takes account of technical specifications (such as quantity of materials and labour hours needed to make the product) and the prices and wage rates expected to prevail during the period for which the standard costs are to be used.

In arriving at a standard cost for each product, the company must consider the performance attainable from existing facilities. Standard performance is usually identified under two headings: an ideal standard and an attainable standard. These are defined by the CIMA in the following way:

Ideal standard. A standard which can be attained under the most favourable conditions. No provision is made for machine breakdowns, etc.

Attainable standard. A standard which can be attained if a standard unit of work is carried out efficiently. Allowances are made for normal shrinkage, waste and machine breakdowns. This standard represents a performance which is capable of achievement.

The comparison of actual performance against either of these two standards, and the analysis of cost variances according to their cause, provides the basic framework for cost control.

Activity 1	The comparison of actual performance against an ideal standard usually results in unfavourable cost variances because actual performance is unlikely to be able to match up to the ideal. Proponents of the ideal standard claim that the resulting unfavourable variances will remind management of the need for improvement in all phases of operations. Despite this, ideal standards are very rarely used in practice. See if you can think why this might be and make a note of your ideas here.

Attainable standards represent targets that are capable of achievement and any variances between actual performance and these standards are, theoretically, capable of being controlled. In exercising control, management establishes a system of responsibility accounting. This involves assigning responsibility for the control of costs to departmental managers who may then be called upon to explain any variations between actual performance and standard.

Responsibility accounting is very closely linked to variance analysis. If we look at any cost variance, we will find that there are two basic causes: variances in the price of resources used, and variances in the utilisation of those resources. Consider the following example on material costs:

The standard raw material cost of one unit of finished product has been set for the next accounting period:

1 kilogram of raw material CDS at a standard price of £2 per kg = £2

During the accounting period concerned, the company made 100 units of the finished product. This consumed 110 kg of raw material CDS which had cost the company £217 to purchase.

The standard material cost for 100 units of finished product is £200, yet these materials have cost £217. The difference of £17 (the 'total material cost variance') is the total negative (adverse) effect on profit and loss from purchase and use of the raw materials on the 100 product units.

Activity 2	If you look more closely at the detail you will notice this total variance is the result of two separate causes. Describe the two causes (but do not attempt to make any accounting measurements at the moment).

These two variances are known as the material price variance and the material usage variance.

The responsibility for explaining these two variances rests with different departmental managers. The production manager is responsible for explaining the usage variance, whereas the price variance is the responsibility of the purchasing manager.

You should be able to analyse the total variance of £17 in the above example between the price variance and the usage variance. The following notes are given to clarify how the convention applies to this example.

The price variance is the difference between the amount that the company was charged for the 110 kg, and the amount it would have been charged if these materials had been purchased at the standard price.

The usage variance relates to the difference between the actual quantity of raw materials used and the standard quantity that should have been used. This difference is measured at the standard price.

Where actual costs are lower than the standard we refer to the variance as favourable, where they are higher we refer to the variance as unfavourable or adverse.

| **Activity 3** | Calculate the material price variance and the material usage variance for the above example, and identify these variances as favourable or adverse.

Material price variance:

Material usage variance:

 |

A first glance at this analysis might suggest that the purchasing department have done rather well for the company, whereas the production department can be criticised for having been careless in the use of materials. But quite often there is an inter-relationship between the two variances that might explain why one is favourable and the other is adverse.

| **Activity 4** | See if you can think of a common factor that might explain why the price variance was favourable and the usage variance was adverse.

 |

Note that standards should be constantly reviewed. If a variance is shown to have been caused by the use of an out-of-date standard, the standard cost will be revised.

2 The relevance of standard cost for stock valuation

We tend to think of 'actual cost' as something derived from the recording of a past transaction, whereas 'standard' cost seems to be an amount that someone has thought up in advance of the transaction. This might make us sceptical of the idea of using standard costs as a basis for stock valuation.

However, as we saw in the use of overhead absorption rates, using a standard for application of costs into stock balances until any reasons for variations from standard are fully analysed and accounted for can provide excellent control and analysis of variances.

In any system of cost accounting the amounts entering into the cost of products for materials and labour are not necessarily the same as the actual expenditure incurred on these two items. The basic concept is that the cost of manufactured products should only include costs that arise in the normal course of business.

Activity 5	You have come across a limited number of examples of this concept in previous chapters. Make a note here of any circumstances you can think of when actual expenditure on direct materials, and direct labour, are treated as abnormal and excluded from product costs. Example of abnormal cost excluded from product costs Direct materials Direct labour

These costs will finish up as expenses in the profit and loss for the period. It should therefore be fairly clear that although a company incurs actual costs in the course of manufacturing, this expenditure does not always finish up as a part of the cost of products. To maintain a correct balance (and realistic costs per product unit), some costs will be written off to profit and loss and not charged into stock valuations.

In all systems of cost accounting it is necessary to make a judgement of what represents a normal cost and what should be classed as abnormal. In standard costing, this judgement is made as part of a structured process of determining standards for the next period. By maintaining stock values effectively at standard, a cost accounting system highlights and explains variances that enable effective management control.

3 Outline of the book-keeping in a standard costing system

We will restrict the explanation of the book-keeping to material costs, although you should be able to see how the same principles can be applied to labour costs.

Most companies identify material price variances when the materials are purchased. The price variance is separated at this point and debited (or credited) to a price variance account. The raw materials stock account is debited with the standard price of the stock purchased, all stock-holdings registered in the account are then recorded at the standard price.

Activity 6	A new business has adopted standard costing. Its first transaction was to make a credit purchase of 100 units of raw material at a total cost of £220. The standard price for this material had been set at £2 per unit. Indicate how this transaction would be recorded in the books by entering the appropriate figures in the ledger accounts set out below this activity box. This is quite easy to do; the raw materials stock account is debited with the actual cost, the price variance is debited to the price variance account and credited to the raw material stock account, and creditors must be credited with the full amount due to them for the purchase.

Raw material stock	Price variance	Creditors

The charge of £20 recorded in the price variance account will subsequently be charged to profit and loss.

When the production department require materials for a particular production run they will be issued with the quantity of raw materials they require. This is debited to the work-in-progress account at standard price.

If additional materials are required to complete the production run (e.g. when some of the materials are wasted) the production supervisor will have to sign an 'excess materials requisition' and the standard price of this issue is debited to a usage variance account. If some of the original materials are returned to store, the usage variance account is credited.

Activity 7	The next transaction for the company in Activity 6 was to issue 40 units of raw material to production. Based on standard quantities, this should have been sufficient for the number of products being made but, due to excessive spoilage, the production department had to draw another 10 units of raw material from store in order to complete the batch. Indicate how these transactions would be recorded in the books by entering the appropriate figures in the ledger accounts shown below this box. The raw material stock account has been repeated for the sake of convenience.

Raw material stock	Work-in-progress	Usage variance
(100) £200		

Notice how the raw material stock account is maintained at standard price, thus eliminating the need to adopt a policy (such as FIFO) for pricing the issues. You can also make a useful observation by focusing your attention on the usage variance account.

The balance of the £20 charge to the usage variance account is transferred to profit and loss at the end of the financial period.

Activity 8	Make a note here of what you notice about the pricing of the usage variance account in this form of variance analysis.

The remaining sections in this chapter are concerned with variance analysis, and are based on a single set of details for one company which are set out in Appendix 1 at the end of this chapter.

4 Cost variances – materials and labour

You will find the analysis of cost variances for materials and labour to be the easiest part of any problem. You have already used the basis for analysing material cost variances; labour cost variances are calculated in a similar way although the terminology is slightly different.

When calculating cost variances from a mass of data, you must focus your attention on the actual quantity of goods produced, not on the quantity that the company expected to produce according to its budget.

We will deal with material cost variances first.

Total material cost variance
This is the difference between the material costs incurred and the standard material cost of the units produced.

Price variance
This is based on the whole quantity purchased.

Usage variance
This is measured at standard price.

Activity 9	For the example in Appendix 1, calculate variances for material costs and indicate whether they are adverse or favourable. Use the working guidelines following this activity box.

Total material cost variance:
    The standard material cost for the 10,200 units produced is   £
    The actual material cost incurred in producing 10,200 units was   £____
    Difference = total material cost variance (adverse/favourable)   £____

Material price variance:
    At standard price, the 39,000 kilos used would have cost   £____
    The 39,000 kilos actually cost   £____
    Difference = the price variance (adverse/favourable)   £____

Material usage variance:
    The standard quantity needed to produce 10,200 units is kilos
    The actual quantity used in producing 10,200 units was   ____ kilos
    Difference = quantity variance   ____ kilos

Quantity variance at standard price = £   (adverse/favourable)

Make sure that the sum of the material price variance and the material usage variance agrees with the total material cost variance. If they do not agree, check your calculations again before referring to the Key.

It is a good idea to calculate the price variance first because this might remind you that the usage variance is measured at standard price.

Notice how there are two stages in calculating the usage variance: the first stage calculates the difference in quantity between what should have been used and what was actually used, the second stage evaluates this quantity variance at the standard price.

The direct wage cost variance uses the same convention as for materials. The equivalent of the material price variance is known as the rate variance, and the equivalent of the usage variance is known as the efficiency variance.

Activity 10	Before considering the terms of the convention in relation to wages, see if you can answer the following two questions:
	1. Will the wage rate variance relate to the standard hours for the goods produced, or the actual hours worked?
	2. Will the efficiency variance be measured at the actual wage rate or at the standard wage rate?

The convention can now be summarised in the following way:

Total wage cost variance
This is the difference between the direct wages cost incurred and the standard wages cost of the units produced.

Rate variance
This is based on the total hours worked.

Efficiency variance
This is measured using the standard wage rate.

Activity 11	For the example in Appendix 1, calculate variances for direct wages costs and indicate whether they are adverse or favourable. Use the working guidelines following this activity box.

Total wages cost variance:
    The standard direct wages cost for 10,200 units is   £
    The actual direct wages cost incurred was   £ _____
    Difference = direct wages cost variance (adverse/favourable)   £ _____

Wages rate variance:
    At standard rate, the 21,500 hours taken would have cost   £
    The 21,500 hours actually cost   £ _____
    Difference = the rate variance (adverse/favourable)   £ _____

Efficiency variance:
    The standard hours allowed to produce 10,200 units is hours
    The actual hours taken to produce 10,200 units was   _____ hours
    Difference = time variance   _____ hours

    Time variance at standard rate = (adverse/favourable) £

As with materials, you should ensure that the sum of the two 'sub'-variances agrees with the total wages cost variance.

5 Cost variances – overheads

You have encountered the total overhead cost variance in previous chapters; it was not described as such because we were not dealing with standard costing. The total overhead cost variance is the difference between the overheads incurred and the amount absorbed. In previous chapters this was described as overheads under- or over-absorbed.

In standard costing, if overheads are under-absorbed (a debit balance) this is described as an adverse variance; if they are over-absorbed (a credit balance) the variance is described as favourable.

There is a slight variation in the way overheads are absorbed in the case of standard costing, and it is vital that you understand this concept because it is at the heart of the variance analysis for overheads.

In standard costing, overheads are absorbed on the basis of the standard hours for the goods produced, not the actual hours taken. This is simply another way of stating that absorption is based on a standard amount per unit produced, irrespective of how long it took to produce that unit. Consider the following example:

The standard time allowed for the production of one unit is one hour.
The overhead absorption rate is set at £4 per hour.
The actual time taken to produce one unit was two hours.

Activity 12

Make a note of the amount of overhead that will be absorbed into the cost of production for this unit.

Note how this leaves an overhead under-absorbed of £4 and this may form part of what is known as the efficiency variance.

It is normal practice in the case of standard costing to maintain separate accounts for variable overheads and fixed overheads.

We can now return to our work on the example in Appendix 1. It will not be possible to work at the same pace on overheads as you did with materials and labour. The activities are designed to enable you to sort out the analysis on a piecemeal basis. We will deal with variable overheads first.

The first figure to calculate is the total variance. This, as stated earlier, is the amount of variable overhead under- or over-absorbed, and can be found by comparing the amount actually spent on variable overheads with the amount absorbed. In the case of standard costing, absorption is based on a standard amount per unit produced, irrespective of how long it actually took to produce that unit.

Activity 13	Calculate the total amount of variable overhead under- or over-absorbed. Use the following guidelines for the calculation, and identify whether the total variance is favourable or adverse:

The amount actually spent on variable overheads was   £

The amount absorbed on production of 10,200 units was   £ ____

Total variance (adverse/favourable)   £ ____

The total amount spent on variable overheads must vary with something. In the absence of any details to the contrary, it is normally assumed that variable overheads vary with the number of hours worked. These hours might be machine hours or labour hours. The variance analysis proceeds on much the same lines as for direct wages.

Activity 14	Analyse the total variable overhead cost variance by completing the guidelines set out below this activity box. Indicate whether the variances are adverse or favourable.

Spending variance:

    At standard rate, the 21,500 hours would have cost   £

    The amount actually spent on variable overheads was   £ ____

    Difference = the spending variance (adverse/favourable)   £ ____

Efficiency variance:

    The standard hours allowed to produce 10,200 units is   hours

    The actual hours taken to produce 10,200 units was   ____ hours

    Difference = time variance   ____ hours

    Time variance at standard rate = (adverse/favourable) £

The spending variance may be called an expenditure variance, although it is better to call it a spending variance in order to avoid confusion with the way the expenditure variance on fixed overheads is calculated.

The first figure to calculate on fixed overheads is the total variance, i.e. the amount over- or under-absorbed. This is the difference between the expenditure incurred and the amount absorbed.

Activity 15	Calculate the total fixed overhead cost variance, and indicate whether this is favourable or adverse, by completing the following guidelines:

The actual expenditure on fixed overheads was   £

The amount absorbed on production of 10,200 units was   £ ____

Total variance (adverse/favourable)   £ ____

This now gives us a total against which we can agree the individual variances in the analysis. This total is analysed into two separate variances which are called expenditure and volume. Volume can then be sub-divided into capacity and efficiency variances.

The expenditure variance, as stated earlier, is the difference between the expenditure incurred and the budgeted fixed overheads for the period. You will quite often find that the budgeted fixed overhead for the period is not given directly in the question, you have to determine the amount from related data. This applies to the problem in Appendix 1.

Activity 16	Refer to the details in Appendix 1 and calculate how much had been budgeted for fixed overheads for the month of December. Make a note of the amount here:

Having determined this figure, it is then quite easy to calculate the expenditure allowance.

Activity 17	Calculate the expenditure variance, and indicate whether the variance is favourable or adverse, by completing the following: Expenditure incurred on fixed overheads £ Budgeted expenditure for the period £ Expenditure variance (adverse/favourable) £

So far we have established that the total variance is £2,800 favourable and that £2,000 of this relates to a favourable expenditure variance. This leaves a balance of £800 (favourable) which is sometimes labelled as an activity (or volume) variance. It arises because the fixed overhead absorption rate (FOAR) of £4 per unit was based on 10,000 hours, thus giving £40,000 expected absorption of cost into product units. The overhead actually absorbed is 10,200 units at £4 per unit, £40,800. The difference of 200 units at £4 per unit accounts for the £800 over-absorbed.

However, a single activity variance is not very helpful to management because it hides two underlying factors that have contributed to the variance. These two factors can be described as follows:

Production capacity

The company was budgeting to work 20,000 hours and yet 21,500 hours were actually worked. This situation will produce a favourable capacity variance because the company had the capacity to produce more units than the number specified in the budget.

Production efficiency

The standard time allowed for 10,200 units is 20,400 hours, and yet 21,500 hours were actually taken. This results in an adverse efficiency variance because the time taken to produce the units was longer than the standard time allowance.

In both cases, the variance is measured at the standard fixed overhead absorption rate of £2 per hour.

Activity 18	Analyse the favourable activity variance of £800 by calculating the capacity variance and the efficiency variance. Use the working schedules set out below, and indicate whether the variances are adverse or favourable.

Capacity variance:

Budgeted hours for the period		hours
Actual hours worked	_____	hours
Additional capacity	_____	hours

Additional capacity at £2 per hour = (adverse/favourable) variance of £

Efficiency variance:

Standard hours for the		
10,200 units produced		hours
Actual hours taken	_____	hours
Time variance	_____	hours

Time variance at £2 per hour = (adverse/favourable) variance of £

Notice how this analysis of the activity variance enables management to see the effect of taking longer to produce the goods than the standard time allowed. This information is not apparent from the activity variance (of £800 favourable) because the amount of overhead absorbed is related to the standard hours for the goods produced, not the actual time taken.

Summary

This summary concentrates on variance analysis. You have been learning the subject on the basis of observing a common thread and a basic convention. The alternative to this is to learn a formula for each variance. But there is every chance that a formula (even if you can remember it) will let you down. There will always be situations where formulae cannot really be used.

The main learning points in this chapter are:

■ cost variances are calculated for the actual quantity of goods produced, not on budgeted quantities

■ the common thread is that all variances between standard (or budgeted) amounts and actual amounts stem from two causes: prices and quantity

■ in the case of costs:

> price variances are manifest in material prices, wage rates, and hourly rates for variable overheads

> quantity variances are manifest in material usage, and hours worked for both labour and variable overheads.

■ the basic convention is that price variances are related to the entire quantity (resources used or goods sold) and that quantity variances are measured at a standard rate.

Appendix 1

Details for activities in Sections 4 and 5 of the chapter.

A company produces a single product and uses a standard costing system for which the following standard costs apply:

STANDARD COST CARD	£
Direct material: 4 kilos at £2 per kilo	8
Direct wages: 2 hours at £5 per hour	10
Variable overhead: 2 hours at £1 per hour	2
Fixed overhead: 2 hours at £2 per hour	4
	24

Budgeted production for December is 10,000 units.

The actual results for December were as follows:

Production: 10,200 units

Actual materials consumed: 39,000 kilos costing £84,180

Actual direct wages cost: 21,500 hours costing £107,190

Actual variable overhead cost: £23,650

Actual fixed overhead cost: £38,000

The above details are to be used in the activities for calculating appropriate cost variances.

Key to Chapter 5 activities

Activity 1

They are likely to have an adverse effect on employee motivation. Setting standards that are impossible to achieve will only lead to frustration.

Activity 2

The actual price of materials is different to standard (110 kg should cost £220 at the standard price of £2 per kg, not £217), and more materials have been used than the standard quantity (110 kg as against the standard quantity of 100).

Activity 3

Price variance:	110 kg should have cost	£220
	110 kg actually cost	£217
	Variance	£3 favourable

Usage variance:	100 units of finished product should use	100 kg
	100 units of finished product actually used	110 kg
	Excess usage	10 kg
	10 kg at £2 = £20 adverse	

Activity 4

The cheaper materials were of poor quality resulting in a higher than normal wastage during production.

Activity 5

Direct materials: abnormally high wastage or any other avoidable difference from expected costs.
Direct labour: avoidable idle time due to inefficient scheduling or any other avoidable event that produces a variation from expected costs.

Activity 6

Raw material stock		Price variance		Creditors	
£220	£20	£20			£220

Activity 7

Raw material stock				Work-in-progress				Usage variance	
(100)	£200	(50)	£100	(50)	£100	(10)	£20	£20	

Activity 8   It has been measured at standard price.

Activity 9   Total material cost variance:

Standard material cost of 10,200 units	£81,600
Actual material cost	£84,180
Adverse variance	£2,580

Material price variance:

39,000 kilos used should cost	£78,000
39,000 kilos actually cost	£84,180
Adverse variance	£6,180

Material usage variance:

10,200 units should use	40,800	kilos
Actual quantity used	39,000	kilos
Quantity variance	1,800	kilos (favourable)

1,800 kilos at £2 per kilo = £3,600 favourable

Activity 10
1.   The rate variance relates to actual hours worked.

2.   The efficiency variance is measured at standard rate.

Activity 11   Total wages cost variance:

The standard direct wages cost for 10,200 units	£102,000
Actual direct wages cost	£107,190
Adverse cost variance	£5,190

Wages rate variance:

21,500 hours should have cost	£107,500
21,500 hours actually cost	£107,190
Favourable rate variance	£310

Efficiency variance:

10,200 units should take	20,400	hours
10,200 units actually took	21,500	hours
Time variance	1,100	hours

Adverse efficiency variance 1,100 at £5 = £5,500

Activity 12   The amount absorbed will be (1 × £4) £4.00

Activity 13

Expenditure	£23,650
Absorbed (10,200 × £2)	£20,400
Total variance	£3,250 adverse

Note that this is a debit balance (under-absorbed) and if any variance is represented by a debit balance, the variance is adverse.

Activity 14

Spending variance:

21,500 hours should cost	£21,500
Actually spent	£23,650
Adverse spending variance	£2,150

Efficiency variance:

10,200 units should take	20,400	hours
10,200 units actually took	21,500	hours
Time variance	1,100	hours

Adverse efficiency variance 1,100 × £1 = £1,100

Note that the sum of the spending variance, £2,150 adverse, and the efficiency variance, £1,100 adverse, is the total variable overhead variance of £3,250 adverse.

Activity 15

Actual expenditure	£38,000	
Overheads absorbed (10,200 × £4)	£40,800	
Total variance	£2,800	favourable

Note that this is a credit balance (over-absorbed) and if any variance is represented by a credit balance, the variance is favourable.

Activity 16

10,000 units at £4 per unit = £40,000 (or 20,000 hours at £2 per hour)

Activity 17

Actual expenditure	£38,000	
Budgeted expenditure	£40,000	
Total variance	£2,000	favourable

Activity 18

Capacity variance:

Budgeted hours for the period	20,000	hours
Actual hours worked	21,500	hours
Additional capacity	1,500	hours

Capacity variance (1,500 × £2) = £3,000 favourable

The variance is favourable because by working longer hours than budgeted hours the company had the capacity to produce more units.

Efficiency variance:

10,200 units should take	20,400	hours
Actual hours taken	21,500	hours
Time variance	1,100	hours (adverse)

Efficiency variance 1,100 × £2 = £2,200 adverse

Introduction to Part 4: Reports and Returns

The amount of information available for analysing and assessing the performance of an entity will depend on whether the assessment is being made by external users (e.g. investors or their advisors) or internal users such as management. The purpose of the analysis may also differ.

External users such as shareholders or lending institutions are likely to be concerned with some kind of management of their investment portfolios. This might involve assessing the safety of existing investments or considering whether to make or increase an investment in a particular entity. Management and other internal users will be assessing performance in order to control operations and provide the best possible returns for the investors.

Most large organisations are separated into divisions such as departments, branches, or separate companies within a group. Each division might have its own divisional manager who is allowed to act with a degree of local autonomy. Central management, having delegated local control to divisional managers, will require information on which to assess the performance of each division. This information will be used for control purposes and also for rewarding divisional managers according to their performance. One of the problems with decentralisation is that divisional managers might make decisions that are in the best interests of their own division but are unfavourable to the company as a whole. This has led to the development of specialised techniques in assessing divisional performance which consider the motivational effect of the indicators used.

In this module we will look at the analysis and use of information by external users and by internal users, and at how information can be presented in the form of statistical reports.

Chapter 1

Information assessment by external users

Introduction

As financial accounting has much earlier origins than cost and management accounting, many of the performance appraisal techniques were developed within the framework of financial statements for external users, such as shareholders and lending institutions. It is fitting, therefore, to start this subject by considering the techniques available to an external user whose main source of information is the annual financial statements published by the company. When you come to study Chapter 2 you will find that many of the same concepts and techniques are applied to internal accounting reports.

Objectives

After completing this chapter you should be able to:

■ calculate accounting ratios in accordance with any specification given to you

■ carry out your own analysis of financial statements in a discriminating and informative manner

■ discuss limitations of the analytical techniques used

■ form opinions on the information revealed by accounting ratios and give appropriate advice in a written report to an external user of financial statements.

1 The level of skills involved

As part of your skills development for this analytical aspect of financial accounting, you will be using a tool called ratio analysis. But the tool itself is probably less important than the way in which it is used. Accounting ratios simply provide additional information by setting out the relationship between two items in the financial statements. The analytical skills involved are not so much a matter of knowing how to calculate ratios (these are simple enough) but being able to make judgements on the relevance of the information which they reveal.

In making these judgements, you must not expect too much from the ratios themselves; they have their limitations in terms of what they can tell us about an entity's performance. We use them as a tool in our search for more information, but they tend to raise questions rather than provide answers. Any opinion formed simply from figures produced in ratio analysis can only be tentative. Persons within and outside the organisation must be questioned to find out what the figures really mean and how they should be viewed in the context of organisational performance.

During your initial study of this subject you are likely to concentrate on methodology (such as how the ratios are calculated) but you must keep in mind that the information is produced to help users make decisions. You might have to help in these decisions by giving your opinion in a written report and so you must try to develop the judgmental skills involved. Your written communication skills must be good too.

Even at the methodology level you will find the subject is by no means an exact science; there are different bases that could be used when measuring a particular ratio. The inference of this is twofold, namely:

- ratios must be calculated in accordance with the methodology prescribed by those who have requested them – this could be an external agency such as a trade association

- when forming opinions on accounting ratios provided by others, it might be necessary to accept that the information has limited value unless you are given details of how the ratio has been calculated.

2 The role of accounting ratios

Most people think of profit as an indicator of performance, but a single figure for profit will not enable us to make an objective judgement on the profitable use of resources. If we compare profit in the current year with profit in the previous year and notice it is up by so many percent we might think that the entity had been more profitable during the current year, but in making this judgement we are looking at profit in absolute terms rather than in relative terms. Profit must be related to something.

If you were to compare the profit of Sainsbury's with the profit of a small local shop, it would not help you to assess which of the two entities had used its resources more profitably by measuring the difference in profit. Even by intuition you would realise that the amount of profit is relative to the size of the business. For example, a profit of £50,000 is good if the business invested £100,000, but not very good if the business invested £10,000,000. The same concept applies when you are comparing the results of a single entity over a period of years, profit may change in absolute terms but so does the size of the business. In assessing profitability we need to look at the changes of profit in relative terms.

The same approach applies when it comes to assessing the financial management of an organisation. Take debtors' balances as an example – we might notice that the debtors' balance has increased by 50% in comparison with the previous year. This information by itself has little value; debtors are relative to sales and if sales have increased by 50% then we may expect debtors to increase by 50%. It is the change in debtors in relation to the change in sales that will tell us something, not changes in a single balance sheet figure. Accounting ratios provide us with a tool for measuring these relative changes.

| Activity 1 | You have just completed the draft accounts of businessman and are discussing them with him before they are typed. He notices that they show a net profit of £50,000 and says: 'That's pretty good isn't it, that's a 43% increase on last year's profit of £35,000?' It sounds as if he has done well, but he may not have done. You will have to compare the profit with something else in the accounts before you can comment.

What could the profit be related to in order assess his performance? You might be able to think of two items. Make a note here of any that occur to you and then check your ideas with those in the Key.

1.

2.
 |

The second item in the Key is the most useful and normally forms a starting point for any analysis on operating performance. It is the basis of a ratio called the 'primary ratio' and measures what is known as 'the return on capital employed' (ROCE), or return on investment (ROI). You can get an idea of its relevance by thinking about something at a personal level. Suppose you were lucky enough to win £1,000 in a raffle and decided to invest the money in a building society. You have worked out that you will be credited with £90 interest at the end of the year. That interest is a return on the amount of capital you have invested.

Activity 2	The relationship between the £90 interest and the £1,000 invested is normally expressed in a particular way. Make a note of this relationship and work out how it would be expressed in numerical terms.

What you have done is use a ratio. You have divided one figure by another and expressed the result as a percentage. This forms the basis of all ratios, although the way in which the result is expressed varies according to the type of ratio being measured. If you now think of the net assets of a business as the investment, and the profits earned as a return on that investment, you can see the underlying concept of the primary ratio.

In the case of your investment in a building society you looked at the ratio as follows:

$$\frac{interest}{investment} = \frac{90}{1,000} \times 100 = 9\%$$

You use exactly the same approach for a business when measuring the return on capital employed (the primary ratio). Interest earned on investment simply becomes profit earned on net assets, since net assets (as you will remember from your work with balance sheets) perfectly match the owners' investment in the business.

Activity 3	When you look at the current year's balance sheet for the businessman in Activity 1, you find that the net assets are shown as £250,000. Calculate this businessman's return on capital employed.

We have now found something a bit more useful than the profit alone, but we are still in a weak position if we were asked to assess the profitability of this business. We could tell the client that there is a return of 20% on the capital invested, but this might prompt him to say: 'So what, is that good or bad?'

How can we answer this question? He has certainly done better than the (imaginary) investment in a building society (9%) which might be some comfort. But we are being asked to assess how well this particular business has done – not compare it to an alternative type of investment.

In just the same way as single figure in the accounts is not very informative, an accounting ratio looked at in isolation is not very useful. We need some kind of benchmark against which the ratio can be compared.

Activity 4	See if you can think of something useful against which the 20% return could be compared. Four different types of comparison are sometimes made in practice, but you might not be able to think of all four. Make a note here of any that do occur to you and then check your ideas with those in the Key.
	1.
	2.
	3.
	4.

We will use the previous year's figures in the next activity.

Activity 5	When you look at the previous year's balance sheet for the businessman in Activity 1, you find that the net assets employed in that year were £140,000. How would you now respond to his comment that this year's results (profits £50,000) were much better than last year when the profits were £35,000?

This idea of calculating the ratio, and then making a comparison, forms the basis of ratio analysis. But it is only a starting point. For example, in Activity 5 you have come to the conclusion that the return on capital employed (ROCE) is down by 5% on what it was in the previous year. This information is useful but we can help the client further by finding the factors which have caused the drop in profitability. Our search for this information requires a secondary analysis of the primary ratio.

We can analyse the primary ratio (ROCE) into secondary ratios in something often referred to as the performance pyramid:

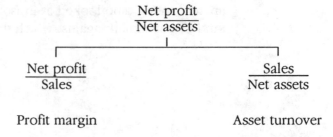

$$\frac{\text{Net profit}}{\text{Net assets}}$$

$$\frac{\text{Net profit}}{\text{Sales}} \qquad\qquad \frac{\text{Sales}}{\text{Net assets}}$$

Profit margin   Asset turnover

Note that when you multiply the secondary ratios together, the result is the primary ratio, (ROCE). A fall in ROCE from one year to the next (as with the business in Activity 5) may result from:

1   earning a smaller profit on each £1 of sales

2   producing less sales revenue from each £1 of net assets, or

3   a combination of both.

You can see this when you look at the pyramid. You will learn how to calculate and use the secondary ratios in Section 6.

3 Ratio classification and structure

There are literally dozens of ratios that could be calculated and the subject is constantly developing. In recent times there has been a trend towards showing the relationship between accounting figures and non-financial data, such as:

■   the amount of sales revenue per employee

■   sales revenue per square metre of shop space.

Some companies (for example, Marks and Spencer plc) publish this kind of information in their annual report to shareholders, but because of its interest to management it is covered in Chapter 2. In this chapter we will concentrate on the more traditional type of analysis available to external users.

It is important to approach the study in a structured way. There is a kind of hierarchy (or pyramid) of ratios within which the individual ratios can be organised. If you fail to appreciate this structure, the whole subject can seem disjointed. Perhaps this does not matter if you are simply calculating ratios according to some specification, but if you are carrying out your own ratio analysis you must be aware of the relationship between different ratios.

Unfortunately there is no generally agreed way of classifying ratios under separate headings. The following division holds the subject together quite well and will be used throughout this chapter, but it is not by any means the only classification.

a)   **Business performance ratios**. These include the return on capital employed, sub-divided into the secondary ratios of net profit percentage and asset turnover. The components of the ratios will vary slightly, depending on the viewpoint from which the analysis is being made.

b)   **Working capital ratios**. The ratios dealt with here are those which are concerned with the control of working capital. They are used by management for planning and control and by external analysts. Strictly speaking, these ratios are a continuation of the ratio hierarchy established in (a) above, but because of the way in which they are expressed they tend to be thought of as a separate group.

c) **Solvency ratios**. These ratios, the current ratio and acid test (quick) ratio, are often of interest to external users such as creditors and banks.

Another class of ratios are **financial capital ratios**. These ratios are concerned with a company's financial structure in terms of the proportion of loans to equity. They are of interest to all providers of capital, particularly the equity investor group. They tend to be put under a general heading called 'gearing ratios'. They are, however, beyond the scope of this book, and so we will not be considering them.

A further class of ratios can be described as **investor ratios.** These are used by investment analysts and make use of stock market information such as share prices and dividends paid to investors. They include: earnings per share (EPS), the price/earnings ratios, dividend yield, and earnings yield. These ratios are beyond the scope of NVQ Level 3.

4 Expression of ratios

All ratios are the result of dividing one number by another. The way in which the result of the arithmetic is expressed can be varied in order to provide information which is easier for the user to understand. Where the two figures result in a fraction (as in Activities 2 to 5) they are normally expressed as a percentage. The idea of information in the form of a percentage return is something to which most people can relate.

In many ratios we will be dividing a larger number by a smaller one. In these cases there are various ways in which the result can be expressed. Consider the following:

$$\frac{12,000}{2,000}$$

This could be expressed as 600%, but percentages are not always the clearest or most useful way of expressing this kind of information.

A pure ratio is expressed as a value to one. In the above, 12,000 divided by 2,000 is six and so we would state the ratio as 6:1. Traditionally, this form of expression is used for the solvency ratios mentioned in (c) above.

Sometimes the two figures are expressed in terms of the number of 'times' the smaller goes into the larger. This expression is often used when the larger figure represents an annual amount from the profit and loss account, and the smaller figure is a balance from the balance sheet. For example, if cost of sales for the year is £12,000 and stock is £2,000 we could state that stock is turned over six times a year.

Some of the ratios in this category are understood more readily when they are converted into a time period such as days or months. Another way of stating that stock is turned over six times a year is to say that stocks (on average) are being held for two months before being sold.

Activity 6	By simple observation (not by calculation) see if you can find any useful relationship between the following two figures from a set of accounts: Sales for the year (all on credit) £365,000 Debtors at the end of the year £30,000 If you find it difficult to see anything, think about the fact that a year is made up of 365 days.

This ratio is usually called the 'debtors' collection period' and gives an indication of how long (on average) debtors are taking to pay. If the figures had not been so apparent, the number of days' sales in debtors would have to be calculated. To do this you could find one day's sales (by dividing £365,000 by 365) and then divide this into £30,000. But this two-stage calculation can easily be resolved into a simple formula, as you will see in the sub-section on working capital analysis.

5 Limitations of ratio analysis

You must constantly be alert to the limitations of ratio analysis. You will discover several as you work through the activities. It is quite easy to become besotted by numbers (particularly those derived from mathematical formulae) and in order to encourage you to set out with a more cautious approach, we will look at a few of the problems now.

You have already seen that judgements on the information revealed by a ratio are quite difficult to make unless we have a benchmark for comparison purposes. The two common types of comparison are:

1) **trend analysis**; comparing the current year with previous years

2) **inter-firm comparison**; comparison with similar ratios in other firms that are operating in the same line of business.

In both cases the comparison calls for caution over the way in which the information revealed is interpreted.

| Activity 7 | A businessman is trying to convince you to buy his business. He shows you the latest figures and says: 'Look, you can see the business is expanding, turnover is up, this year's turnover is £107,000 against a turnover of £100,000 in the previous year.' How would you interpret this? Do you think there been an increase of 7% in the volume of trade conducted by this business? |

Inflation is one of the most important factors to take into account when looking at financial trends. Unless some adjustment is made for the effects of inflation, the comparison is misleading. You will see in Chapter 3 how index numbers can be used to establish changes in real terms rather than in money terms.

It is also important to remember the effects of unit price increases. Higher unit prices can lead to higher sales revenues even if sales volume is falling.

| Activity 8 | You find that the return on capital employed in your own business is 40%. You read in a trade journal that the average return on capital for other companies in your line of business is 30%. On the face of it, you seem to be doing much better than average. But are you? See how many factors you can think of that might account for the variation. Aim at finding two. Think about two things: inflation (again), and the fact that accounting is not an exact science. Note your ideas here and then check with the Key. |

The second point made in the Key can be demonstrated by comparing two companies of equal size and earning equal profits before depreciation. Consider the following example:

Company A's fixed assets were purchased 10 years ago and are being written off over 15 years. Company B's fixed assets were purchased during the current year and are also being written off over 15 years. The rate of inflation on the type of fixed asset used has averaged 10% over the last 10 years. The following is a summary of each company's financial statements:

	Company A	Company B
Fixed assets at cost	30,000	75,000
Aggregate depreciation	20,000	5,000
Net book value	10,000	70,000
Net current assets	5,000	5,000
	15,000	75,000
Profit before depreciation	8,000	8,000
Depreciation	2,000	5,000
Net profit	6,000	3,000
Return on capital employed	40%	4%

Comment:

The primary ratio suggests that Company A was much more profitable than Company B, yet the variation stems from nothing more than the different ages of each company's assets. In all other respects, the two companies have identical operating results.

Another problem in making inter-firm comparisons is related to the way in which the ratios are calculated. In Section 1 we mentioned that different ideas exist regarding the components of a particular ratio. In order to ensure that like is being compared to like, it will be necessary to know how other firms have calculated their ratios. Many trade associations publish averages of accounting ratios compiled from returns made by businesses operating in their sector, and the International Chamber of Commerce produces a publication called Performance Indicators. These publications usually state the basis of the ratio. If you are required to prepare returns to one of these organisations, you must ensure that the ratio is made according to the specification. We will look at the most common variations.

6 Practice in ratio calculation and interpretation of results

Most of the work in this section will be based on the financial statements for a company called Overload Ltd. These statements are set out in Appendix 1.

In ratio analysis we express the result of a ratio to the nearest significant number. Nothing is gained by telling someone that their return on capital is 31.2469% – the subject is concerned with interpretation and communication, not with the precision of calculations. If a return on capital did work out at 31.2469%, we would either report this as 31% or 31.25% depending on how important we thought the extra 0.25% was to those using the analysis. You will have to use your own judgement on this, there are no hard and fast rules.

The type of comment that can be made after calculating an individual ratio is not usually very helpful. It is better to wait until all the key ratios have been calculated before drawing any conclusions.

Business performance ratios

The primary ratio

The purpose of the primary ratio is to determine the return on capital employed (ROCE). Different versions of this ratio are used in practice. There are different interpretations of what is meant by profit and what is meant by capital. As a starting point, think about the problem of profit. When you look at a company's profit and loss account you may find many different references to profit. The item we have so far called 'net profit' is often called 'operating profit', and there are various other profits such as 'profit before tax', 'profit after tax' (and sometimes profit before and after extraordinary items). Which one of all these different profit figures should we use in the ratio?

It is generally agreed that taxation can distort the analysis and so it is common practice to use profit before tax.

Let's consider what we mean by capital. If we regard capital as all forms of long-term finance provided to the business to enable it to acquire net assets, then the long-term loans can be considered to be part of the capital. If we consider that loans are part of the capital, then the interest paid should be treated as part of the profit earned on that capital. On this basis, the formula for ROCE will be:

$$\frac{\text{profit before tax and interest}}{\text{total assets less current liabilities}}$$

where the interest is interest on long-term loans only.

The top of this ratio represents the returns to the types of capital provided (share capital and loans) which will be on the bottom of the ratio.

The fraction is then expressed as a percentage. Note that the denominator is the same thing as the sum of share capital, reserves, and long-term loan capital. In other words total capital employed includes long-term loans. The numerator is usually the same figure as the amount described as 'operating profit' in a company's profit and loss account.

Activity 9	Calculate ROCE for Overload Ltd on the basis that capital includes long-term loans.
	1991 1992

The only comment we could make at this point is that the return is down by 5.5%

The return on capital employed is sometimes looked at from the viewpoint of the owners. In the case of a company this is referred to as the **return on equity**; for a sole trader it is simply the return on the proprietor's capital. If this concept of capital is used, the profits will be **after interest** but before tax. The basis of the formula may then be:

$$\frac{\text{profit before tax}}{\text{total assets less total liabilities}}$$

The denominator, as your knowledge of balance sheets will confirm, is the same as the sum of share capital and reserves.

It is quite common to work this calculation before and after tax. This gives both a perception of the tax charge and the true, final percentage earnings or returns for the owners.

Activity 10	Calculate ROCE for Overload Ltd using pre-tax profits and the equity capital basis.
	1991 1992

The return is greater under this basis (although the trend is the same) because the loan capital is costing the company 10% but the cash received from the loan has been invested in the business and is earning a return in excess of 10%. This results in a gain for the equity shareholders.

Sometimes the capital base for ROCE is taken to be total assets, i.e. fixed assets plus current assets. Because a balance sheet balances, total assets equal creditors due within one year plus creditors due after one year plus capital and reserves.

A more frequent variation occurs when the assets include investments. If a company is holding surplus funds and invests these in short-term securities, most analysts would exclude the investment income from profit and exclude the investments from the capital. The return on the investments is then measured as a separate ratio. The ROCE for business activities is then in reality 'operating profit' to 'operating assets' as follows:

$$\frac{\text{operating profit}}{\text{operating assets}}$$

The term 'operating profit' is used to identify profit before investment income and interest charges, i.e. profit from general business trading. If this figure is used for the numerator, the operating assets will be total assets excluding investments less current liabilities. (Loan capital is treated as part of the capital and is not deducted in arriving at operating assets.)

The problem of different bases for ROCE is not a matter of establishing which one of them is correct; the idea of correctness does not exist except in terms of ensuring calculations are made according to any specification given to you. If it is left to you devise your own approach to an analysis, you should select one of the bases and state your definitions of profit and capital. You should bear in mind who will read the report and what kind of analysis the readers will want. Information on the basis used is just as important as the ratio itself.

The important points to keep in mind are as follows:

■ the appropriate figure for profit will depend on how capital is defined

■ if loans are treated as part of the capital, profit should be profit before interest (operating profit)

■ if loans are excluded from capital, and therefore the owners' investment is all that is considered, profit should be profit after interest and before or after tax

■ whatever basis is used in the primary ratio, the same components must be used for the secondary ratios

■ when making comparisons (such as a trend analysis or inter-firm comparisons) ensure that all ratios have been prepared on the same basis.

Inter-firm comparisons are difficult if information on the basis used for ratio analysis is not available. Limitations of the comparison in this respect should be mentioned in any reports that you make.

In this chapter we will think of capital employed as being total assets less current liabilities. In other words we will define capital as being the sum of equity and long-term loans. The return (net profit) will, therefore, be represented by profit before tax and interest. This basis is frequently used by accountants but you must not think of this basis as being the 'correct' basis: it is simply one of many different bases used. It does, however, provide some idea of the level of percentage returns earned by the management on **all** the investment finance used in an organisation. Total assets less current liabilities tends to reflect the net trading or operating assets of the organisation. ROCE using total assets less current liabilities reflects over percentage trading returns.

The secondary ratios

The purpose of the secondary ratios is to isolate causes of the variation in ROCE. In the case of Overload Ltd, we know that ROCE has fallen during 1992 and we must now look for possible explanations. Before looking at the formulae used, deal with the following activity:

Activity 11	When we write down the primary ratio and the two secondary ratios alongside each other, we find something interesting. What do you notice about the following?

Primary ratio | **Secondary ratios**

ROCE | Net profit margin | Asset turnover or efficiency

$$\frac{\text{Operating profit}}{\text{Net assets}} \qquad \frac{\text{Operating profit}}{\text{Sales}} \qquad \frac{\text{Sales}}{\text{Net assets}}$$

The net or operating profit to sales ratio is usually referred to as the net profit margin and the sales to net assets as the asset turnover or efficiency ratio. The profitability ratios are expressed as a %, the asset turnover as a multiple or 'number of times'. You will see how to make use of this information in a moment.

Activity 12

Calculate the two secondary ratios for Overload Ltd. Make sure that you use the same components for profit and net assets as used in Activity 9. Summarise the results of your calculations here.

	Primary ratio		Secondary ratios			
			Net profit margin		Asset turnover	
	1991	1992	1991	1992	1991	1992
	29.5%	24%				

Activity 13

After checking Activity 12 with the Key, make sure that multiplying together the two secondary ratios gives the primary ratio. Set out your calculations here.

1991	1992

The relevance of the asset turnover ratio is difficult to see when expressed as so many times. A more informative interpretation of this ratio is to say that in 1991 each £1 of net assets produced £3.57 in sales, whereas in 1992 each £1 of net assets produced £4 in sales. This kind of interpretation gives an indication of how efficiently the assets have been utilised. The asset turnover ratio is sometimes called the asset utilisation ratio.

If you use this approach, the link between the primary and secondary ratios can be explained to the user in an informative way. If we take the figures of Overload Ltd for 1992 as an example, an explanation to the user could take the following form:

Each £1 of net assets produced £4 in sales; the profit earned on these sales is 24p (i.e. 6% x £4). This 24p represents 24% of the £1 of net assets used to generate the sales.

We can continue the analysis by breaking down each secondary ratio into its constituent parts. The profitability ratio can be analysed further by expressing each key figure in the profit and loss account as a percentage of sales; the asset to turnover ratio can be calculated for individual classes of asset. This produces a kind of pyramid (or family tree) of ratios. The following diagram (in which the terms 'net profit' and 'net assets' have been used for the sake of convenience) gives some idea of the structure:

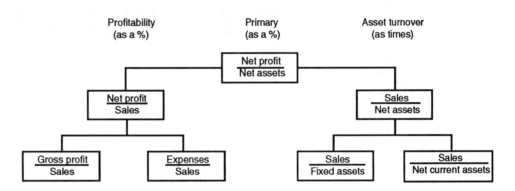

This is only the top part of the pyramid; it should be fairly clear that each of these can be divided again. Notice that the net profit ratio is the gross profit percentage less the expense to sales percentage. Since expenses are usually grouped under functional headings (distribution, administration, etc.) each group can be expressed as a percentage of sales.

In our analysis of Overload Ltd, it looks as if asset turnover may not be a problem, in fact there seems to be a slight improvement. In our search for an explanation of the fall in ROCE, we may initially turn our attention to the net profit margin and the profit and loss account, i.e. the left-hand side of the pyramid.

| Activity 14 | Calculate the two additional profitability ratios for Overload Ltd and reconcile these to the net profit margin percentage. |

	1991	1992
Gross profit margin		
Expense to sales		
Net profit margin		

We are now starting to get some idea of the changes in Overload's operations which explain its fall in ROCE. The most striking feature is the fall in gross profit percentage, although the fact that the ratio of expenses to sales has remained much the same is equally disturbing.

In the case of Overload Ltd, turnover has increased by 45% and expenses have increased at almost the same rate – hence the expense to sales ratio has remained fairly static over the two years.

A variation in the gross profit percentage is something that demands serious attention. We would normally expect it to remain fairly static each year, although the rate itself will depend upon the type of trade and the pricing policy. The fall from 25% to 22% in the case of Overload is quite significant and should be explored further by discussion with management.

Activity 15

An increase in turnover, accompanied by a fall in the gross profit margin, quite often suggests a deliberate marketing strategy by the business. Make a note of what you think this strategy might be.

Activity 16

Some of the following events will cause the gross profit percentage to fall, others will not. Consider each event and indicate whether or not it would cause a fall in gross profit percentage.

Will gross profit % fall with:

1. an increase in the price of purchases
    that is not passed on to customers?   Yes/No
2. reduction of selling prices assuming no
    corresponding reduction in purchase prices?   Yes/No
3. increase in bad debts?   Yes/No
4. increase in outward delivery costs?   Yes/No

The variation might also result from book-keeping errors (this is why auditors pay such close attention to the gross profit ratio) or a change in the type of trade. The gross profit percentage represents an average. If the company deals in many different kinds of product, each with a different margin, a change in the 'mix' of products sold will cause the average to change.

We should now turn our attention to the right-hand side of the pyramid, the asset turnover ratios. You will find that the fixed asset turnover ratio works out at 5.8 for 1991 and 7.13 for 1992. This indicates that fixed assets were being used more efficiently during 1992; each £1 of fixed assets produced £7.13 in sales, compared to £5.80 in the previous year.

If you do the same thing on net current assets you will find the variation does not appear very significant; 9.4 in 1991 to 9.1 in 1992. But it is the individual components of working capital that should be examined at this stage, not the overall position.

Working capital analysis

We could calculate the asset turnover ratio for each type of current asset but, as stated earlier, these ratios are more informative if expressed in terms of a time cycle. It still seems to be a common practice to measure the stock turnover ratio in terms of 'times' per annum. Cost of sales is used in the formula – not sales. This particular form of stock turnover ratio is normally found by dividing cost of sales by the average stock (an average of the opening and closing stock) as follows:

$$\frac{\text{cost of sales}}{\text{average stock}}$$

Activity 17	Calculate the stock turnover ratio for Overload Ltd using the above formula. The opening stock for 1991 is given in the notes to Appendix 1.
	1991 1992

This particular ratio attempts to measure the average rate of stock turnover for the year. As you can see it has slowed down. We would normally think of this as an unhealthy sign since it suggests an unnecessary build up of stocks on the shelf. This ratio tends to be affected by booms and recessions. During a boom period, firms tend to overstock and the stock turnover ratio falls. If this is not properly controlled, the firm might find itself short of liquid funds and unable to pay its bills. The trend is usually in the opposite direction during a recession because firms tend to run down existing stocks in order to conserve cash.

It is usually more informative to look at the closing stocks and convert the ratio into one that shows how many days (or weeks or months) the stock is likely to remain on hand before being sold. This is the stock turnover cycle and to find the answer in days the ratio becomes:

$$\frac{\text{Closing stock}}{\text{Cost of sales}} \times 365$$

We would use a multiplier of 12 for an answer in months, and 52 for an answer in weeks.

Activity 18

Calculate the closing stock turnover cycle (in days) for Overload Ltd.

1991	1992

The closing stock turnover cycle is sometimes called the average stock-holding period.

The increase in Overload's stock holding period is quite significant (about 50%) and warrants further enquiry. But it is usually better to wait until the full analysis has been carried out before drawing conclusions on any one particular trend. It is the ability to see a relationship between trends in different ratios that helps the analyst to ask the right questions.

The approach used to calculate the stock holding period is also used for debtors and creditors. In these cases we are attempting to measure how long debtors are taking to pay, and the length of credit period being taken to pay creditors. The following formulae are used:

Debtors' collection period: $\dfrac{\text{debtors}}{\text{sales}} \times 365$

Creditors' payment period: $\dfrac{\text{creditors}}{\text{purchases}} \times 365$

Note that these are trade debtors and trade creditors.

Activity 19

Calculate these periods for Overload Ltd. (You will have to calculate purchases from the cost of sales information.)

	1991	1992
Debtors' collection period		
Creditors' payment period		

Before trying to draw any conclusions from this we need to be careful over how we interpret the extension of the debt collection period. There could be a perfectly reasonable explanation.

Activity 20	Make a note of **any** factors that might explain the extension of the debt collection period.

The last point in the Key is another example of why we must be careful over the way we interpret ratios that are based on averages. The same point applies to creditors and stock.

Consider, for example, a company that produces nothing except fireworks for the UK market. You would expect to find a considerable difference in its balance of stocks as between (say) the end of September and the end of November. At the end of September it would have a high level of stocks and precious little cash. At the end of November it is likely to have very low stocks but a high level of debtors and cash. If the accounting period is the end of September, we could easily draw the wrong conclusion from the stock turnover ratio if we compared this company with another company in this sector whose accounting date was 30 November.

As regards the creditor payment period, an extension of this may be a deliberate policy; taking longer to pay creditors is one way of obtaining interest-free finance. But this kind of policy can be taken too far and sometimes an extension of the creditor payment period may prompt questions about whether the company was getting into difficulty over payment of its debts. In an extreme case, the company might find creditors are refusing to supply further goods until their outstanding accounts have been paid.

In the case of Overload Ltd, the lengthening of the debt collection period requires further enquiry because (as with stock) if it is not closely controlled the firm may run into difficulty over payment to creditors.

The net cash cycle

The three operating cycles identified in Activities 18 and 19 (stock, debtors, and creditors) can be put together in order to find what is known as the net cash cycle. For Overload Ltd, the net cash cycle would be calculated as follows:

	1991 Days	1992 Days
Stock	30	45
Debtors	34	42
	64	87
Less creditors	26	42
Net cash cycle	38	45

The net cash cycle is mainly used as tool for budgeting because it enables the firm to forecast the amount of cash needed to finance the trading cycle. Stock arrives, it is held for a short while before being sold, and there is a further delay before the customers pay. The firm needs sufficient cash to enable it to meet all payments in the period between arrival of the stock and receipt of cash from the debtors.

Using the 1992 figures of Overload as an example, the stock comes in and remains on the shelf for 45 days; then it is sold but the firm has to wait another 42 days before any money is received. In the meantime it has had to pay for the stock (three days before it was sold) and pay all operating expenses for the 87 days. This period of 87 days is known as the **net operating cycle** for Overload Ltd, i.e. the combination of stock turnover and debtors.

Firms aim to keep both cycles as short as possible in order to reduce the amount of money invested in working capital. Entrepreneurs consider that money tied up in working capital is 'dead' money. It is necessary for most businesses to carry a certain amount of working capital, but business activity is not likely to expand simply by investing more in working capital. (On the other hand, if the trade does expand the amount invested in working capital will have to be increased.)

By contrast, if more money is invested in fixed assets such as productive plant, the business (and profits) are likely to expand. By reducing the amount invested in working capital to its optimum level, funds can be released for purchase of fixed assets. Investment in working capital can be reduced by keeping the net operating cycle as short as possible.

Activity 21	Make a list of the various ways in which a business might be able to reduce the length of its net cash cycle.

You are not likely to get a chance of making use of the net cash cycle until you study some of the more advanced aspects of financial management. The main reason for introducing the concept here is to allow a note of caution to be added to the way we interpret the solvency ratios, which are dealt with next.

Solvency ratios

Solvency or liquidity ratios are quite easy to calculate but difficult to use. There are two common ratios, one is called the 'current ratio' and the other the 'quick asset ratio' or 'acid test'. Cash flow forecasts and statements (as prescribed by SSAP 10) are much more useful, but are not covered at this level of your study.

The current ratio is quite simply current assets divided by current liabilities, as follows:

$$\frac{\text{current assets}}{\text{current liabilities}}$$

The result is usually expressed as a value to 1, although there is no reason why it should not be expressed as a percentage.

Activity 22	Calculate the current ratio for Overload Ltd, for 1991 and 1992. Express the result as a ratio, not a percentage.
	1991 1992

A traditional reaction to this would be that the trend shows a slight deterioration (by about 23%: 0.61/2.67) and thus a warning sign that the company might soon experience cash flow problems.

But a reduction in the current ratio could be the result of careful planning. We cannot assume (without more information) that a fall in this ratio is an unhealthy sign; it might be the result of skilful management. If we take the traditional view, then presumably we would have to interpret an increase in the current ratio as a healthy sign. But an increase might be the result of poor financial management (e.g. lack of control over the build up of stocks and debtors to a point where excessive amounts are being invested in working capital). If the information contained in the working capital ratio is so ambiguous, then why do we try to use it?

Part of our difficulty stems from traditional literature. When these ratios were discussed in earlier text books, there was a tendency to try and prescribe norms. In just the same way as we would say that a healthy person should have a body temperature of 98.7°F (or 36.9°C), the earlier writers on accounting set out norms for solvency ratios. A typical comment was that in a healthy business there should be a current ratio of 2:1, although no reason was ever put forward to explain why. This particular norm seems to have resulted from an observation of successful companies at the time. It was inferred that since these companies had survived, then a ratio of 2:1 was a key to their survival.

We now accept that ratios cannot be used in this way; ratios simply describe a relationship between two figures, they are not used in a prescriptive sense. The current ratio depends more on the type of industry (and its net cash cycle) than anything else. We learn more by comparing a company's current ratio to the industry average than by comparing it to these so called norms.

A retail store may sell its goods for cash in a much shorter time than the period of credit allowed by its suppliers. It will have a negative cash cycle and is quite happy to operate with negative working capital.

Activity 23	The published balance sheets of two public companies are included at the end of this chapter as Appendix 2 and Appendix 3. One of these balance sheets is for Sainsbury's and the other is for ICI, although there is nothing to say which one is which. You should refer to them now and see if you can identify (in the context of what you have just been learning) which balance sheet is likely to be Sainsbury's and which is likely to be ICI's.

	Delete as appropriate
Appendix 2 is the balance sheet of	Sainsbury/ICI
Appendix 3 is the balance sheet of	Sainsbury/ICI

Good financial management will attempt to keep working capital as low as possible, while at the same time wishing to avoid the possibility of losing trade (by not having the materials or goods on hand when needed) and losing the goodwill of suppliers by not paying them within a reasonable time.

The acid test (or quick) ratio

The acid test (or quick) ratio is similar to the current ratio except that those current assets which will take a long time to turn into cash are excluded. It is normally computed as follows:

$$\frac{\text{Current assets less stock}}{\text{Current liabilities}}$$

It suffers from similar defects to the current ratio in that it is difficult to interpret without further examination. Current liabilities might include a bank overdraft which theoretically could be called in at short notice but in reality is a continuing source of finance. Current liabilities also include taxation which may not be payable for another nine months.

Contrary to what many people think, a large cash balance is not necessarily a healthy sign. It might indicate favourable trading but it could indicate poor financial management since funds are not being used to their best advantage. Money in the bank does not earn any profit.

The acid test ratio tends to vary with booms and recessions, usually in the opposite direction to that which you would expect. In times of prosperity the ratio tends to fall because the increased activity often leads to larger stocks but less cash; in a recession, firms conserve resources by running down their existing stocks.

The trends in Overload Ltd might be the result of a boom. There was a substantial expansion in trade during 1992 and if you measure the acid test ratio you will find that it has fallen from 1.7:1 at 31 December 1991, to 1.1:1 at 31 December 1992. From the working capital analysis we found that there was a significant increase in the stock holding levels by the end of 1992.

The trends revealed by the analysis of Overload Ltd might be interpreted as the first sign of a classic disease known as 'overtrading'. This can occur where the business has underestimated the amount of working capital needed to finance expansion. The business might be successful in profit terms but unless it can pay its debts as they fall due, it is technically insolvent. A build up of non-cash assets (such as stock) can result from undue optimism over trading prospects and insufficient attention to the control of working capital.

On the other hand, we might be misjudging the position if we always assumed that a build-up of non-cash items in the working capital chain was a symptom of overtrading. It could be that the business has moved from a position that was much too conservative in the past. Allowing additional credit to customers is a way of attracting trade, and buying stocks in larger quantities is a way of reducing purchase costs. We would be able to improve our interpretation of the trends in Overload Ltd if we could compare its performance with other firms in the same line of business.

7 Drawing conclusions and constructing the report

Throughout this chapter the ratios for Overload Ltd have been calculated on a piecemeal basis. In order to draw conclusions and compose a report it will be necessary to prepare a summary of the ratios. This summary is usually included as an appendix to the report. Sometimes the simple process of producing the summary provides a clearer picture of the points that need to be brought out in the report. If ratios provided by a trade association are available, it might be appropriate to include these in the summary to enable comparisons to be made.

The report will have to be written in the context of the terms of reference – who requested it and for what purpose? The terms of reference often include information which calls for comment in the report. In many cases, the purpose of the report has an influence on the type of analysis undertaken. In the case of Overload Ltd, we have calculated ratios without knowing why the information was required. There is a self-assessment case study at the end of this chapter which puts the analysis of Overload Ltd into a context that will enable these ratios to be used.

Most students tend to be apprehensive in forming conclusions from ratio analysis. This might partly be due to lack of experience, but could stem from the fact that students tend to expect more from the technique than it is able to provide. Understanding and accepting the limitations is part of the learning process, and in very nearly every case it will be necessary to comment on these limitations in the actual report. Ratio analysis should always be followed by investigation and interpretation.

Furthermore, you must not be distracted by accounting ratios to the extent that you fail to use your common sense during the analysis. We do not need ratios to tell us that the company has valuable assets that could be used as a security for a loan, or that the balance sheet does not tell us how much the business is worth, or that directors have taken out profits in the form of a salary. Factors such as these might have a significant bearing on the way we report to those who have asked for our advice.

In order to give you an opportunity to practise preparing a full report, the exercises at the end of this chapter include a self-assessment case study based on Overload Ltd. This case study requires you to construct a report in the context of the situation described.

A suggested report for the case study relating to Overload Ltd is provided. Even if you do not attempt the case study you will find it worthwhile reading through the report to see the kind of comment that can be made. The report is far more comprehensive than anything that would be expected from a student. You will also find that it includes comment on matters not discussed in this chapter, such as the valuation of a business as a going concern.

8 Returns for external agencies

In this chapter we have been concentrating on the types of information and reports required by external users. Many external agencies require particular pieces of information presented in a certain way, and find that the best way to achieve this is to issue forms or returns for completion.

Such agencies include trade associations and government agencies and departments. A good example of such an organisation is the government's Central Statistical Office (CSO), which gathers enormous amounts of information on many varied returns issued to organisations in all sectors of the business community. The Office of Population Censuses and Surveys collects and analyses data on British society. We will be looking at the work of these two organisations again in Chapter 3.

Earlier in this chapter we stressed the importance of working to any specifications that have been laid down for the report you are preparing. This is equally important when preparing a return for an external agency. You may well find that some instructions on how to complete the return are included with it – possibly up to several pages of instructions if the subject is very complex. Alternatively there may be a note on the return advising you to obtain a copy of a leaflet which explains how to fill it in, which you should read before attempting to complete the return. For example, the form from which we show an extract, the Quarterly Inquiry into Capital Expenditure, is accompanied by two sides of notes in very small type.

PLEASE COMPLETE AND RETURN THIS FORM BY   31/03/96

IMPORTANT –   Please read the enclosed notes before completing this
              form. If you do not have precise figures available give
              the best estimates you can.
              All values should be shown to the nearest £ thousand.

FV		CE		

		Day	Month	Year

1. PERIOD (see note 1)

Period covered by the return –   From

08	/	/

To

09	/	/

2. LAND AND BUILDINGS (see note 2)

2.1 New building work or other constructional
    work of a capital nature (excluding the cost of land and of new dwellings– – – – – – – – – – –

10	

2.2 Acquisition of land and existing buildings –

20	

2.3 Proceeds of land and buildings disposed of –

30	

3. VEHICLES (see note 3)

3.1 New and second-hand acquisitions   –

40	

3.2 Proceeds of vehicles disposed of   –

50	

When you look at the extract from the Quarterly Inquiry into Capital
Expenditure, you will see that the first point the CSO makes is the date by
which the form should be returned. This is quite common in returns for
external agencies, and its prominence is a pointer to its importance to the
agency. Customs and Excise, for example, issue VAT returns to all VAT-
registered traders. Most organisations complete VAT returns quarterly, and
in an attempt to even out the workload, the return dates are spread
throughout the year. It is therefore important to Customs and Excise that
the returns are returned on time. The CSO publishes many of the statistics
calculated from the information it obtains, and it therefore needs the
information in good time to analyse it and get it to press.

There is list of some sources of government statistical information and
examples of the types of information contained in these publications in
some of the appendices to Chapter 3.

Summary

The important learning points in this chapter are as follows:

- conclusions regarding an entity's performance cannot be made from a single accounting figure viewed in isolation

- single figures are absolute measurements, accounting ratios are relative measurements

- accounting ratios attempt to find a relationship between two figures, and this relationship should be expressed in a way that can be understood by the user

- the information contained in a ratio has more meaning when compared to the same ratio in previous years, or the same ratio in another firm

- caution is needed over the interpretation of ratios, as distortions arise through various factors such as inflation, accounting policies, definition of terms, the use of averages, and the nature of many businesses

- there is a hierarchy (or family tree) of ratios which inter-relate

- ratios are meant to be descriptive, not prescriptive

- since most ratios can be calculated in a number of different ways, it is important that any figures produced for others (such as external agencies) are calculated in accordance with the methodology specified.

Appendix 1

Financial statements for Overload Ltd

Profit and loss accounts year to	31 Dec 1991	31 Dec 1992
Turnover	400,000	580,000
Cost of sales	300,000	452,400
Gross profit	100,000	127,600
Distribution costs and admin. expenses	67,000	92,765
Operating profit	33,000	34,835
Interest paid and similar charges	5,000	5,835
Profit before tax	28,000	29,000
Taxation	4,200	4,350
Profit after tax	23,800	24,650
Dividends	nil	nil
Profit retained	23,800	24,650

Balance sheets at	31 Dec 1991		31 Dec 1992	
Fixed assets		69,310		81,335
Current assets				
Stock	25,000		56,550	
Debtors	37,260		66,740	
Bank	6,000		500	
	68,260		123,790	
Creditors falling due within one year				
Creditors	21,370		55,775	
Taxation	4,200		4,350	
	25,570		60,125	
Net current assets		42,690		63,665
Total assets less current liabilities		112,000		145,000
Creditors falling due after more than one year				
10% debenture 1994		50,000		58,350
		62,000		86,650
Capital and reserves				
Ordinary shares capital		10,000		10,000
Profit and loss account		52,000		76,650
		62,000		86,650

Stock at 31 December 1990 was £23,000. Depreciation charges in 1992 were £7,000 and there were no sales of fixed assets during that year.

Appendix 2

BALANCE SHEETS

At 31 December 1985

			GROUP	
			1985	1984
		Notes	£m	£m
ASSETS EMPLOYED				
FIXED ASSETS				
Tangible assets		12	3,533	3,629
Investments: Related and other companies		14	287	442
			3,820	4,071
CURRENT ASSETS				
Stocks		15	1,750	1,740
Debtors		16	1,950	2,102
Investments and short-term deposits		17	576	865
Cash		17	221	146
			4,497	4,853
TOTAL ASSETS			8,317	8,924
CREDITORS DUE WITHIN ONE YEAR				
Short-term borrowings		18	(511)	(383)
Current instalments of loans		21	(131)	(207)
Other creditors		19	(1,961)	(2,084)
			(2,603)	(2,674)
NET CURRENT ASSETS (LIABILITIES)			1,894	2,179
TOTAL ASSETS LESS CURRENT LIABILITIES			5,714	6,250
FINANCED BY				
CREDITORS DUE AFTER MORE THAN ONE YEAR				
Loans		21	1,208	1,311
Other creditors		19	76	127
			1,284	1,438
PROVISIONS FOR LIABILITIES AND CHARGES		20	332	279
DEFERRED INCOME: Grants not yet credited to profit			198	196
MINORITY INTERESTS			405	508
CAPITAL AND RESERVES ATTRIBUTABLE TO PARENT COMPANY				
Called-up share capital		22	657	628
Reserves:	Share premium account		591	415
	Revaluation reserve		89	122
	Other reserves		312	327
	Profit and loss account		1,877	2,294
	Related companies' reserves		(31)	43
	Total reserves	11	2,838	3,201
Total capital and reserves attributable to parent company			3,495	3,829
			5,714	6,250

Appendix 3

Balance sheets 22nd March

	Note	Group 1985 £m	1984 £m
Fixed assets			
Tangible assets	1	1,069.3	876.2
Investments	2	55.6	48.8
		1,124.9	925.0
Current assets			
Stocks		174.4	177.3
Debtors	5	37.4	27.4
ACT recoverable	6	5.8	6.5
Cash at bank and in hand		48.6	37.2
		266.2	248.4
Creditors: due within one year	7	(643.5)	(578.4)
Net current liabilities		(377.3)	(330.0)
Total assets less current liabilities		747.6	595.0
Creditors: due after one year	8	(73.1)	(13.4)
Deferred income	9	(13.6)	(17.8)
Minority interest		(7.4)	(7.5)
		653.5	556.3
Capital and reserves			
Called up share capital	10	175.5	174.2
Share premium account	11	11.8	5.6
Revaluation reserve	12	31.9	34.0
Profit and loss account	13	434.3	342.5
		653.5	556.3

Self-assessment case study

Case study – Overload Ltd

The share capital of Overload Ltd is owned entirely by two brothers who are also the directors. You have been approached by a Mrs Firty who is interested in acquiring the company and intends to make an offer to the two brothers to acquire their shares.

You have no access to information on Overload Ltd other than the financial statements which Mrs Firty has obtained and given to you for the purposes of this case study (the financial statements are those used throughout the chapter). You may make any reasonable assumptions considered appropriate.

Mrs Firty has shown the financial statements to a friend who has told her that the balance sheet shows the business is worth £145,000 according to the latest figures, but that Mrs Firty might be able to buy the company for less than this, since it is running short of cash and therefore cannot have been very profitable during 1992.

Mrs Firty has given you a schedule of accounting ratios for firms operating as merchants in the same line of business as Overload Ltd. She had obtained this information from a cousin who works for the trade association; details are set out below.

Mrs Firty knows very little about accounting and does not really understand the significance of some of the ratios. You have had a short meeting with her during which you explained the key points in the financial statements and gave her a brief idea of how accounting ratios are used. She has now asked you to analyse the financial statements and give her a report on the company's financial affairs so that she can begin negotiations with the directors.

You are required to write the report. Group your comments in the report under suitable headings.

Schedule of ratios obtained from the trade association:

Return on capital	32%
Asset turnover	4 times
Gross profit	24%
Net profit	8%
Stock turnover ratio	7.3 times
Debt collection period	36 days
Creditors' payment period	30 days
Current ratio	2.8:1

The average rate of inflation for the industry's products during 1992 was 6%.

Self-assessment activity

Jane Winters is currently considering which of two companies she should choose for the investment legacy from her late father's estate. The choice lies between purchasing all the share capital of A Limited and purchasing 40% of the share capital of B Limited. Whilst neither A Limited nor B Limited has paid any dividends in recent years, it is anticipated that the companies will resume dividends in the next year or two.

The summarised final accounts of the companies for their last completed financial year are as follows:

Trading and profit and loss accounts

	Company A		Company B	
Sales		160,000		240,000
Cost of sales:				
Opening stock	10,000		70,000	
Purchases	140,000		160,000	
	150,000		230,000	
Closing stock	30,000		50,000	
		120,000		180,000
Gross profit		40,000		60,000
Less:				
Establishment expenses	10,000		14,000	
Administrative expenses	12,000		18,000	
Sales and distribution expenses	6,000		9,500	
Interest expenses	3,000		500	
		31,000		42,000
Net profit		9,000		18,000

Balance sheets

	Company A		Company B	
Fixed assets		80,000		180,000
Current assets:				
Stock	30,000		50,000	
Debtors	6,000		20,000	
Balance at bank	4,000		10,000	
	40,000		80,000	
Creditors: Amounts falling due within one year				
Trade creditors	10,000		20,000	
		30,000		60,000
		110,000		240,000
Creditors: Amounts falling due after more than one year				
10% loan stock		30,000		5,000
		80,000		235,000
Represented by:				
Ordinary share capital		60,000		160,000
Retained earnings		20,000		75,000
		80,000		235,000

Required:

a) Prepare a schedule of appropriate accounting ratios or financial ratios using the information given on the two companies, A Limited and B Limited, to permit a comparison between these companies in each of the following areas: Profitability, Effective use of resources, Short-term solvency, Long-term solvency.

   Answers should include eight ratios or other statistics, each one of which should be shown to two decimal places. Taxation is to be ignored.

b) A report to Jane Winters drawing attention to the comparative strengths and weaknesses of each of the companies A Limited and B Limited as revealed in the answer to a) above and making reference to other significant matters which should be borne in mind by Jane Winters when making her investment decision. Note: Assume that the report is from a financial adviser.

(AAT Intermediate, Paper 5, Accounting, Jun 92)

Key to Chapter 1 activities

Activity 1   You may have thought of:
1. Sales (most students tend to think of this one first)
2. Capital invested or employed in the business (or net assets).

Activity 2   The most likely is the rate of interest on the investment. In this case, 9%. You may also have considered inflation. Profits may be thought of as earnings made on behalf of the business investors. If inflation had been very high over the past year, say 50%, the profits earned would not have kept pace with inflation.

Activity 3   20%, i.e. $\dfrac{50,000}{250,000} \times 100$

Activity 4
1. The same ratio in the previous year (this is called a trend analysis)
2. The same ratio in other firms operating in the same line of business (this is called an inter-firm comparison)
3. With the ratio that was expected (e.g. from the budgeted figures).
4. The return that might be earned by other businesses of similar risk even if not in the same line of business. (This will be important to investors.)

Activity 5   You would have to tell him that he had not done as well as last year, the return on capital invested (i.e. net assets) for that year was 25%.

Activity 6   The debtors represent sales for 30 days. This could be interpreted as meaning that 30 days sales are outstanding, or (put another way) that debtors are taking 30 days to pay.

Activity 7   We need to know how the price of the goods has changed over the year. If the type of goods dealt with by this firm have been subject to an inflation rate of (say) 8%, there has been a reduction in trade in real terms, i.e. sales volumes are down. Alternatively, he might have sold the same volume but increased the unit selling price by 7%.

Activity 8
1. Use of accounting figures: results can vary depending upon the accounting policies adopted.
2. Age of assets: use of older assets may mean a lower denominator in the fraction (lower net book values in the balance sheet) and a lower depreciation charge in the profit calculation. This means, all else being equal, a higher value for ROCE.

Activity 9   For 1991: 33,000/112,000 = 29.5%   For 1992: 34,835/145,000 = 24%

Activity 10   For 1991: (28,000/62,000) = 45%   For 1992 (29,000/86,650) = 33.5%

Activity 11   Multiplying the two secondary ratios together gives you the primary ratio. You can see this by cancelling out sales in the two secondary ratios. Indicate this in the Activity box by including the arithmetic signs, as follows:

Primary ratio		Secondary ratios	
$\dfrac{\text{Net profit}}{\text{Net assets}} \times 100\%$	$=$	$\dfrac{\text{Net profit}}{\text{Sales}}$	$\times$ $\dfrac{\text{Sales}}{\text{Net assets}}$

Activity 12

Profitability: 1991 (33,000/400,000) = 8.25%
1992 (34,835/580,000) = 6%
Asset turnover: 1991 (400,000/112,000) = 3.57 times
1992 (580,000/145,000) = 4 times

Activity 13

1991 8.25% x 3.57 = 29.5% (allowing for rounding)
1992 6% x 4 = 24%

Activity 14

	1991	1992
Gross profit	$\dfrac{100,000}{400,000} = 25.00\%$	$\dfrac{127,600}{580,000} = 22\%$
Expense to sales	$\dfrac{67,000}{400,000} = 16.75\%$	$\dfrac{92,765}{580,000} = 16\%$
Net profit	$\dfrac{33,000}{400,000} = 8.25\%$	$\dfrac{34,835}{580,000} = 6\%$

Activity 15   Cutting sales prices in order to attract a larger volume of trade.

Activity 16

1. Yes.
2. Yes.
3. No. The bad debts expense is not part of cost of sales.
4. No. The cost is part of selling and distribution costs.

Activity 17

1991 (300,000/24,000) = 12.5 times
1992 (452,400/40,775) = 11.1 times

Activity 18

1991 (25,000/300,000 x 365) = 30 days
1992 (56,550/452,400 x 365) = 45.6 days

Activity 19

Debtors collection period:

1991   (37,260/400,000 x 365) = 34 days
1992   (66,740/580,000 x 365) = 42 days

To calculate the creditors payment period, we first need to calculate the figure for purchases from the cost of sales information:
Cost of sales = opening stock + purchases - closing stock
so Purchases = cost of sales - opening stock + closing stock

1991   Purchases = 300,000 - 23,000 + 25,000 = 302,000
1992   Purchases = 452,400 - 25,000 + 56,550 = 483,950

Creditors payment period:

1991   (21,370/302,000 x 365) = 26 days
1992   (55,775/483,950 x 365) = 42 days

Purchases can be found by adding the stock increase to cost of sales (if they were bought but not sold, the stock will increase).

Activity 20

Some possible explanations:
1. Poor credit control
2. A change in the mix between cash sales and credit sales
3. Overload has offered more credit to increase sales
4. There could be one large debtor who is taking a long time to pay whereas the others have been paying up on time.

Activity 21

Reducing the period between purchase and anticipated demand (the jargon used here is to buy stock 'just in time'). Reducing the period of credit granted to customers. Agreeing longer credit periods with suppliers.

Activity 22

1991 (68,260/25,570) = 2.67:1   1992 (123,790/60,125) = 2.06:1

Activity 23

Appendix 2 is ICI, and Appendix 3 is Sainsbury's. Note that the balance sheet in Appendix 2 has a positive working capital (of about 1.7:1) whereas the balance sheet in Appendix 3 has a negative working capital. ICI will have a long operating cycle between the receipt of raw materials and receipt of cash from customers. It will need positive working capital. Sainsbury's will sell its goods (mainly for cash) long before it has to pay its suppliers and can operate on negative working capital.

Key to self-assessment case study

Overload Ltd

Name
Address

Dear Mrs Firty

re: Overload Ltd

Thank you for consulting me in respect of the above, and I hope that you found our initial meeting helpful. I have now carried out an analysis of the financial statements for the year ending 31 December 1992 and my report on these is set out below. The ratios to which I refer are summarised in a separate schedule attached to this report.

1. Value of the business

I realise you have not asked me to advise you on the price you should pay for the shares, but since the information in my report is directed towards helping you in this respect, I feel obliged to include some comment. I am mainly concerned to clarify your friend's comments regarding the value of the business, and have two initial points to make:

(a) Balance sheets are not drawn up in order to show what a business is worth. For example, the amount shown for fixed assets may be based on what the company originally paid for these assets several years ago, less amounts which have been written off against profit. This procedure is used in order to measure the profit, not to value the assets.

(b) Your friend has referred to the wrong figure when saying the balance sheet shows a value of £145,000. This figure is before deducting the loan of £58,350. This loan is repayable in 1994 and the balance sheet value of net assets (total assets less all liabilities) is £86,650.

In negotiating a price for the business, you really need to think of the total amount paid as an investment which earns a return in the form of profits. If you use this idea as a basis you need to determine the rate of return you are looking for on your investment, and also estimate the amount of profit that the company is likely to generate in the near future.

If you use the latest profit as a starting point you will see that after interest payments this amounts to £24,650. If you are looking for a 32% return (the industry average) on your investment, this profit represents 32% of £77,031. I merely put this to you as an example of how you might be able to value the business; you will have to take account of my later comments regarding maintaining future profits at an acceptable level.

2. Growth

The company enjoyed substantial growth during 1992, having increased its turnover on the previous year by 45%. Even with inflation rates in the industry running at 6%, this constitutes an increase in the volume of trade. The increase in turnover should, however, be viewed in the light of my comments below on the possibility that the company has stimulated sales by reducing prices and offering credit terms which are more generous than those offered by its competitors.

3. Return on capital

As mentioned earlier, this is a key factor in determining the price that you might wish to pay for the company. It is also a good indicator of the company's profitability. I have set out, on the attached schedule, the return on total capital for Overload Ltd but it is difficult to make a comparison with the industry average. I cannot be sure from the information provided if the return shown for the industry has been calculated on the same basis as my figures.

Capital employed is quite often viewed from two different angles. Looked at from inside the business, capital is usually considered to be the total capital as represented by the proprietor's capital plus long-term debt. But a proprietor of the business would view the long-term debt as a liability rather than as a part of capital.

The proprietor's view of return on capital is usually referred to as the return on equity rather than the return on capital. I have included the return on equity in my schedule, but I suspect the industry average refers to the return on total capital. You should check with your cousin on this in order to be sure.

You friend was quite right to point out that Overload Ltd was less profitable during 1992 but it is not the reduction in the bank balance (to which I shall refer later) that gives an indication of this, it is the fall in return on capital. You will see from my schedule that the company suffered a serious reduction in its return on capital during 1992 when compared to the previous year. This reduction is almost entirely due to the trading factors to which I refer in Section 4 of my report.

You must, however, be cautious over how you interpret the return on capital in the case of a private company. The directors can obviously determine the amount of their remuneration and quite often this reflects a withdrawal of profit in addition to a payment for services. I have no information on the directors' remuneration and cannot tell whether the amount charged is reasonable for the services they provide.

4. Trading profitability

My analysis of the fall in return on capital for 1992 shows that it is almost entirely due to trading factors rather than arising from a less efficient use of the company's assets. You may be interested to learn how this kind of conclusion can be reached.

You will notice that the schedule produced by your cousin includes a ratio called 'asset turnover'. This reflects the relationship between net assets and turnover. This ratio tells us the value of sales produced by each £1 of net assets. For example, if you look at the industry average you can determine that each £1 of net assets produced £4 in sales. You will also see that the percentage of profit on sales is 8% and so the amount of profit earned on sales of £4 would be 32 pence. This 32 pence has arisen from an investment of £1 in net assets; hence the return on capital being stated at 32%.

When the return on capital falls, this could arise from either a fall in the amount of sales produced by each £1 of net assets (a less efficient use of assets) or a fall in the amount of profit earned on each £1 of sales. In the case of Overload Ltd, you will see that there is a slight improvement in the asset turnover ratio; in 1992 each £1 of net assets produced £4 in sales, whereas this was only £3.57 in 1991.

The fall in the company's net profit as a percentage of its turnover (from 8.25% to 6%) raises a serious question that you should investigate further; a fall in the gross profit margin.

As regards the fall in gross profit margin, there could be several explanations for this but I suspect that it results from a deliberate policy of price cutting in order to stimulate sales. This might explain the considerable growth in trade during 1992.

Unfortunately the additional gross profit earned by the increased turnover has not materialised very much by way of increased profits (from £28,000 in 1991 to £29,000 in 1992) mainly because the running costs have risen in step with the increased turnover. This seems rather strange since a fair proportion of these costs (staff salaries, office expenses, etc.) would not normally increase with an increase in the turnover.

This could be explained by the fact that these costs include a high proportion of costs that do vary with turnover, such as sales commissions and delivery expenses. It might also be explained by an increase in directors' remuneration which, as suggested earlier, may have been increased in order to obtain a tax advantage. The expenses will also include a higher depreciation charge than in the previous year due to the additional fixed assets purchased.

When it comes to considering the price you will offer to acquire the company, you will have to estimate how much profit it is likely to generate in the future. I have set out a few pointers on this in Section 6 of this report.

5. Financial management

The company seems to have managed its affairs reasonably well during 1992. The current ratio is slightly less than the industry average. This is mainly a reflection of the longer period being taken by Overload Ltd to pay its creditors.

The trend in the debt collection period is not a good sign and requires further investigation. It could (as suggested earlier) be part of a deliberate policy to encourage trade, or may be an indication that the company is starting to accumulate bad debts. You really need to examine the debtors in more detail because if some have to be written off as bad, this will clearly affect any estimates of future profits and, therefore, the price you would pay for the company.

As regards the stock turnover ratio, I have converted the figure that your cousin provided into one that shows how many days (on average) stock is held before being sold. Unfortunately, the stock used for this ratio might be different to those in my calculations. The ratio is sometimes calculated on average stock (average of opening and closing stock) and sometimes on closing stock. I have set out both calculations on the schedule. You will notice that the company is holding its stock for a much shorter period than the average within the industry. This suggests that stocks have not been acquired too far in advance of anticipated demand.

You might be concerned with the increase in this ratio between 1991 and 1992 (from 30 days to 45 days) but this quite often happens during a period of rapid expansion. It is a point that needs watching but since the company seems to be operating well within the industry average, it should not be the cause of too much alarm.

The increase in net working capital by the end of 1992 is very much in line with the increase in trade for that year. At the end of 1991 the net amount invested in stocks and debtors less creditors was 10.7 pence for each £1 of sales; at the end of 1992 the amount was 11 pence. This increase is related to the extension of debt collection and stock holding periods.

There is no need to be too concerned with the fall in the bank balance (you will notice I have excluded it from my working capital analysis in the previous paragraph). Most businesses try to keep their cash balance as low as possible because it is uneconomical to hold large amounts of uninvested cash. In any case, the balance sheet only shows the balance of cash at a particular date, and cash balances are subject to many peaks and troughs resulting from factors which fall outside of the day-to-day trading transactions.

6. Profit forecasts and general points

In assessing future profits, you will need to consider the role played in the business by the two brothers. If they are going to retire following your acquisition of their shares, you should try to assess the likely impact this will have on the company's profits. There are at least two factors to think about in this respect; (1) customer loyalty, and (2) management salaries.

It could be that the reputation of the firm rests largely on the skills and personality of the two directors, and there might be a loss of trade should they depart. On the other hand, it is quite likely that the cost of employing a manager to take their place will be less than the amount currently being charged for directors' remuneration.

I trust you will find this report helpful in your negotiations. Should you require any further assistance, or there are any points in my report which are not clear to you, please do not hesitate to get in touch.

Yours faithfully

Schedule of ratios attached to the report

Overload Ltd	1991	1992	Industry
Return on total capital employed	29.5%	24%	32% (see Section 3)
Return on equity	45%	33.5%	? (see Section 3)
Asset turnover	3.57	4	4
Gross profit margin	25%	22%	24%
Expense to sales ratio	16.75%	16%	16% (24% - 8%)
Net profit to sales margin	8.25%	6%	8%
Stock turnover cycle:			
- using average stock	29 days	33 days	50 days (see
- using closing stock	30 days	45 days	Section 5)
Debt collection period	34 days	42 days	36 days
Creditor payment period	26 days	42 days	30 days
Current ratio	2.67:1	2.05:1	2.8:1
Working capital			
for each £1 sales	10.7 pence	11 pence	? (not given)

Author's guidance notes: The working capital for each £1 of sales was calculated as follows: 1991 42,690/400,000; 1992 63,665/580,000. Conversion of the stock turnover ratio into days was simply 365/7.3.

Key to self-assessment activity

Jane Winters

(a) Selected ratios

Description	Formula	A Ltd	B Ltd
1. Return on total capital	$$\frac{\text{Profit before interest}}{\text{Total assets less current liabilities}}$$	10.91%	7.71%
2. Gross profit margin	$$\frac{\text{Gross profit}}{\text{Sales}}$$	25%	25%
3. Expenses to sales ratio	$$\frac{\text{Total expenses less interest}}{\text{Sales}}$$	17.5%	17.3%
4. Net profit to sales	$$\frac{\text{Profit before interest}}{\text{Sales}}$$ *(Notice how Ratio 4 is Ratio 2 less Ratio 3.)*	7.5%	7.7%
5. Asset utilisation (sales per £1 of assets)	$$\frac{\text{Sales}}{\text{Total assets less current liabilities}}$$	£1.45	£1.00
6. Stock turnover	$$\frac{\text{Cost of sales}}{\text{Average stock}}$$	6 times	3 times
7. Debtor collection period	$$\frac{\text{Debtors x 365}}{\text{Sales}}$$	14 days	30 days
8. Creditor payment period	$$\frac{\text{Creditors x 365}}{\text{Purchases}}$$	26 days	46 days

Other ratios could include the current ratio (4:1 in both companies) and acid test ratio (1:1 in A Ltd, 1.5:1 in B Ltd).

(b) The report to Jane Winters.

The following points should be brought out in the report:

Context:

Discuss that an acquisition of 100% of the equity gives total control, whereas an acquisition of 40% would be classed as a minority interest. A 40% interest might give Jane effective control if the remaining shares are widely dispersed, but can only guarantee giving her the ability to exercise significant influence over the company.

Profitability:

The return on capital is quite low in both companies. In A Ltd it is barely more than the 10% being paid on the loan capital, in B Ltd it is substantially less than the rate of interest. On the face of it, Jane could probably earn as much (if not more) from her inheritance by investing it in long-term debenture stocks. Such an investment would carry less risk than either of the two proposals.

As it stands, if Jane is looking for a return of, say, 20% on her investment, the business of A Ltd is only worth (£12,000/0.2) £60,000 compared to a book value of £110,000. On the same basis the total worth of B Ltd is (£18,000/0.2) £90,000 compared to a book value of £240,000 (a 40% interest would be valued at around £36,000). Both valuations assume profit could be maintained at a constant level into the foreseeable future.

Although Jane might have some knowledge which leads her to think that profits can be improved, both proposals should be rejected if the asking price does not give her the return required.

Comparisons:

The lower profitability in B Ltd is mainly due to a less efficient use of assets (£1 of sales from each £1 of assets, compared to A Ltd's £1.45 of sales from each £1 of assets).

The debt collection period in A Ltd is considerably less than B Ltd, suggesting that A Ltd has a higher proportion cash sales than B Ltd.

Caution:

Conclusions should not be drawn from the results of a single year.

The author wishes to make it clear that this answer is purely his own work, and that the AAT are not in any way responsible for it.

Chapter 2

Information assessment by internal users

Introduction

The ratios in Chapter 1 were studied from the viewpoint of an external user. If the company is a relatively small and simple organisation (e.g. no branches or divisions), management can use the same kind of approach for monitoring and controlling the performance of the company. In particular, management will (or should) pay close attention to the ratios used for the working capital analysis. Management of working capital is crucial if a company is to operate at an optimum level of profitability. The failure of many businesses can often be linked to insufficient attention being given to the management of working capital.

But in view of the more detailed information available to management, performance can be monitored by techniques other than the use of financial ratios. For example, in Chapter 5 of Part 3 you learned how to calculate cost variances in a standard costing system. The procedure that you learned there is part of an information system to provide management with a means of monitoring production performance.

The cost variances are usually summarised in a single report which, together with sales variances, will provide a reconciliation between budgeted profit and actual profit. This report is an example of responsibility accounting and provides management with a tool for what is known as 'management by exception'. Where actual results are relatively close to targets set by central management, no action is needed. If there are significant variances, departmental managers (e.g. those in production, purchasing, or marketing) have the responsibility of investigating and explaining variances to central management. As a source of information, cost variances are similar to accounting ratios in that they direct management's attention to problem areas – they do not provide answers.

The information system might also be able to provide quantitative data of a non-financial nature. It should be possible for the system to provide data regarding production volumes, either in physical units or in standard hours. (Note that a 'standard hour' is a measurement of work, not of time.) This has led to the development of ratios that apply specifically to management accounting, such as production volume ratios, capacity or usage ratios, and efficiency or productivity ratios.

Finally, performance assessment in a large, divisionalised, company must usually recognise the motivational effect of any indicators used. In these cases, the information system plays an important role in the harmonisation of the different interests of each divisional manager. This harmonisation process is sometimes called 'goal congruence'.

You can get some insight into the problem of goal congruence if you think about a divisional manager who has seen a business opportunity that would increase the total profit of the company but would reduce the profits of his or her own division. If the performance appraisal system is so rigid that the sole criterion for measuring divisional performance is profit, the new business opportunity might be lost. In cases where supplies (of goods or services) are made from one division to another, there are problems of determining a transfer price that allows the performance of the supplying division to be measured but, at the same time, does not penalise the transferee division.

The subject of divisional performance appraisal and transfer prices is discussed more fully in Sections 4 and 5 of this chapter, but you will find that there are no easy answers to many of the problems. At this stage of your professional development you need to be aware of the problems so that you can recognise how they affect any performance reports that you might be asked to prepare.

Objectives

After completing this chapter you should be able to:

- prepare variance reports that reconcile budgeted profit with actual profit where a standard costing system is used

- calculate productivity ratios

- prepare performance reports for organisations whose total results are derived from sectional activity

- discuss some of the problems inherent in calculating profit for different segments of the whole business

- calculate performance ratios that make use of non-financial data

- prepare performance reports for divisionalised companies in accordance with the methodology devised by central management

- discuss the strengths and weaknesses of the various performance indicators used when measuring divisional performance

- contribute to any discussion regarding the suitability of transfer prices.

1 Variance reports

Cost variances are not simply written out on an odd sheet of paper for management to consider. They are usually part of a formal reporting system that explains the difference between budgeted and actual profit. Such reporting systems usually identify performance variances under two main headings, namely:

■ sales variances

■ cost variances.

In the following text and activities we will ignore overheads for non-production departments (such as administration) so that we can concentrate on budgeted and actual profit comparisons at the gross profit level. Variances between budgeted costs and actual costs for departments such as administration must be incorporated into the variance report, but it is not necessary to include them in order to see how the reconciliation statement works.

Activity 1	Refer to Appendix 1 and calculate the total actual production cost for the 10,200 units produced. Make a note of the amount here.

Admittedly the company had planned to produce 10,000 units but in considering the performance of the production department we need to consider the difference between the budgeted (or standard) cost of the 10,200 units actually produced, and the actual cost of those 10,200 units. This can be calculated as follows:

10,200 units at budgeted (standard) cost was (10,200 x £24)	244,800
10,200 units at actual cost (Activity 1)	253,020
Total cost variance (adverse)	8,220

Management will need to know the factors that have caused this variance. From your work on the cost variances in Chapter 5 of Part 3, you will find that the above amount was analysed under the following headings:

	Adverse	Favourable
Materials:		
Price	6,180	
Usage		3,600
Labour:		
Rate		310
Efficiency	5,500	
Variable overhead:		
Spending variance	2,150	
Efficiency	1,100	
Fixed overheads:		
Expenditure variance		2,000
Capacity variance		3,000
Efficiency	2,200	
	17,130	8,910

Net adverse = 8,220

Activity 2	Identify which managers will be responsible for investigating and explaining the following variances to central management: Manager Material price Material usage Labour rate Labour efficiency

Notice how responsibility accounting is not concerned with finding someone to blame for the variance, but in making someone responsible for explaining the variance so that central management can take remedial action should that be thought necessary.

The schedule of cost variances set out above will enable the company to identify causes of the difference between actual production costs for the units produced and their budgeted cost. These cost variances partly explain why budgeted profit differs from actual profit, the remaining difference is explained by the sales variances.

Activity 3	See if you can identify two variances in relation to sales that will cause actual profit to differ from budgeted profit. The thought process is similar to how you identified the two factors that caused the raw material cost variance.

Notice how these two factors, price and quantity, form a common thread throughout variance analysis. The same basic convention as used for cost variances is also applied to sales variances. In general terms this can be described as follows:

- **sales price variances** are related to the whole quantity sold

- **sales volume variances** are measured at a standard rate.

In Chapter 5 of Part 3 the standard cost of each unit was given as £24. The budgeting process will also involve establishing a budgeted (or standard) selling price for each unit. If we assume that the standard selling price was £40, a summary of the budgeted figures is as follows:

standard cost per unit	£24
standard selling price	£40
standard gross profit margin per unit	£16

The two types of sales variance are measured in terms of their effect on the total anticipated or budgeted gross profit. When measuring sales variances we assume that each unit sold has a cost equal to its standard cost.

In order to make sense of how the variance report works you need to think about how the budgeted profit would have been calculated. In this explanation we are ignoring overheads for the non-production departments and so budgeted profit will be gross profit, i.e. total budgeted gross profit margin. The remaining activities for this section are based on the above example and assume the following quantities:

Budgeted sales 10,000 units at £40 each

Actual sales quantity 10,200 units at £42 each

Activity 4	1. Calculate the total budgeted gross profit or margin. You should set this out on two lines as follows: Budgeted sales revenue Budgeted cost of sales _____ Total budgeted margin/gross profit _____ 2. Calculate the total margin or gross profit actually earned (you have already calculated actual production costs for Activity 1).

We now have the two figures that will be reconciled by the variance report. The difference between them is explained by the sales variances and the cost variances. The variance report commences with budgeted margin/gross profit, followed by the sales variances.

In the case of **sales price variances**, the impact on the total budgeted gross profit or margin can be measured directly be comparing actual sales price with the standard sales price. In the above case the units were sold for £42 each and the impact on the total gross profit margin for each unit sold is £42 - £40 = £2.

Activity 5	Calculate the sales price variance and make a note of the amount here. Remember that price variances are related to the entire quantity sold.

With **sales quantity variances**, however, it is essential to measure this at the standard margin per unit. It would be wrong to use the standard selling price because this would be ignoring the fact that each additional unit sold did cost something to make. Since cost variances are not the responsibility of the sales department we assume a standard cost and measure the quantity variance at standard margin.

Activity 6	Calculate the sales volume variance and make a note of it here.

You are now in a position to set out a variance report reconciling budgeted profit with actual profit. In the next activity you will be asked to complete the report in the format specified. In practice many different types of format are used but they are all based on much the same idea. In the format provided here, a sub-total is required after adding the sales variances to the budgeted total gross profit margin. This sub-total is described as **actual sales revenue less the standard cost of sales** and represents the margin that would have been achieved if the goods sold had cost the same as their standard cost. Since the actual production costs of these units was different to standard, the actual margin earned for the period can be found by deducting the adverse cost variances and adding the favourable ones.

Activity 7	Complete the variance report set out below this box, using figures from Activities 4, 5 and 6, and from the text above Activity 2.

Variance report for the period ending .....

Budgeted sales (10,000 x £40)

Standard cost of budgeted sales (10,000 x 24)   _____

Budgeted margin/gross profit

Add favourable sales variances:

    Sales price variance

    Sales volume variance   _____

Actual sales revenue less standard cost of sales

Cost variances

    Materials:

        Price

        Usage

    Labour:

        Rate

        Efficiency

    Variable overhead:

        Spending variance

        Efficiency

    Fixed overheads:

        Expenditure variance

        Capacity variance

        Efficiency   _____   _____

                            ======   ======   Net   _____

Actual margin/gross profit   =======

2 Productivity ratios

In the standard costing activities for Chapter 5 of Part 3, you calculated the fixed overhead cost variances. Although these were reported in the variance statement as cost variances, the data regarding production activity might be equally useful to management if given in the form of a ratio. This can be done even if no standard costing system exists.

These ratios use a concept known as a standard hour. A standard hour is defined as the output expected in one hour at normal or standard efficiency. A standard hour is a measurement of work, not a measurement of time. If a unit should take one hour to make (at standard efficiency) and 100 units were produced, we would say that 100 standard hours of output were produced. If it actually took 120 hours to produce this work we would say that the efficiency or productivity of the workers was 83.33% (100/120), i.e. the efficiency or productivity ratio was 83.3%.

In the standard costing exercise, the fixed overhead variances were initially identified under two main headings: expenditure variance and volume (or activity) variance. We can ignore the expenditure variance in this section and concentrate on the volume variance for which the productivity ratios are calculated. The volume variance was sub-divided under two headings, namely:

- **efficiency variance**, which arises when the hours taken to produce the goods differs from the standard hours allowed to produce those goods

- **capacity variance**, which arises when the total number of hours worked in the period differs from the number of hours budgeted to be worked.

The total of these two variances is the **volume (or activity) variance** which is the difference between the standard hours of actual output and the budgeted standard hours for the period. The same idea is used in calculating labour control ratios. The labour control ratios express figures for overall production volume (or activity) with a breakdown into efficiency/productivity and capacity. The three ratios are expressed as percentages and are calculated using the following fractions:

Production volume/ activity ratio $\dfrac{\text{Standard hours worth of production}}{\text{Budgeted hours for the period}}$

This ratio is often simply called the PV ratio.

Efficiency/productivity ratio $\dfrac{\text{Standard hours worth of production}}{\text{Actual hours worked}}$

Capacity ratio $\dfrac{\text{Actual hours worked in period}}{\text{Budgeted labour hours for the period}}$

The capacity ratio is also known as the usage ratio.

The production volume ratio is the product of the efficiency and capacity ratios. This is easier to see when you set the three fractions out alongside each other, as follows:

Production volume		**Efficiency**		**Capacity**
Standard hours produced	=	Standard hours produced	x	Actual hours worked
Budgeted hours for period		Actual hours worked		Budgeted hours for period

Notice how 'actual hours worked' can be cancelled to give the product for the activity ratio.

We can use the details from the standard costing exercise to practise calculating these ratios. The details are repeated here as follows:

Budgeted hours for the period (10,000 x 2)	20,000
Actual output measured in standard hours (10,200 x 2)	20,400
Actual hours worked	21,500

Activity 8

Calculate the three labour control ratios, and ensure that the product of the efficiency and capacity ratios is equal to the activity ratio.

Production volume ratio   Efficiency ratio   Capacity ratio

Now practise using the idea on a problem outside the context of standard costing.

Details for the activities:

A manufacturer produces a range of three products for which the standard times and budgeted production quantities were as follows:

Product	Standard hours per unit	Number of units budgeted
Aye	10	2,000
Bee	1	8,000
Cee	2	8,000

During the period, 43,000 hours were worked and the following production achieved:

Aye	1,800 units
Bee	8,000 units
Cee	12,000 units

Activity 9	As a starting point, calculate the total budgeted hours for the period and the total standard hours of actual output. 1. Total budgeted hours for the period 2. Total standard hours of actual output

Activity 10	Now calculate the three productivity ratios and check that they reconcile. Work to one decimal point for the percentages.

3 Sectional activity

Many large-scale enterprises (and some of the smaller ones) derive their total profit from sectional activity. The way in which an enterprise is divided into sections will vary, and the following table gives an indication of the most common bases adopted:

Basis of division	Examples
By activities or products	(a) retail store with several departments (b) manufacturing and merchandising (c) manufacture or sale of different products
By geographical location	(a) supermarkets and chain stores with several branches (b) coal mining from different pits
By legal separation	separate companies are formed for each division – each company being part of a 'group' under the control of a holding company

We will look at some of the problems associated with producing financial reports for sectional activity in the context of departmental trading. You must keep in mind, however, that the same principles apply to any kind of business (mining, manufacturing or selling) where total profit is derived from a number of different sections (or divisions).

The information system will be set up in order to determine the profit contributed by each department.

Activity 11	Think about why management might wish to know the results of each department. Aim at finding two reasons and make a note of them here: 1. 2.

The problem faced by the accountant is mainly one of classification (and coding) of departmental costs, and departmental income, in order to prepare the profit reports for each department. Up to a point there will be little difficulty in identifying the costs incurred by a particular selling department.

Activity 12

Make a note of the types of cost that can easily be identified as directly attributable to a particular selling department in a departmental store. Aim at finding three, but be satisfied with two before you turn to the Key for help if needed.

1

2

3

A cost accountant refers to these items as 'allocated costs' because there is no doubt that they are directly related to a particular department. These costs would not have been incurred if the department did not exist.

The term 'allocation' is used in order to differentiate between the accounting treatment of costs directly attributable to departments, and the treatment of certain costs that relate to the business as a whole and have to be 'apportioned' to the different departments. The process of cost apportionment is used when departments are sharing the benefits derived from certain types of expenditure that cannot be allocated to any one department. These non-specific costs are shared out and charged to all departments on a pro-rata basis.

Activity 13

There will be many costs that are not specific to any one department, but where each department receives a benefit from that expenditure. Make a note of some of the costs that you consider might fall under this heading.

These costs are not specific to the department. Notice that we talk about costs specific to a department being *allocated* to departments, and costs that are not specific being *apportioned*. The basis used for apportionment of non-specific costs should bear some relationship to the benefits received by each department from the costs concerned. It is not difficult to find an appropriate basis for estimating the benefits received. You worked on something similar in Chapter 4 of Part 3 when dealing with overhead absorption.

Activity 14	See if you can think of a reasonable basis for apportioning each of the following types of indirect cost to different departments:

	Apportionment basis
1. Occupancy costs such as rent, rates, light and heat	
2. Insurance of total trading stock	
3. A floor supervisor overseeing several departments	
4. Advertising costs	

Although these apportionments appear to be based on some kind of logic, they are purely accounting apportionments based on a policy decision. The practice of cost apportionment is arbitrary and can sometimes produce information that is misleading to management and it might be preferable to leave them out of the departmental report. You will get some idea of how cost apportionment can distort accounting information by working on a simple (imaginary) example. The details for the example are as follows:

A departmental store has three sales departments: Jewellery sales, ladies' clothes, and a restaurant for customers. The following data is available.

Departmental accounting data	Jewellery	Ladies' clothes	Restaurant
	£	£	£
Sales	60,000	250,000	120,000
Cost of sales	36,000	130,000	70,000
Departmental salaries	12,000	40,000	30,000
Other allocated expenses	1,000	4,000	10,000

Statistical data

Floor area in square metres	40	260	100
Number of employees	2	5	3

Other costs

Occupancy costs (rent, rates, insurance, etc.) of the whole building were £60,000; salary of shop floor supervisor for jewellery and ladies' clothes departments £14,000.

Activity 15	Prepare the departmental profit statements using apportionment bases that seem to be appropriate. You can work this activity by completing the tabulation set out below this box.

	Jewellery		**Ladies' clothes**		**Restaurant**	
Sales		60,000		250,000		120,000
Cost of sales		36,000		130,000		70,000
Gross profit		24,000		120,000		50,000
Departmental salaries	12,000		40,000		30,000	
Allocated expenses	1,000		4,000		10,000	
Occupancy costs						
Supervisor's salary						
Profit or (loss)						

Check your figures with the Key before going on to the next activity.

Activity 16	A manager reviewing the departmental figures concludes that the restaurant should be closed because it is causing the company to lose money. Consider whether or not the restaurant is losing money and make a note of your observations.

One of the problems inherent in cost apportionment is that many of the costs are 'fixed'. In other words, the cost would be incurred whether a particular department existed or not. A part of these costs might be saved if the department is closed, but most of them (rent, rates, heating, etc.) would continue at the same level as before the closure. Closing down a department would simply load these costs on to the remaining departments.

Costs which can be saved by closing down a segment are often called *avoidable costs* since such costs will not be incurred if the department does not exist. Costs which will continue even though the department is closed down are then referred to as *unavoidable costs*. It is a pity that this concept is not understood more widely, particularly by politicians who often talk about product costs in industries such as coal mining as if the 'cost' of a product is something known with certainty.

The 1984/85 miners' strike was precipitated by the proposed closure of the Cortonwood pit in Yorkshire. The National Coal Board (NCB) claimed that the pit was uneconomic and produced figures (based on the 1981/2 profit and loss account) to show that the operating costs of producing a tonne of coal were greater than the net sale proceeds. These figures revealed a loss of £6.20 per tonne. Yet on a subsequent analysis (November 1984) it was shown that some of the operating costs included in the calculation of this loss were unavoidable costs, such as an apportionment of the NCB's overheads and management services. These costs would continue to be incurred even after closure of the pit. When the unavoidable costs were taken out of the equation, each tonne of coal from the pit was shown to be contributing £5.75 to the NCB's profits.

The problem of apportioning common costs to separate divisions for the purposes of measuring divisional performance has led to the development of ideas such as divisional contribution and controllable divisional overheads. A full study of these principles is not necessary at this stage of your professional development, but you should be aware of the problems, and exercise caution on any divisional performance indicators where the costs include apportionments of central services.

The idea of divisional contribution is quite interesting. Contribution is the difference between sales income and the direct costs of earning that income. We think of this difference as contributing to indirect costs and profits. If you look at the figures of our department store more closely, you will see that the restaurant is making a contribution of £10,000. This contribution will be lost if the department is closed.

The contribution from each department can be calculated as follows:

	Jewellery		Ladies' clothes		Restaurant	
Sales income		60,000		250,000		120,000
Cost of sales	36,000		130,000		70,000	
Salaries	12,000		40,000		30,000	
Allocated expenses	1,000		4,000		10,000	
		49,000		174,000		110,000
Contribution		11,000		76,000		10,000

A report produced on this basis will show the total contribution as £97,000. From the total contribution there will be deductions for the fixed occupancy costs of £60,000, and the shop floor supervisor's salary of £14,000, giving a total profit of £23,000. The profit for the whole business does not change but the report now shows a contribution of £10,000 from the restaurant, and so there is less likelihood of management being led into making a wrong decision.

In view of the practical difficulties of determining profits from individual sections, performance indicators other than profit are often used. In the case of firms whose total profit is derived from different branches, the performance of each branch can be measured by indicators such as:

- sales revenue per employee

- sales revenue per square metre of floor space.

You can practise using this idea on our departmental store.

Activity 17	Using the details provided for Activity 16, calculate sales revenue per employee and sales per square metre of floor space.

	Sales per employee	Sales per square metre
Jewellery		
Ladies' clothing		

In the case of a departmental store (where different departments have different requirements) these ratios are not necessarily used for departmental comparisons. They tend to be used for comparing results of a particular department over a period of years. In the case of branches, they are often used for comparisons between the branches.

4 Divisional performance appraisal

This subject is usually studied on an advanced course in management accounting and is associated with the problems of decentralisation in complex (often diversified) organisations. In the context of performance appraisal, decentralisation refers to situations where a high degree of managerial decision making is delegated to divisional managers. This leaves central management with the task of monitoring and controlling the entire group of divisional units.

The information system in a decentralised organisation aims to achieve a number of things but you should be able to identify the following three objectives:

1. **To provide feedback for central management.** This will enable central management to assess the performance of divisional managers and consider the economic worth of the division as an operating unit.

2. **To encourage initiative and provide motivation.** The appraisal system must be such that local managers are allowed to operate with a reasonable degree of autonomy, and with the assurance that their performance is being measured in a way that is perceived to be fair.

3. **To promote goal congruence.** In an ideal world, the goals of local management will coincide with the overall goals of the company (known as perfect goal congruence). This is not always the case and so the appraisal system must help local management to direct operations in a way that fulfils the company's objectives.

At NVQ level 3 it is sufficient to be aware of the problems in order to recognise their relevance to any reports you are asked to prepare.

The subject is related to the idea of responsibility accounting. In Section 1 you saw how various managers were responsible for explaining cost variances arising in their departments. In those cases the financial responsibility of the managers related to costs, and in the context of responsibility accounting we would refer to their departments as cost centres. In divisional organisations, financial responsibility (and hence performance appraisal) extends beyond costs. Two types of financial responsibility centres (other than standard cost centres) that are frequently found in practice are as follows:

■ profit centres

■ investment centres.

Profit centres relate to divisions where managers are responsible for a combination of costs and revenues. Investment centres are divisions where managers are responsible for the best combination of costs and revenues in relation to the capital employed in their division. Both types of responsibility centre involve a measurement of divisional profit and so some of the problems are common to both.

You have already seen the problems of measuring the profits of a particular segment of the business. If divisional profit is to be used for performance appraisal, the main difficulty is associated with costs over which the divisional manager has no control. It is important to ensure that managers are made responsible only for those costs over which they have control. This has led to a concept of 'controllable profit' which is often used a starting point for performance appraisal in both profit centres and investment centres.

Activity 18	See if you can identify some costs over which a divisional manager would have no control and should, therefore, be left out of account when calculating controllable profit.

Roughly speaking, controllable profit for each division results from the following:

Divisional revenue		X
Less divisional variable costs		X
Divisional contribution		X
Less: fixed overheads controllable by the division	X	
depreciation on assets controllable by the division	X	
		X
Controllable profit		X

In the case of an investment centre, there are usually other deductions from controllable profit in order to determine the profit that should be related to the capital invested. You will recall from Chapter 1 that since profit is an absolute figure it might be more appropriate to consider profit in relation to the assets that have generated that profit. But if divisionalised companies simply use the return on capital employed (ROCE) as an indicator of divisional performance, it might lead to local managers making decisions that are not in the best interest of the company as whole.

There are several problems associated with using ROCE as an indicator of divisional performance but some of them require an understanding of topics that you will not cover until you reach a more advanced stage of your studies. You will be able to recognise one of them now because it relates to something that you covered in Chapter 1. You might recall an example (following Activity 8 in Chapter 1) where two companies were earning the same profits before depreciation but the assets of one company were 10 years older than the other. We can use the same idea to understand one of the problems in measuring ROCE for divisions. The example is repeated below, except that divisions have been substituted for companies.

Division A's fixed assets were purchased 10 years ago and are being written off over 15 years. Division B's fixed assets were purchased during the current year and are also being written off over 15 years. The following is a summary of each division's financial reports:

	Division A	Division B
Fixed assets at cost	30,000	75,000
Aggregate depreciation	20,000	5,000
Net book value	10,000	70,000
Net current assets	5,000	5,000
	15,000	75,000
Profit before depreciation	8,000	8,000
Depreciation	2,000	5,000
Net profit	6,000	3,000
Return on capital employed	40%	4%

In Chapter 1 we considered this in relation to the problem of comparing the performance of two companies. The problem is somewhat different when measuring divisional performance because we are often thinking about the motivational aspects of the performance indicators used. If we use the wrong indicator, we might motivate a divisional manager to make decisions that are simply aimed at maximising that indicator.

The above example is highly contrived in order to demonstrate a point. In reality it is likely that the new fixed assets in Division B will be more efficient than those in Division A and should produce higher profits. But it would require a considerable increase in profitability in order to bring the ROCE of each division into line with each other.

Activity 19	Imagine that you are the divisional manager of A and that you are considering whether or not to renew the fixed assets of your division. You realise that at the end of the first year with the new assets, the balance sheet of your division will be the same as that in Division B, but the profits before depreciation will be £20,000 instead of £8,000. A full year's depreciation is charged in the year of acquisition. Your performance is being monitored on the basis of ROCE. Consider whether you would decide to go ahead with the renewal and make a note of your calculations and observations here.

Note that if you had decided to go ahead with the replacement, there would have been an increase in the company's overall profits by £12,000. This opportunity has been lost simply because of the way the performance of your division was appraised.

In order to solve this type of problem, divisional performance is often measured on the basis of a concept known as **residual income**. Residual income is usually based on controllable profit less interest imputed to the division at a rate specified by central management. Residual income is an absolute amount (not relative) and the idea is that divisional managers will decide in favour of any project that produces income in excess of the rate of imputed interest because the excess will go to swell the residual income of their division.

5 Transfer prices

Traditionally, the subject of transfer prices has been associated with the problem of measuring performance in divisionalised organisations – often in the context of vertically integrated groups of companies, such as where a manufacturing division transfers goods to a trading division. But its application to performance appraisal is much wider, and transfer prices become necessary in most organisations where there is an internal transfer of goods or services between departments. Examples of these transfers include the provision of computer services to the user departments, the provision of photocopying services by a central reprographic department, and provision of vehicle maintenance services. You will probably find many other examples in your own organisation.

The provision of these services could be made 'free' or as a 'favour' to the department receiving the benefit, but this will not enable central management to assess the financial performance of the supplying and receiving departments. For example, a garage that has a car repair section and a car sales section is likely to make use of the car repair section to service cars being held for sale. If no accounting record is made for this service, management have no way of checking on the resources used in running the car sales department, and an inaccurate record of profitability in the car repair section.

One way of keeping a record of the internal transfer is to give it a price and to charge this out to the department receiving the benefit. In general terms, a system of transfer pricing is an internal book-keeping procedure and does not affect the total profit of the firm. If goods are transferred from one division to another at a price in excess of cost, the total profit (assuming the goods have been sold by the receiving division) is merely split between the two divisions. In some cases, however, a system of transfer pricing can affect profitability by influencing decisions at a local level. For example, a divisional manager might decide to purchase externally rather than accept an internal transfer, even when this reduces the overall profit of the company.

There is no easy answer to how a transfer price should be calculated but it is important to appreciate the limitations of using transfer prices when making decisions. Consider the following example:

> A local authority is deciding whether to continue providing 'day care' services from its own resources or whether to purchase them from an outside agency. For internal accounting purposes, the local authority has determined a charge-out rate (the transfer price) based on the cost of providing day care services.

In this situation a wrong decision might be made by comparing the external agency's fees with the internal charge-out rate. The decision should be based on comparing the agencies fees with the costs that will be saved by the local authority. These cost savings might not be the same as the charge-out rate, even though it is based on cost. Quite often these costs include apportionments of costs that will continue even if a department is closed. As with many decisions it is necessary to distinguish between avoidable and unavoidable costs.

A full study of transfer pricing involves certain aspects of economic analysis in order to determine a theoretical optimum price. In practice this analysis is not always feasible and management will choose a method that meets most of their objectives in terms of performance appraisal and goal congruence. The methods used fall into three classes, namely:

■   cost-based prices

■   market-based prices

■   negotiated prices.

Cost-based prices are based either on some variant of cost such as variable cost, full cost (i.e. variable cost plus absorbed fixed overheads), or standard cost; or they are based on cost plus a profit 'mark-up'. Where the transferor is a profit (or investment) centre it is not appropriate to use any of the variants of cost. One of the problems with a 'cost plus' basis is that there is no incentive for the transferring division to control costs. In fact it encourages inefficiency because the higher the cost, the greater will be the profit added. The whole cost of being inefficient is passed on to the transferee.

Market-based prices can only be used if a market exists for the products concerned. This is not always the case with certain types of intermediate product. If a market does exist then market-based prices usually meet most of the objectives of a transfer pricing system because they create a truly competitive environment and encourage operational efficiency. They are not entirely free of problems. There might not be anything to prevent the purchasing division from buying externally (to the detriment of the whole company) unless there is a directive to deal internally.

Negotiated prices require the intervention of central management. They are used when either of the other two bases cause a conflict or are inappropriate for performance appraisal. A good example is an adjusted market price which recognises that the transferring division does not incur any marketing costs. In these circumstances an unadjusted market price might not be a perfect indicator of the value of goods transferred.

Summary

The important learning points in this chapter are as follows:

- accounting ratios can be used by management to monitor performance in a small organisation

- a standard costing system can be used to measure performance when responsibility accounting is based on cost centres

- responsibility accounting includes the preparation of performance reports that signify the department responsible for explaining variances

- productivity ratios can be calculated if standard hours are established

- profit measurement for sectional activity can be misleading when apportioned costs are included

- departmental profits are more useful to management when they are based on the concept of departmental contribution

- responsibility accounting in divisionalised companies often involves establishing investment centres

- central management must recognise the motivational effect of indicators used to measure divisional performance

- profit measurements in profit centres should be based on controllable profit

- a measurement of divisional performance based on ROCE might lead divisional managers into being reluctant to renew the assets of their division

- alternative measures such as residual income will achieve better goal congruence

- transfer prices are used as a means of recording inter-departmental transfers

- there is no single method for determining a transfer price, management must select one that meets their objectives of measuring departmental performance and achieving goal congruence

- accounting technicians must be constantly aware of the motivational aspects of any performance reports which they prepare.

Appendix 1

A company produces a single product and uses a standard costing system for which the following standard costs apply:

STANDARD COST CARD

	£
Direct material: 4 kilos at £2 per kilo	8
Direct wages: 2 hours at £5 per hour	10
Variable overhead: 2 hours at £1 per hour	2
Fixed overhead: 2 hours at £2 per hour	_4_
	24

Budgeted production for December is 10,000 units.

The actual results for December were as follows:

Production: 10,200 units

Actual materials consumed: 39,000 kilos costing £84,180

Actual direct wages cost: 21,500 hours costing £107,190

Actual variable overhead cost: £23,650

Actual fixed overhead cost: £38,000

Key to Chapter 2 activities

Activity 1   £84,180 + £107,190 + £23,650 + £38,000 = £253,020.

Activity 2
Material price	–	purchasing manager
Material usage	–	production manager
Labour rate	–	personnel manager
Labour efficiency	–	production manager

Activity 3   Sales price and sales volume.

Activity 4

Budgeted sales revenue (10,000 x £40)	400,000
Standard cost of budgeted sales (10,000 x 24)	240,000
Budgeted margin	160,000
Total margin/gross profit actually earned:	
Sales (10,200 x £42)	428,400
Actual costs of 10,200 units	253,020
	175,380

Activity 5   10,200 x £2 = £20,400 favourable

Activity 6   200 x £16 = £3,200 favourable

Activity 7

Budgeted sales (10,000 x £40)		400,000
Standard cost of budgeted sales (10,000 x 24)		240,000
Budgeted margin		160,000
Add favourable sales variances:		
Sales price variance		20,400
Sales volume variance		3,200
Actual sales revenue less standard cost of sales		183,600
Cost variances as defined in earlier text	Net	8,220
Actual margin		175,380

Activity 8   Production volume/activity ratio 20,400/20,000 = 102%

Efficiency ratio 20,400/21,500 = 95% (rounded)

Capacity usage ratio 21,500/20,000 = 107.5%

As a cross-check, the product of the efficiency and capacity ratio is 107.5% x 95% = 102% (the PV ratio, allowing for rounding).

Activity 9

1. (2,000 x 10) + (8,000 x 1) + (8,000 x 2) = 44,000 hours

2. (1,800 x 10) + (8,000 x 1) + (12,000 x 2) = 50,000 hours

Activity 10

PV/activity ratio: 50,000/44,000 = 113.6%

Efficiency ratio 50,000/43,000 = 116.3%

Capacity ratio 43,000/44,000 = 97.7%

Activity 11

1. For control purposes (measuring departmental performance), i.e. to compare actual performance with plans and take action where appropriate to stimulate the most advantageous corporate performance by, for example, removing inefficiencies.

2. Calculation of departmental bonuses.

Activity 12

Examples are:

1. Cost of goods sold by the department.

2. Salaries of employees working in the department.

3. Depreciation of any equipment used by the department.

Activity 13

Occupancy costs (rent, rates, insurance, lighting and heating), advertising, shop floor supervisor's salary.

Activity 14

Suitable bases could be:

1. Relative floor area

2. Value of stock held by the department

3. Number of employees in each department

4. Departmental sales for the period.

Activity 15

	Jewellery		Ladies' clothes		Restaurant	
Sales		60,000		250,000		120,000
Cost of sales		36,000		130,000		70,000
Gross profit		24,000		120,000		50,000
Departmental salaries	12,000		40,000		30,000	
Direct expenses	1,000		4,000		10,000	
Occupancy costs	6,000		39,000		15,000	
Supervisor's salary	4,000		10,000		–	
		23,000		93,000		55,000
Profit or (loss)		1,000		27,000		(5,000)

Activity 16

Possibly not. It is possible that the £15,000 occupancy costs apportioned to the restaurant would have to be paid whether the restaurant existed or not. Also, the availability of a restaurant may encourage customers to shop at the department store.

Activity 17

Jewellery: Sales per employee (60,000/2) £30,000. Sales per square metre (60,000/40) £1,500

Ladies' clothes: Sales per employee (250,000/5) £50,000. Sales per square metre (250,000/260) £962.

Activity 18

These costs are usually identified under the following headings: apportioned costs (such as the apportionment of central services) and depreciation of fixed assets. The investment (or disinvestment) in fixed assets at a division may be the subject of centrally co-ordinated management control and would be outside the control of a divisional manager.

Activity 19

The profit will be (20,000 - 5,000) £15,000. This represents a ROCE of (15/75) 20%, which is much lower than the present ROCE of 40%. The renewal of fixed assets is, therefore, likely to be declined. Senior management will use current cost.

Chapter 3
Statistical reports

Introduction

The term 'statistics' is used in two ways, namely:

- a numerical science that uses numbers in various ways, such as estimating the results of the next general election from a small number of voters

- a group of facts that are expressed numerically, such as the number of people who are unemployed.

The study of statistics as a numerical science is quite extensive, particularly for subjects such as sampling and the mathematical laws of probability. It is not necessary for you to study these matters for Unit 7 because the competence required at this level is concerned mainly with the preparation and presentation of reports. The skills involved include the presentation of information in graphical form, which is normally considered to be part of the subject called statistics. You are, however, expected to have a basic knowledge of two topics that will help you to understand the relevance of certain reports that you might be asked to prepare:

- index numbers

- time series analysis.

Statistics as a means of presenting facts in numerical form is something that we all encounter virtually every day via the press, television or radio. Nearly every day we are given statistics relating to unemployment rates, crime rates, inflation rates, increase (or decrease) in retail sales, imports and exports, birth rates, and even the decline in church attendance. The raw data for these statistics has to be collected by someone and sorted in some way so that it can be turned into information. Sometimes the information is useful to particular groups in society such as the government and businesses; sometimes it is simply published because someone considers it to be newsworthy.

The largest collector of statistical data is the government. Every month the Central Statistical Office (CSO) publishes a booklet called 'Monthly Digest of Statistics'. Most central libraries, and libraries attached to colleges and universities, keep copies of this publication. If you get the opportunity to look at a copy, you will find that most of the information is based on data that must have been supplied by the business community, other government offices, and local government offices. Wherever you work, there is every likelihood that at some time you will be involved in preparing and providing data for a statistical survey carried out by various external agencies such as the CSO or a trade association.

Objectives

After completing this chapter you should be able to:

■ tabulate and present quantitative data in accordance with a specification

■ give advice on the most appropriate way of presenting quantitative data so that it provides useful information to those for whom it is intended

■ give advice on sources of statistical data

■ select appropriate data from tabulations prepared by others (including external agencies) and convert it into information that is relevant to users' needs

■ prepare graphs and charts in a way that is intended to inform the reader rather than deceive

■ calculate index numbers according to an agreed specification

■ use index numbers for making useful comparisons between variables

■ calculate moving averages to assist in identifying trends in a time series.

1 Use of statistics in business

Your practical involvement with statistics as an accounting technician is most likely to be in providing statistical data for an external agency. Sometimes management use statistical information (such as that published by the CSO) when planning business operations, and you might be asked to advise on the best source of information.

Activity 1	If your company is contemplating producing a text book aimed at students preparing for an 'A' level examination, information will be needed to help in deciding the number of copies to produce. Make a note of the type of information, and of its source, that might be useful in this respect. 1. Statistical information 2. Source

When it comes to making use of statistics as a numerical science, there are a number of techniques that could be applied to business situations, although some of them are rarely used. Two applications where the scientific approach tends to be rejected in favour of less sophisticated techniques are as follows:

- stock control, where statistical techniques could help management to determine economic order quantities and the frequency of placing orders

- production cost behaviour, where the statistical techniques of correlation and regression could be used to analyse production costs (particularly overheads) between fixed and variable.

Activity 2	Make a note of why you think management prefer to use less sophisticated techniques.

Companies often make use of statistical data prepared by external agencies, such as index numbers published by the CSO, but this is not the same thing as using statistics as a science to assist with the management of the business. The statistical techniques that are most frequently applied to business situations are as follows:

- market research, where statistical surveys are used to determine customers' wants and the effectiveness of advertising methods

- quality control, where inspection of finished goods as they come off the production line is often done on the basis of a statistical sample

- auditing, where statistical sampling methods have been developed that help the auditor to form an opinion of the entire group of items (such as sales invoices) from conditions found in a sample taken from that group.

2 Presentation of data as information

Raw data is turned into useful information when that data is sorted in some way and then presented in a form that can be understood by, and is useful to, those for whom it is intended. After selecting and collecting the data, the first step is usually to tabulate the numbers according to some useful classification.

Appendix 1 to this chapter gives an example of tabulated data taken from Section 2 (Population and vital statistics) of the Monthly Digest of Statistics published by the CSO. Data in tabulated form can be thought of as information, but in most cases it is used as raw data for subsequent analysis. The analysis is then used to produce information in a form that can be understood and used by others.

A lot of the tables in the CSO publications contain data that can be purchased from the CSO in computer readable format. The four-letter code at the top of each column in Table 2.1 in Appendix 1 is an identifier to allow computer access to the data in that column, and quite often to additional data that has not been published. This service makes it easier to carry out various types of mathematical analysis on the data and to produce information in an easily readable form such as a graph.

Although an analyst will find information in the form of tabulated data (such as Table 2.1) quite useful, it will look like a meaningless jumble of figures to the general public. Communication requires a consideration of various factors, including:

- the type of data

- the amount of data

- the audience.

The last point is usually the most important. The way in which we communicate with someone who has not studied accounting will differ from the way in which we communicate with an accountant. It also requires a consideration of the purposes for which the information might be used.

The publishers of newspapers will consider they are communicating news to the general public. Almost every day you can find examples of statistical data in a newspaper presented in the form of a graph or chart. Presentation of data in the form of graphs and charts requires a great deal of care in order to inform rather than mislead. For example, the demographic data from Table 2.2 could be presented in the form of a bar chart, as shown on the next page:

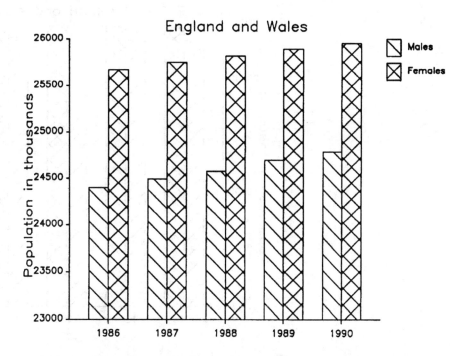

England and Wales

There is nothing incorrect in any of the measurements used to produce this chart, but it is deceptive. It also fails to communicate certain trends that might be of interest to the reader.

Activity 3	See if you can identify a misleading feature of this chart, and also identify an item of information that might be of interest to readers which is not clearly communicated by the bar chart.

1. Misleading feature

2. Information not clear

If the chart had used zero as the bottom scale-point for the Y-axis (the one on the left), the chart would have been drawn as shown on the next page:

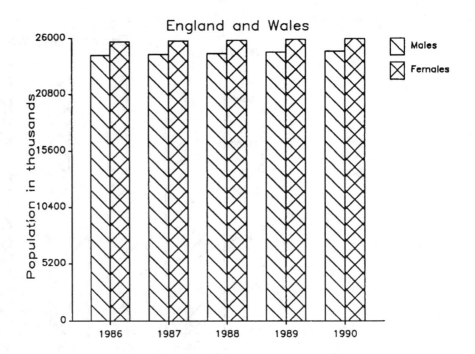

This gives a less deceptive picture of the population split between males and females but it does not enable the reader to see whether the difference between the two is growing larger or getting smaller.

Activity 4	See if you can think of a type of graph that might enable the trend in this population difference to be seen, and make a note of it here.

If we were to produce a line graph on which the population for each sex was plotted, we might be able to see whether the two lines were converging or diverging. If you did this for the example being considered, it would look something like the graph shown on the next page. As you can see, it requires a very sharp eye to notice whether the two lines are getting closer together or simply staying at an equal distance apart.

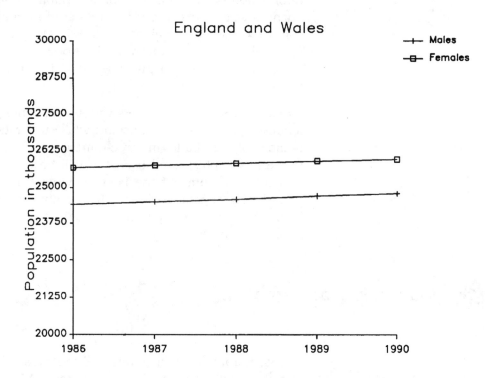

A better approach would be to measure the difference between the two sexes and then plot this on a line graph. This would result in a graph being presented on the following lines:

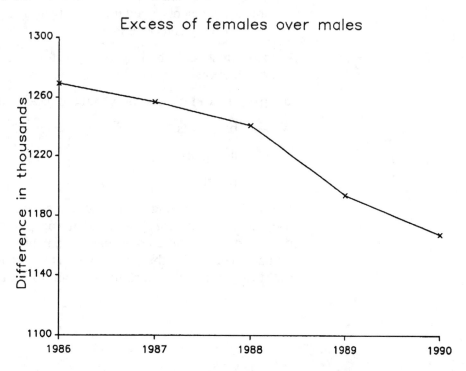

The trend information is now clear for everyone to see. The fall could have been made even more dramatic by contracting the scale on the Y-axis. This series of four charts, all based on the same raw data, shows how important it is to select the relevant data and to present it in a form that provides useful information to the user.

Information in the annual reports of public companies includes the annual financial statements (profit and loss account and balance sheet) which the company is legally required to publish. Many companies include additional financial data on voluntary basis. Appendix 2 to this chapter shows the additional information given by Marks and Spencer plc in their annual report for 1991.

As you can see, this includes various accounting ratios which might be of interest to those who understand what such ratios mean. It also includes a number of bar charts (in three-dimensional form) that might be of interest to the less sophisticated user. We will be using the data contained in this appendix for some of the later activities. The bar charts were originally published in separate colours which cannot be reproduced here, but colour is another way of separating data into sets so that users can see the information more clearly.

3 Graphical presentation

Charts, graphs, and diagrams are the most common way of presenting numerical data in an easily readable form. You have seen examples of this in Section 2. Charts and diagrams fall into the following categories:

- **pictograms** that use images (such as people, horses, aeroplanes, etc.) to convey quantities of the subject being measured – each complete image represents a certain quantity and anything less than this is shown as a partially complete image

- **histograms** which give a pictorial presentation of a frequency distribution

- **graphs and charts**, of which the most common are as follows:

    - bar charts

    - line graphs

    - pie charts.

We will not be dealing with pictograms, although you quite often see them used in newspapers. The population split between males and females discussed in Section 2 could have been shown as a number of images (and partial images) for the two sexes. Histograms are used in the study of statistical sampling and are not relevant to Unit 7.

Using computers

In the past, graphs and charts had to be drawn by hand on graph paper. Today, virtually all published graphs and charts are created by computer software. The most common method is to use a spreadsheet package. Spreadsheets allow data to be entered and manipulated in the spreadsheet itself, and for specified data in the spreadsheet to be plotted on a graph or chart. The programs usually include features that enable labels and legends to be appended, provide options regarding the scale points, and allow the graph to be printed (or saved for use in a word-processing program). All of the graphs and charts in this chapter were created by using a spreadsheet.

If you have not already done so, you should try to obtain some experience at using a spreadsheet and its graphing facilities. The best way of learning is to experiment. If you are unable to get your hands on a personal computer at work (or at home) you might find that a local college or university has open learning facilities that you can join.

Bar charts

Bar charts show quantities as a bar, drawn vertically or horizontally. There are three basic forms of bar chart, namely:

- a simple bar chart

- a stacked (or component) bar chart

- a compound (or multiple) bar chart.

In a simple bar chart the magnitude of an item can be seen by the height (or length) of the bar. In a stacked bar chart the total of an item is divided into components to show the make-up of that total. In a compound bar chart the total of an item is divided into components that are shown as separate bars, and these are then grouped together side-by-side. In all cases the chart often shows measurements for a series of time points, such as a year, so that trends and changes over a period of time can be seen.

Activity 5

Refer to the extract from Marks and Spencer's 1991 annual report in Appendix 2 and identify the two types of bar chart presented there. Make a note here of the information presented in each type of chart.

1. Simple bar charts have been used for:

2. Stacked bar charts have been used for:

As mentioned earlier, the originals were in colour which helps with the separation in the stacked bar chart. A black and white image of a stacked bar chart has to rely on some kind of shading or cross-hatching for each component in the bar. A simple stacked bar chart for the analysis of turnover by business activity could be presented as shown on the next page:

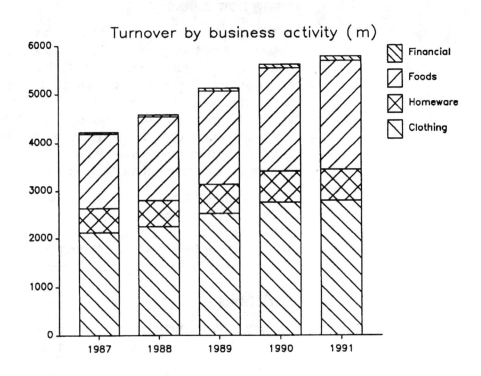

<table>
<tr><td></td></tr>
</table>

Activity 6	Review the above chart and make a note of any sales information which it does convey to you, and of any sales information which is not clear from the chart. 1. Information conveyed 2. Information not clear

A better comparison between the individual components over a series of years can be achieved by using compound bar charts. These use one bar for each component which are then grouped together for each time point. The sales analysis for Marks and Spencer would be presented in this type of chart as shown on the next page:

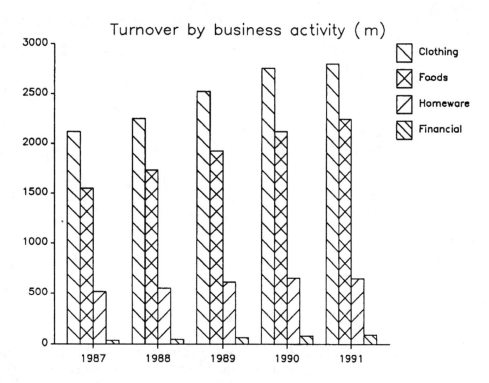

The problem of proportions is sometimes dealt with by stacked bar charts that show the percentage of the total for each component. In a time series (such as Marks and Spencer's analysis of turnover) the height of all the bars would be equal but the size of components within each bar will change if there has been a significant change in the make up of the total. A more common way of showing proportions of a total is to use a pie chart.

Pie charts

Pie charts give the image of a pie cut into slices, and are a useful way of presenting information that draws attention to the make-up of a whole. If you have to draw one by hand the proportions are related to the 360 degrees in the circumference of a circle. Lines are then drawn from the points plotted on the circumference to the centre of the circle. They are, however, easily produced by a spreadsheet program on a computer. Most programs allow one (or more) of the segments of the pie to be 'exploded' for visual effect when a particular feature requires emphasis. The following pie chart shows how Marks and Spencer's turnover for 1991 is divided according to business activity. The proportion relating to financial services has been exploded for the purposes of illustration.

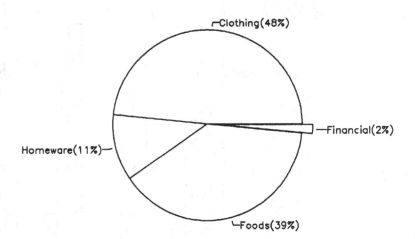

Percentage of 1991 turnover by activity

Notice how the computer program has calculated the percentages as well as drawn the chart. You will sometimes find that the percentages in pie charts produced by computers do not add to 100, and a little fine-tuning is needed before publishing the chart. (You might also have noticed that there is a warning in the CSO tables that figures may not add due to rounding.)

Although the bar charts for Marks and Spencer's turnover enable general trends to be seen, they do not reveal the relative trends for each type of business activity. Apart from a 'blip' on foods (which dropped slightly in 1991) we cannot see if any of the activities are growing at a faster rate than the others.

Activity 7

Trends over a period of time can be seen quite easily on a line graph. The slope of the line gives some indication of the rate of change. See if you can think of a way of presenting Marks and Spencer's turnover so that growth rates for each activity can be compared visually.

A chart produced on this basis could be presented as follows:

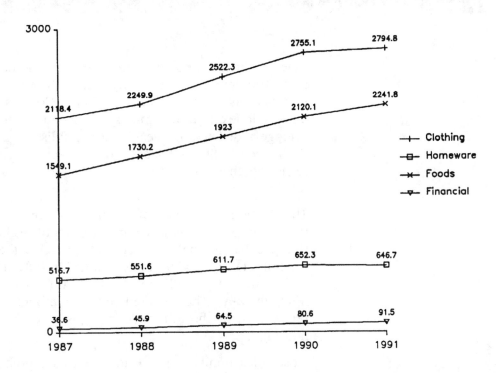

Although the relative trends are slightly blurred by the growth in clothing sales between 1988 and 1989, it does seem clear from the graph that the highest increase in sales revenue is in foods. If you measure the percentage change from 1987 to 1991, you will find that clothing sales have grown by 32% and food sales by 45%. This might be a reflection of the recession; people must continue to eat – clothing is less important when spending money is short. Note that the highest percentage increase is in financial services – 151% over the five-year period.

Activity 8	It is wrong to assume that an increase in the total revenue from the sale of a particular type of produce represents an increase in the sales volume of that product. Make a note here of why this is so (you considered this in Chapter 1).

4 Index numbers

Index numbers measure changes in an economic variable over a period of time. The time period can vary, although most indices are calculated on a monthly basis. The Retail Price Index (RPI) is perhaps the most widely known index number and is published by the CSO every month. An average index for the year is also published. The Financial Times Stock Exchange (FT-SE) 100 share index can change by the minute. Information regarding changes in the FT-SE 100 index is available to contributors on a real-time basis.

The RPI is an indicator of general rates of inflation and is of interest to many groups such as government (for policy decisions) and trade unions (for pay bargaining). You should note that there is no such thing as a general rate of inflation; rates of inflation differ for each product or service and so the rate of inflation that we suffer will depend on the things we normally buy. The detailed index numbers published by CSO give a breakdown of the RPI under various categories such as food, clothing, housing, etc.

Most index numbers are related to a base number of 100. A base date is chosen from which the base number applies. The RPI has a base number of 100 referenced to 13 January 1987. The FT-SE 100 share index (usually called the 'footsie' 100 share index) has a base number of 1,000 referenced to the start of trading on 1 January 1984. Index numbers for a subsequent point in time can be calculated by relating the change in an economic value (such as a price) to a change in the base number.

Example

A simple price index is to be calculated on the sales price of a box of widgets based on the data given below. The base period is 1987 and a base number of 100 is to be used.

	Price
1987	£1.00
1988	£1.10
1989	£1.12
1990	£1.15
1991	£1.20

In this example the index numbers can be seen without having to resort to calculations. The index numbers for widgets would be 1988 = 110, 1989 = 112, 1990 = 115, 1991 = 120. If it had been necessary to perform calculations the basic approach is as follows:

$$\frac{\text{Price in year}}{\text{Price in base year}} \times 100 = \text{index number}$$

The index numbers are usually expressed to one decimal place.

Activity 9	Calculate a simple index number for a particular commodity where the base year is 1987 and the prices of that commodity were as follows:

Year	Price	Calculations and index number
1987	60p	
1988	61p	
1989	63p	
1990	66p	
1991	70p	

Consumer price index numbers are usually calculated for a composite package of generic items. For example, an index number for food will take account of the different types of food that people buy. A typical mix is established and an average index number can then be calculated for that group. This average must give some weight to the relative quantities consumed, otherwise a food index number will be equally influenced by changes in the price of (say) Christmas cake as it is for daily items such as bread.

When weights are not assigned to individual items, the index is sometimes called an unweighted index, or an implicitly weighted aggregate index because the weights are implied by the price of individual items. An item costing £2.00 in a particular group is likely to have more influence on an unweighted index than an item costing £0.10.

There are various ways of computing a weighted average index number. In the case of consumer goods, the weights are usually related to typical quantities purchased. In some cases the typical quantities relate to those in the base period, in others the weightings are adjusted to take account of subsequent changes in spending patterns. The technical considerations in selecting appropriate weights are beyond the scope of the knowledge required for Unit 7. Appendix 3 to this chapter gives an extract from the general index of retail prices (Table 18.2) published by the CSO, from which you can see the weights given to food items.

A weighted index is calculated for each period by multiplying the price of each item in the group by its weight (such as typical quantity purchased). These values (representing the amount typically spent) are then totalled and divided by the corresponding total for the base period to obtain an index number.

You can practise doing the calculations on some simplified data. The activities are in two stages so that you can see the progress of the calculation. The data is as follows:

		Average price for one item during the year			
Item	Typical quantities	Base year 1988	1989	1990	1991
A	100	£0.10	£0.11	£0.12	£0.14
B	20	£1.00	£1.05	£1.15	£1.20
C	40	£0.50	£0.60	£0.62	£0.63

Activity 10

The first step is to calculate a value for each commodity for each time period. This value is simply the quantity times the price. The values are then aggregated for each time period. Carry out this step by completing the following table.

Commodity	1988	1989	1990	1991
A				
B				
C				
Total				

The index number is then found by:

$$\frac{\text{total in time period}}{\text{total in base period}} \times 100$$

Activity 11

Calculate the index numbers

1988	1989	1990	1991
100			

Although the underlying assumptions in consumer price indices are often questioned, the index numbers do provide useful information and are frequently used in relation to business activity. There are two applications which you will readily appreciate, namely:

■ pay negotiations, where negotiators will want to convert old wage rates and proposed new rates into comparable earnings in *real* (purchasing power) terms

■ inflation adjustments so that trends in real terms can be assessed, and future results predicted.

As you know from Chapter 2, increases in the amount for sales can arise from both quantity increases and price increases. If we are trying to assess the real (volume) increase in sales over a period of time, it will be necessary to remove the inflationary element in the total monetary value for sales.

Consider the following example:

Sales in 1991 were £100,000

Sales in 1992 were £121,000

On the face of it there seems to be a 21% growth. But if the index number for the commodities being sold was 100 in 1991 and 110 in 1992, we would realise that part of the £121,000 relates to price increases. The real growth can be calculated by restating the 1992 sale figure in terms of 1991 prices as follows:

$$£121,000 \times \frac{100}{110} = £110,000$$

This shows a growth of 10%. The alternative approach is to restate the 1991 figures to 1992 prices and then measure the increase. This would result in sales for 1991 being restated to £110,000 (at 1992 prices) and the increase of (121,000 - 110,000) £11,000 can be seen to be 10% of the 1991 amount.

Appendix 4 to this chapter is a further extract from the RPI tables (Table 18.1) published by the CSO which gives the annual averages up to 1991. The figures for Marks and Spencer's sales for the years 1987 to 1991 can all be restated to their 1987 prices by dividing the sales figure given for each year by the relative index number for that year and multiplying the result by the index number for 1987. This gives a constant pound value by reference to 1987 prices. The sales figures for foods are given on the line graph following Activity 7.

Activity 12	Calculate Marks and Spencer's foods sales for 1988 to 1991 based on the purchasing power of the £ in 1987.
	1988
	1989
	1990
	1991

After making this adjustment on food sales, the deflated figures can be plotted on a graph alongside the actual sales figures reported, as follows:

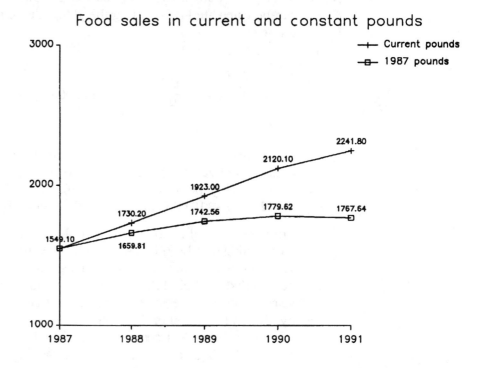

Food sales in current and constant pounds

As you can see, the inflation-adjusted figures show a somewhat different trend to the unadjusted figures. The same trend would have been produced by adjusting the figures to 1991 prices. The alternative forms of inflation adjustment can be plotted on a graph as follows:

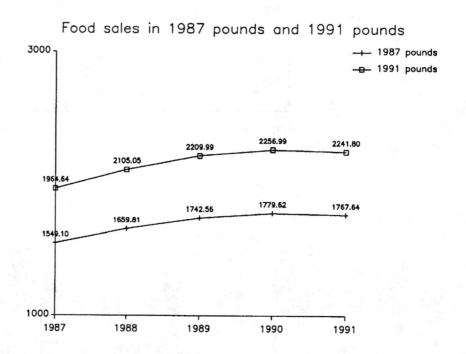

Food sales in 1987 pounds and 1991 pounds

Both sets of figures show a drop in real terms between 1990 and 1991 of 0.07%. Although this kind of information might be more useful than when inflation was ignored, you need to keep in mind that the adjusted figures are only approximate. Index numbers use averages and there are many limitations in the use of averages. You cannot be certain that the volume of food sales between 1990 and 1991 has dropped by 0.07%.

A further use of index numbers is to compare a company's growth in a particular market with the national growth in that market. This will show whether the company's 'market share' is increasing or decreasing. This comparison is possible because the CSO's monthly digest of statistics includes index numbers showing the growth (in combined volume and value, i.e. in two revenues) in retail sales. An extract from this index for food retailers is as follows:

1987	113.5
1988	122.8
1989	133.8
1990	147.1
1991	157.6

These numbers are based on average weekly sales and a base of 100 in 1985. If we use these index numbers to plot Marks and Spencer's share of market growth since 1987, we can produce the following graph:

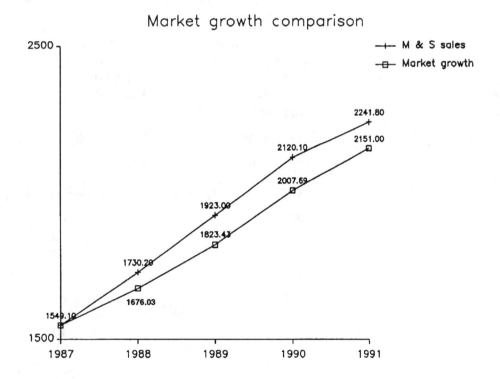

Market growth comparison

As can be seen, between 1987 and 1990 the growth in Marks and Spencer's food sales was greater than growth in the market place. Between 1990 and 1991 Marks and Spencer's growth in food sales was less than growth in the market. Market share is another performance indicator, but it needs to be interpreted with care. There is nothing in this to suggest that Marks and Spencer was less efficient during 1990/1991, it could simply be explained by more food retailers entering the market. In order to measure efficiency in this respect we would need to use ratios such as sales per square metre of floor space and compare Marks and Spencer with other companies in the food retailing industry.

5 Time series analysis

You have already been working with a time series when considering the figures for Marks and Spencer over a period of years. The population analysis in Section 2, and the index numbers in Section 5, were also examples of time series. Much of the interest in time series is in trying to establish if a pattern exists in previously recorded values that might enable future values to be forecast.

Values recorded over a period of time are likely to contain four components which must be smoothed in order to establish a trend. These four components are:

■ secular trends, which represents the long-term underlying growth or decline

■ seasonal variations, such as the increase in sales of suntan lotion during the summer

■ cyclical fluctuations, which occur over much longer periods and are related to booms and recessions

■ irregular movements, which occur at random and are usually unpredictable.

When trying to measure a trend in a time series, several mathematical techniques are available. The easiest and most frequently used approach is to use what is known as a moving average. The more sophisticated techniques such as regression analysis are outside of the scope of the skills required for Unit 7.

The activities will be based on the following data:

The quarterly sales figures (in units) for three years are as follows:

Year	Quarter	Units sold
1990	1	60
	2	90
	3	102
	4	18
1991	1	68
	2	102
	3	110
	4	30
1992	1	78
	2	120
	3	140
	4	62

The first average in the series of moving averages is the average of the first four quarters. The second average in the series drops the first quarter of 1990 and is replaced with the first quarter of 1991. This process is repeated until the last four quarters have been averaged.

Activity 13

Calculate the moving averages for the above time series. There are nine averages in this series. Make a note of the figures here.

The original raw data for the time series can be plotted on a graph, with the trend line (based on the moving averages) superimposed. Each average must be plotted in the centre of the four quarters to which it relates. For example, the average of quarters 1, 2, 3 and 4 would be plotted half-way between 2 and 3. For the example above, the graph would appear as follows:

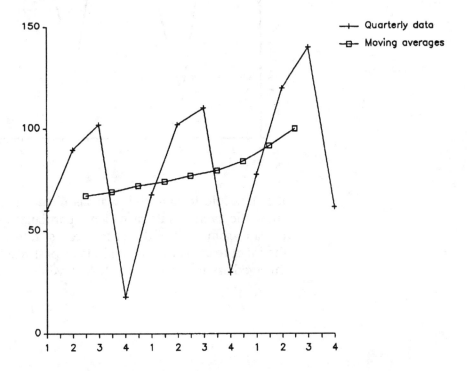

We will now go on to centre these moving averages. To do this you take the average of the first two moving averages and plot that point at the end of the third quarter. You then take the average of the second two moving averages and plot that point at the end of the fourth quarter, and so on.

Activity 14	The first two points in the series of centred moving averages are 68.5 and 71. Calculate the six remaining points.

The trend line with centred moving averages may be superimposed on the graph of the original data like this:

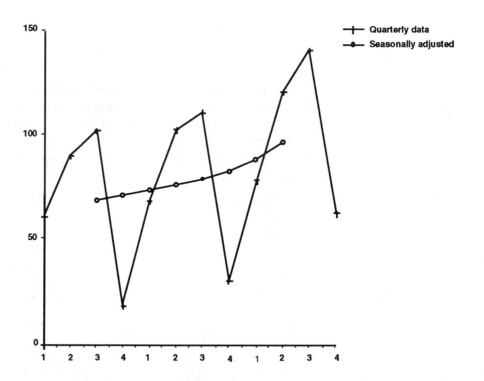

It is possible to take the analysis further by producing index numbers to show the average rate at which a particular quarter in the future is likely to deviate from the trend, i.e. to forecast future results. Forecasting is one of the main reasons for the analysis of past results, but the mathematical skills involved are not required at NVQ level 3.

Summary

The important learning points in this chapter are as follows:

■ statistics is an extensive subject involving the production and use of numeric data

■ competence in this area for Unit 7 is related to the preparation of accurate reports for both internal use and for external agencies

■ the reports must be prepared in accordance with the specification

■ your knowledge of some of the purposes for which the data is used will contribute to the performance criteria of producing accurate reports

■ there can be several stages between the selection of raw data and the point at which data becomes information

■ large volumes of tabulated data are more easily communicated in the form of graphs and charts

■ it is preferable to use computer programs to prepare graphs and charts but care is needed (particularly with scaling) to produce graphs and charts that are not deceptive

■ index numbers show a relation between a current value and a past value

■ index numbers can be computed for internal use

■ the CSO publishes a vast range of index numbers prepared from data supplied by the business community

■ index numbers published by the CSO are often applied to business situations

■ time series analysis is concerned with establishing patterns from past results to facilitate future projections

■ a number of mathematical techniques can be used to isolate a trend from fluctuating data, and the most frequently used device is based on moving averages.

Appendix 1

2 Population and vital statistics

2.1 Mid-year estimates of resident population

Thousands

	England and Wales			Scotland			Northern Ireland			United Kingdom		
	Males	Females	Persons	Males	Females	Persons	Males	Females	Persons	Males	Females	Persons
	BBAE	BBAF	BBAD	BBAH	BBAI	BBAG	BBAK	BBAL	BBAJ	BBAB	BBAC	DYAY
1974	24 075	25 393	49 468	2 519	2 722	5 241	755	772	1 527	27 349	28 887	56 236
1975	24 091	25 378	49 470	2 516	2 716	5 232	753	770	1 524	27 361	28 865	56 226
1976	24 069	25 370	49 459	2 517	2 716	5 233	754	769	1 524	27 360	28 856	56 216
1977	24 076	25 364	49 440	2 515	2 711	5 226	754	769	1 523	27 345	28 845	56 190
1978	24 067	25 375	49 443	2 509	2 704	5 212	754	770	1 523	27 330	28 848	56 178
1979	24 113	25 395	49 508	2 505	2 699	5 204	755	773	1 528	27 373	28 867	56 240
1980	24 156	25 448	49 603	2 501	2 693	5 194	755	778	1 533	27 411	28 919	56 330
1981	24 160	25 474	49 634	2 495	2 685	5 180	754	783	1 538	27 409	28 943	56 352
1982	24 143	25 459	49 601	2 489	2 677	5 167	754	784	1 538	27 386	28 920	56 306
1983	24 176	25 478	49 654	2 485	2 665	5 150	756	787	1 543	27 417	28 931	56 347
1984	24 244	25 519	49 764	2 484	2 662	5 146	760	791	1 550	27 487	28 972	56 460
1985	24 330	25 594	49 924	2 480	2 656	5 137	763	795	1 558	27 574	29 044	56 618
1986	24 403	25 672	50 075	2 475	2 646	5 121	768	798	1 567	27 647	29 116	56 763
1987	24 493	25 750	50 243	2 471	2 641	5 112	773	802	1 575	27 737	29 193	56 930
1988	24 576	25 817	50 393	2 462	2 632	5 094	774	804	1 578	27 813	29 253	57 065
1989	24 669	25 893	50 562	2 460	2 630	5 091	777	806	1 583	27 907	29 330	57 236
1990	24 766	25 953	50 719	2 467	2 636	5 102	780	809	1 589	28 013	29 398	57 411

Figures may not add due to rounding.

Sources: Office of Population Censuses and Surveys;
General Register Office (Scotland);
General Register Office (Northern Ireland)

2.2 Age distribution of estimated resident population at 30 June 1989

Thousands

	Resident population										
	England and Wales		Wales		Scotland		Northern Ireland[1]		United Kingdom		
	Males	Females	Males	Females	Males	Females	Males	Females	Males	Females	Persons
0-4	1 713.8	1 632.4	97.2	92.5	166.7	158.6	69.5	65.7	1 950.7	1 857.0	3 807.7
5-9	1 629.4	1 548.4	93.8	89.0	164.7	157.1	68.2	65.2	1 862.0	1 770.7	3 632.7
10-14	1 517.1	1 434.1	88.6	83.3	158.1	149.7	64.8	62.4	1 739.3	1 645.2	3 384.5
15-19	1 830.1	1 739.0	105.1	100.6	190.1	183.5	70.0	63.5	2 091.2	1 987.8	4 079.0
20-24	2 077.5	2 010.1	113.0	110.6	217.8	208.4	71.8	63.8	2 367.9	2 282.8	4 650.7
25-29	2 058.9	2 023.2	113.1	114.2	210.8	201.8	64.8	60.6	2 333.5	2 285.1	4 618.7
30-34	1 761.4	1 737.0	93.4	91.2	184.2	182.1	54.3	55.3	1 998.2	1 972.9	3 971.1
35-39	1 682.8	1 681.4	92.2	92.6	167.8	168.1	47.5	48.7	1 898.1	1 897.4	3 795.6
40-44	1 821.8	1 812.7	98.8	99.6	172.6	172.8	47.0	47.9	2 041.1	2 033.4	4 074.5
45-49	1 466.6	1 454.9	83.0	82.8	144.0	149.1	43.1	44.6	1 652.6	1 647.2	3 299.9
50-54	1 367.3	1 367.4	77.1	77.6	136.9	145.7	37.7	39.4	1 541.5	1 552.2	3 093.7
55-59	1 293.7	1 323.7	74.1	77.3	131.2	144.3	34.0	37.2	1 458.8	1 505.4	2 964.2
60-64	1 245.2	1 333.3	74.2	81.5	123.1	141.1	31.3	36.5	1 399.7	1 510.8	2 910.4
65-69	1 215.0	1 422.9	73.3	86.2	113.2	142.0	28.0	35.1	1 356.6	1 600.6	2 957.1
70-74	784.9	1 050.7	48.3	65.4	73.2	106.3	20.6	29.2	878.4	1 185.9	2 064.2
75-79	648.3	1 022.9	37.1	60.2	59.1	99.6	15.5	25.4	723.1	1 147.8	1 870.9
80-84	365.7	734.1	20.5	43.0	31.9	70.1	8.5	17.3	405.9	820.9	1 226.8
85 and over	189.3	565.2	10.6	31.9	15.0	50.3	3.8	11.3	208.1	626.6	834.7
0-14	4 860.4	4 614.8	279.6	264.7	489.5	465.3	202.5	193.3	5 552.0	5 272.9	10 824.9
15-64	16 605.4	16 482.8	924.1	928.1	1 678.4	1 696.8	501.5	497.4	18 782.6	18 675.0	37 457.6
65 and over	3 203.3	4 795.8	189.8	286.7	292.4	468.2	76.4	118.3	3 572.0	5 381.8	8 953.8
All ages	24 669.1	25 893.4	1 393.5	1 479.6	2 460.4	2 630.3	780.4	809.0	27 906.5	29 329.7	57 236.2

Figures may not add due to rounding.
1 For Northern Ireland: population at June 1990.

Sources: Office of Population Censuses and Surveys;
General Register Office (Scotland);
General Register Office (Northern Ireland)

Appendix 2

Financial Highlights

TEN YEAR SUMMARY

	1991 52 weeks	1990 52 weeks	1989 52 weeks	1988 53 weeks	1987 52 weeks	1986 52 weeks	1985 52 weeks	1984* 52 weeks	1983* 52 weeks	1982* 53 weeks
Turnover (excluding sales taxes) £m	**5,774.8**	5,608.1	5,121.5	4,577.6	4,220.8	3,734.8	3,208.1	2,862.5	2,509.9	2,204.9
Operating profit £m	**633.5**	627.7	563.7	508.5	434.6	361.0	306.0	277.3	235.8	219.8
Profit on ordinary activities before tax £m	**615.5**	604.2	529.0	501.7	432.1	365.8	304.1	279.3	239.3	222.1
Earnings per share, p	**14.7†**	14.5	12.9	12.2	10.4	8.4	6.9	6.3**	5.2**	4.6**
Dividends per share, p	**6.7**	6.4	5.6	5.1	4.5	3.9	3.4	3.125**	2.55**	2.3**
Shareholders' funds £m	**2,427.4**	2,174.6	1,918.6	2,158.0†	1,578.8	1,452.4	1,325.3	1,226.8	1,140.0	1,063.7
Ordinary shareholders' interests per share, p	**89.4**	80.7	71.7	81.1†	59.4	54.9	50.1	46.6	43.4	40.6†
Capital expenditure £m	**300.4**	280.0	209.7	214.5	247.2	165.2	121.8	120.4	110.5	91.9

†including the effect of the property revaluation during the year
‡Post exceptional charge
* figures have not been restated to show translation using average rates of exchange
** adjusted for scrip issue in 1984

TURNOVER BY BUSINESS ACTIVITY (£m)

PROFIT BEFORE TAX (£m)

DIVIDEND PER SHARE (£m)

EARNINGS PER SHARE (p)

FINANCIAL RATIOS FIVE YEAR SUMMARY

Profitability		1991 52 weeks	1990 52 weeks	1989 52 weeks	1988 53 weeks	1987 52 weeks
GROSS MARGIN	$\dfrac{\text{Gross profit}}{\text{Turnover}}$ %	33.1	32.8	32.5	30.9	30.2
NET MARGIN	$\dfrac{\text{Operating profit}}{\text{Turnover}}$ %	11.0	11.2	11.0	11.1	10.3
RETURN ON EQUITY	$\dfrac{\text{Profit after tax and minority interests}}{\text{Average shareholders' funds}}$ %	17.3	19.0	16.8	17.3†	18.2

† including the effect of the property revaluation during the year

		1991 52 weeks	1990 52 weeks	1989 52 weeks	1988 53 weeks	1987 52 weeks
Dividend cover	$\dfrac{\text{Earnings per share}}{\text{Dividend per share}}$ times	2.2	2.3	2.3	2.4	2.3
Gearing ratio	$\dfrac{\text{Net borrowings}}{\text{Shareholders' funds plus minority interests}}$ %	13.5	16.6	26.9	3.1†	6.8

8   MARKS AND SPENCER p.l.c.

MARKS AND SPENCER p.l.c.   9

Appendix 3

Prices and wages

18.2 General Index of retail prices[1]
Detailed figures for various groups, sub-groups and sections

13 January 1987=100

		Group and sub-group weights in 1992	1992 Feb	1992 Mar	1992 Apr	1992 May	1992 Jun	1992 Jul	1992 Aug	1992 Sep
	Day of month		11	10	14	12	9	14	11	8
All items	CHAW	1000	136.3	136.7	138.8	139.3	139.3	138.8	138.9	139.4
All items excluding mortgage interest	CHMK	924	133.8	134.5	136.7	137.1	137.2	136.7	136.9	137.3
Food	CHBA	152	129.1	129.4	128.9	129.5	129.0	127.2	127.5	127.1
Bread	DOAA	7	135.0	134.9	134.8	135.4	135.2	134.1	133.9	134.6
Cereals	DOAB	4	136.5	136.6	136.8	136.0	135.4	136.1	136.1	135.9
Biscuits and cakes	DOAC	9	132.8	134.4	133.8	135.1	134.8	136.5	136.3	137.6
Beef	DOAD	7	125.1	125.7	124.5	125.5	125.2	123.6	124.3	124.9
Lamb	DOAE	3	115.9	116.1	123.6	122.2	115.2	109.7	109.8	108.3
of which home-killed lamb	DOAF	2	122.6	123.0	129.9	127.9	116.6	109.1	107.3	107.6
Pork	DOAG	3	124.9	127.5	128.3	133.6	130.5	126.4	124.7	123.5
Bacon	DOAH	4	136.8	137.8	137.5	137.8	138.8	137.9	137.6	135.6
Poultry	DOAI	6	111.7	114.2	109.6	112.7	109.7	112.5	113.1	111.1
Other meat	DOAJ	9	123.4	123.5	123.2	124.1	123.9	123.0	123.0	123.0
Fish	DOAK	5	126.6	125.6	124.5	125.8	124.6	126.4	126.5	127.6
of which fresh fish	DOAL	1	143.0	144.7	144.0	145.8	136.4	140.4	139.5	142.0
Butter	DOAM	1	125.3	125.1	127.2	127.0	127.0	126.8	126.5	126.1
Oils and fats	DOAN	2	127.8	127.0	128.3	129.0	128.7	126.7	128.1	128.2
Cheese	DOAO	4	128.7	130.1	130.1	133.1	134.2	132.7	133.8	134.5
Eggs	DOAP	2	119.2	116.8	115.3	116.0	113.9	111.8	112.6	111.7
Milk, fresh	DOAQ	11	136.1	136.5	136.1	136.4	137.6	138.7	139.1	139.8
Milk products	DOAR	3	135.9	136.4	137.6	137.7	138.8	136.1	137.8	135.9
Tea	DOAS	2	152.3	152.9	152.3	151.9	150.9	150.6	150.7	150.8
Coffee and other hot drinks	DOAT	2	91.4	90.9	90.8	91.2	91.4	90.8	91.6	91.3
Soft drinks	DOAU	12	154.7	156.0	156.1	156.2	156.1	155.8	154.9	154.3
Sugar and preserves	DOAV	2	139.2	138.8	137.7	137.6	137.3	136.8	136.5	136.3
Sweets and chocolate	DOAW	13	119.3	119.8	120.1	121.4	121.8	122.7	123.8	123.8
Potatoes	DOAX	7	126.9	126.7	128.6	132.4	122.6	121.2	130.6	126.0
of which unprocessed potatoes	DOAY	3	119.6	118.0	121.9	126.8	103.6	99.8	120.0	110.4
Vegetables	DOAZ	10	121.7	122.0	114.1	111.6	113.0	99.7	98.8	100.0
of which other fresh vegetables	DOBA	7	117.1	117.8	106.2	102.6	105.7	88.0	86.8	89.1
Fruit	DOBB	9	134.9	132.6	133.4	131.1	132.4	121.0	117.9	111.9
of which fresh fruit	DOBC	7	137.6	134.1	135.3	132.0	133.7	119.1	115.1	107.1
Other foods	DOBD	15	133.5	133.6	134.3	134.0	135.0	135.0	134.2	135.4
Catering	CHBC	47	144.8	145.3	146.3	147.2	147.9	148.3	148.8	149.6
Restaurant meals	DOBE	25	144.7	145.1	146.0	146.8	147.3	147.8	148.3	148.8
Canteen meals	DOBF	7	146.5	147.2	148.1	148.7	150.1	150.4	150.4	153.0
Take-aways and snacks	DOBG	15	144.0	144.9	146.1	147.0	147.7	148.2	149.0	149.3
Alcoholic drink	CHBD	80	144.6	145.2	147.1	147.9	148.4	149.2	149.6	150.1
Beer	DOBH	46	148.7	149.1	150.7	151.5	151.9	153.0	153.6	154.3
Beer on sales	DOBI	40	150.5	150.8	152.5	153.2	153.8	155.0	155.7	156.5
Beer off sales	DOBJ	6	136.2	137.1	138.1	139.2	138.7	138.5	139.0	138.8
Wines and spirits	DOBK	34	138.8	139.6	141.8	142.6	143.2	143.7	143.9	144.1
Wines and spirits on sales	DOBL	13	144.4	145.2	147.8	148.7	149.1	149.6	149.8	150.2
Wines and spirits off sales	DOBM	21	134.6	135.4	137.4	138.2	138.8	139.3	139.4	139.7
Tobacco	CHBE	36	137.5	137.5	145.7	146.1	146.1	146.0	145.9	145.9
Cigarettes	DOBN	32	138.1	138.1	146.6	147.1	147.0	146.9	146.7	146.7
Other tobacco	DOBO	4	133.8	133.9	139.5	139.9	139.9	139.9	139.9	140.1
Housing	CHBF	172	156.5	155.1	161.1	161.4	161.1	161.5	161.8	162.1
Rent	DOBP	35	158.5	158.7	168.5	168.7	168.7	168.9	169.1	169.2
Mortgage interest payments	DOBQ	64	189.3	184.3	182.8	183.6	183.5	181.4	182.2	183.2
Community Charge	DOBR	31	120.9	120.9	137.0	136.6	136.6	136.6	136.6	136.6
Water and other charges	DOBS	9	174.1	174.1	191.7	191.8	191.8	191.8	191.8	191.8
Repairs and maintenance charges	DOBT	9	141.8	142.0	143.2	143.5	143.8	144.1	144.5	144.5
Do-it-yourself materials	DOBU	16	140.2	141.5	140.3	141.0	137.5	143.2	143.6	142.8
Dwelling insurance and ground rent	CHMJ	8	190.5	190.0	189.7	189.9	190.2	200.6	200.4	200.0

Indices are given to one decimal place to provide as much information as is available but precision is greater at higher levels of aggregation, ie at sub-group and group levels.

1 *Retail Prices Index 1914-1990* (HMSO Price £10.95 net) contains group and sub-group indices and weights back to 1956, group indices back to 1947, together with cost of living indices as far back as 1914.

Source: Central Statistical Office

Appendix 4

18 Prices and wages

18.1 General Index of retail prices[1]

	All items	All items except seasonal food[2]	Food	Alcoholic drink	Tobacco	Housing	Fuel and light	Durable household goods	Clothing and footwear	Transport and vehicles	Miscella neous goods	Services	Meals bought and consumed outside the home
15 January 1974=100													
Annual averages													
	CBAB	CBAP	CBAN	CBAA	CBAC	CBAH	CBAG	CBAE	CBAD	CBAO	CBAJ	CBAM	CBAI
1982	320.4	322.0	299.3	341.0	413.3	358.3	433.3	243.8	210.5	343.5	325.8	331.6	341.7
1983	335.1	337.1	308.8	366.4	440.9	367.1	465.4	250.4	214.8	366.3	345.6	342.9	364.0
1984	351.8	353.1	326.1	387.7	489.0	400.7	478.8	256.7	214.6	374.7	364.7	357.3	390.8
1985	373.2	375.4	336.3	412.1	532.4	452.3	499.3	263.9	222.9	392.5	392.2	381.3	413.3
1986	385.9	387.9	347.3	430.6	584.5	478.1	506.0	266.7	229.2	390.1	409.2	400.5	439.5
1987 Jan 1	394.5	396.4	354.0	100.0	602.9	502.4	506.1	265.6	230.8	399.7	413.0	408.8	454.8

		All items	Food and catering	Alcohol and tobacco	Housing and household expend- iture	Personal expend- iture	Travel and leisure	All items except seasonal food[2]	All items except food	Seasonal food[2,3]	Non- seasonal food[3]	All items except housing	National ised indust- ries[4]	Consumer durables
13 January 1987=100														
Weights 1991		1000	198	109	353	101	239	976	849	24	127	808		128
Weights 1992		1000	199	116	344	99	242	978	848	22	130	828		127
Annual averages														
		CHAW	CHBS	CHBT	CHBU	CHBV	CHBW	CHAX	CHAY	CHBP	CHBB	CHAZ	CHBX	CHBY
1987		101.9	101.4	101.2	102.1	101.4	102.6	101.9	102.0	101.6	101.0	101.6	100.9	101.2
1988		106.9	105.7	105.7	108.4	105.2	107.2	107.0	107.3	102.4	105.0	105.8	106.7	103.7
1989		115.2	111.9	110.8	121.9	111.2	112.8	115.5	116.1	105.0	111.6	111.5	..	107.2
1990		126.1	120.8	120.5	139.0	117.6	119.8	126.4	127.4	116.4	119.9	119.2	..	111.3
1991		133.5	128.6	136.2	142.2	123.6	128.9	133.8	135.1	121.6	126.3	128.3	..	114.8
1990 Feb	13	120.2	118.1	114.3	129.0	114.7	115.4	120.3	120.9	118.7	116.7	115.3	..	109.1
Mar	13	121.4	118.7	114.8	131.3	115.6	115.9	121.4	122.1	119.6	117.3	115.9	..	109.9
Apr	10	125.1	119.9	118.6	138.5	117.0	118.0	125.1	126.3	123.4	118.0	117.6	..	111.0
May	15	126.2	121.2	120.9	139.8	117.6	118.6	126.3	127.4	123.6	119.4	118.8	..	111.6
Jun	12	126.7	121.3	121.3	140.7	117.5	119.1	126.9	128.0	118.3	120.3	119.1	..	111.5
Jul	17	126.8	120.6	122.4	141.4	116.0	119.6	127.3	128.4	108.1	120.7	119.1	..	109.7
Aug	14	128.1	121.7	123.0	142.5	117.2	121.4	128.5	129.6	112.2	121.4	120.3	..	110.7
Sep	11	129.3	120.3	123.5	143.6	119.3	123.5	129.8	131.1	111.5	121.8	121.6	..	112.5
Oct	16	130.3	122.5	124.4	144.8	120.3	124.6	130.7	132.2	111.8	121.9	122.6	..	113.2
Nov	13	130.0	123.4	124.6	143.8	121.1	123.7	130.4	131.7	114.5	122.4	122.7	..	113.8
Dec	11	129.9	124.1	125.1	143.8	121.1	122.4	130.2	131.4	119.2	122.6	122.6	..	114.1
1991 Jan	15	130.2	124.9	126.0	144.2	118.6	122.8	130.4	131.6	121.2	123.1	122.7	..	110.7
Feb	12	130.9	126.2	126.8	145.0	119.7	123.1	131.1	132.2	125.9	124.0	123.5	..	111.8
Mar	12	131.4	126.4	127.3	145.5	120.9	123.6	131.6	132.8	124.4	124.4	123.9	..	113.0
Apr	16	133.1	128.5	136.9	141.7	123.6	127.5	133.3	134.5	125.6	125.8	127.6	..	115.2
May	14	133.5	128.6	137.9	141.5	124.2	128.9	133.8	135.1	122.5	126.2	128.5	..	116.0
Jun	11	134.1	129.8	138.4	141.7	124.6	129.4	134.3	135.5	126.0	127.1	129.3	..	116.1
Jul	16	133.8	128.8	139.1	141.0	122.3	130.6	134.2	135.4	117.3	126.8	129.2	..	113.2
Aug	13	134.1	129.7	139.6	140.9	122.7	130.9	134.4	135.6	121.6	127.3	129.8	..	113.9
Sep	10	134.6	129.1	140.0	141.3	125.6	131.6	135.2	136.4	114.9	127.4	130.4	..	116.2
Oct	15	135.1	129.4	140.3	141.0	126.7	132.8	135.6	136.9	116.1	127.4	131.1	..	116.9
Nov	12	135.6	130.4	140.8	141.3	127.0	133.1	135.9	137.3	121.3	127.8	131.7	..	117.3
Dec	10	135.7	130.9	141.0	141.6	127.0	132.9	136.0	137.4	122.7	128.0	131.8	..	117.6
1992 Jan	14	135.6	131.9	141.8	141.7	123.5	132.9	135.9	137.1	125.2	129.0	131.6	..	113.2
Feb	11	136.3	132.6	142.3	142.2	124.7	133.7	136.6	137.8	126.0	129.7	132.3	..	114.4
Mar	10	136.7	133.0	142.7	141.9	126.1	134.6	137.0	138.2	124.8	130.2	133.0	..	115.7
Apr	14	138.8	132.8	146.6	144.8	127.3	136.9	139.2	140.7	122.4	130.1	134.4	..	116.2
May	12	139.3	133.4	147.3	145.1	127.5	137.5	139.7	141.2	120.9	131.0	134.9	..	116.4
Jun	9	139.3	133.1	147.6	145.0	127.7	137.8	139.9	141.3	117.4	131.0	135.0	..	116.4
Jul	14	138.8	131.9	148.1	145.0	125.0	137.8	139.6	141.1	105.8	130.9	134.3	..	113.1
Aug	11	138.9	132.2	148.4	145.2	125.0	137.7	139.7	141.2	107.0	131.1	134.4	..	113.5
Sep	8	139.4	132.0	148.7	145.6	128.2	137.7	140.3	141.8	104.0	131.1	134.9	..	116.0

1 Following the recommendation of the Retail Price Index Advisory Committee, the index has been re-referenced to make 13 January, 1987=100. Further details can be found in the April 1987 edition of *Employment Gazette.*

2 Seasonal food is defined as: items of food the prices of which show significant seasonal variations. These are fresh fruit and vegetables, fresh fish, eggs and home-killed lamb.

3 For the February, March and April 1988 indices, the weights for seasonal and non-seasonal food were 24 and 139 respectively. Thereafter the weight for home-killed lamb (a seasonal item) was increased by 1 and that for imported lamb (a non-seasonal item) correspondingly reduced by 1 in the light of new information about their relative shares of household expenditure.

4 From December 1989 the Nationalised Industries Index is no longer published. Industries remaining nationalised in December 1989 were coal, electricity, post and rail.

Source: Central Statistical Office

Appendix 5

The Government Statistical Service (GSS), which includes the CSO and the Office of Population Censuses and Surveys (OPCS), is by far the largest single provider of statistics in Britain. There are so many statistical reports that the GSS actually produces a booklet to guide you to the ones that will be helpful to you. This useful little booklet, which is updated annually, is called *Government Statistics, A Brief Guide to Sources* and can be obtained from the Central Statistical Offices either in London or in Newport.

The publications listed in the guide cover many diverse topics, such as the economy, transport, society and the environment.

Publications listed in the guide include:

Financial Statistics
Key financial and monetary statistics of the UK.

Statistics of Manufacturer's Sales

Housing and Construction Statistics

Agricultural Statistics

Overseas Trade in the UK

Quarterly Transport Statistics

Retail Trade
Summary figures for retail trade and detailed index numbers of sales in various kinds of shops.

Employment Gazette
Includes articles, tables and charts on the labour force employment, unemployment, hours worked, earnings, labour costs, retail prices, stoppages due to disputes, training etc.

Key Population and Vital Statistics

Education Statistics for the UK

Some of the publications listed in the guide are available on computer disk or tape, and on-line access can be obtained to some of the databases.

Key to Chapter 3 activities

Activity 1

1. Number of students sitting 'A' Level in recent exams.

2. The examining bodies.

Activity 2

There could be several reasons such as: distrust through lack of understanding of the techniques, or the costs of using them are considered to exceed the benefits.

Activity 3

1. The female population seems to be about twice that of the male population.

2. It is not possible to see if the population mix between male and female is changing, or how substantial the progressive changes in total population are.

Activity 4

A line graph plotting the total population numbers for both sexes over a period of time.

Activity 5

1. Dividend per share and earnings per share.

2. Turnover by business activity and profit before tax.

Activity 6

1. Income from total turnover is growing, income from financial services is growing.

2. Whether the proportionate composition of the total is changing as between the four types of activity. The absolute value of turnover for each business activity, and whether this is growing/stable/declining, is not easy to discern.

Activity 7

Turnover for each activity plotted on a line graph.

Activity 8

Price increases (inflation) must be taken into account.

Activity 9

1988 61/60 x 100	=	101.7
1989 63/60 x 100	=	105
1990 66/60 x 100	=	110
1991 70/60 x 100	=	116.7

Activity 10   Here is our completed table:

Item	1988	1989	1990	1991
A	10.00	11.00	12.00	14.00
B	20.00	21.00	23.00	24.00
C	20.00	24.00	24.80	25.20
Total	50.00	56.00	59.80	63.20

Activity 11   1989 56/50 x 100 = 112

1990 59.8/50 x 100 = 119.6

1991 63.2/50 x 100 = 126.4

Activity 12   Answer in £000s

1988 1,730.2/105.7 x 101.4 = 1,659.81

1989 1,923/111.9 x 101.4 = 1,742.56

1990 2,120.1/120.8 x 101.4 = 1,779.62

1991 2,241.8/128.6 x 101.4 = 1,767.64

Activity 13   The series of moving averages is: 67.5, 69.5, 72.5, 74.5, 77.5, 80, 84.5, 92, 100.

Activity 14   The six remaining points are: 73.5, 76, 78.75, 82.25, 88.25 and 96.

Introduction to Part 5: Value Added Tax

Value added tax is intended to be a tax on the final consumer, it is not a tax on the business community. Unfortunately, the business community is burdened with the task of collecting the tax and paying it over to Customs and Excise. In general terms, any business that makes what are known as 'taxable supplies' must be registered with Customs and Excise except where the taxable turnover of the business does not exceed a certain limit. This limit has been gradually increased since the tax was first introduced; for 1993/94 it is set at £37,600.

The effect of registration is that the business must keep a record of all the VAT charged to customers (called output tax), and of all the VAT it has been charged by suppliers (called input tax). If output tax exceeds input tax, the difference between the two amounts must be paid over to Customs and Excise on a quarterly basis, accompanied by a VAT return which shows how the figure was calculated.

The records which must be kept include VAT invoices and VAT accounts. The VAT laws state what details must be shown on a tax invoice, and Customs and Excise, in the VAT Guide, suggest how a VAT account should be laid out. Customs and Excise also issue VAT returns. VAT-registered businesses must complete these returns with details of purchases and sales and the VAT thereon.

If any confusion arises over a business's figures on the VAT return, Customs and Excise may send a VAT inspector to investigate the problem. The VAT inspector may ask to check through the VAT account, or even to see individual invoices. If a purchase is not supported by a valid tax invoice, the VAT may not be reclaimed. It is therefore vital for an organisation to keep tax invoices received, and copies of the tax invoices sent out.

We will now look at the records that must be kept and also consider the impact of the Single Market on accounting for VAT.

Chapter 1
Value added tax

Introduction

In this chapter we will consider value added tax (VAT) – what supplies are liable to VAT, and how to prepare VAT accounts, VAT invoices and VAT returns. We will also consider the impact of the single European market on VAT accounting procedures. The contents of this chapter are in line with the requirements of SSAP 5, which we looked at in Part 2 of this book.

Objectives

After you have completed this chapter, you should be able to:

■ keep an accounting record of VAT transactions

■ prepare tax invoices that comply with the VAT regulations

■ ensure that tax invoices received provide adequate evidence of input tax charged

■ discuss the implications of zero rating and exempt supplies

■ make apportionments of input tax for partially exempt traders

■ make claims for bad debt relief and operate the VAT aspects of a cash accounting scheme

■ account for costs where the input tax is 'blocked' (non-deductible)

■ advise a business regarding the elements of proper VAT accounting records

■ complete a VAT account

■ discuss the implications of the single market for accounting for VAT

■ complete a VAT return.

1 How the tax works

Everyone understands what a tax is, but what is meant by 'value added'? The term 'value added' is related to the successive amounts of sales value added to a product as it proceeds down the distribution chain from original supplier to final consumer.

Businesses do not have to work out the value added, they simply charge VAT on the goods sold. The tax added to sales (output tax) less the tax charged on goods and services bought in by the business (input tax) is paid to Customs and Excise and is, in effect, a tax on the value added. There are currently two rates of VAT, a standard rate of 17.5% (1993/94) and a zero rate. The zero rate is charged on certain supplies such as food, text books, exports and children's clothing. You can get some idea of the concept of value added by considering the following simple example.

A trader is registered for VAT and all goods he deals with are subject to VAT at the standard rate of 17.5%. During the year ended 31 December 1992, total sales (exclusive of VAT) were £800,000 and purchases (exclusive of VAT) were £600,000. There were no opening or closing stocks. All transactions are on a cash basis.

For 1992, the output tax amounts to 17.5% of £800,000, i.e. £140,000, and the input tax amounts to 17.5% of £600,000, i.e. £105,000.

The total VAT which this trader will have to pay to Customs and Excise for 1992 is the excess of output tax over input tax, i.e. £140,000 - £105,000 = £35,000.

This trader will record sales at £800,000 and purchases at £600,000, i.e. VAT is not included in cost of purchase or the sales revenue recorded by the business, as required by SSAP 5. In this case, value added is £200,000. The VAT of £35,000 paid over to Customs and Excise represents 17.5% of the £200,000 value added.

This example was highly contrived in order to demonstrate the basic principles of the tax and to show how it is related to the concept of value added. In reality the idea of value added becomes somewhat hazy, because the trader will be charged VAT on many different kinds of inputs, such as motor expenses, telephone, stationery, and even on the purchase of capital equipment, such as a computer. The VAT charged on these inputs will also be offset against the output tax when calculating the amount due to Customs and Excise.

The perception of a tax on value added is also distorted when the goods purchased in any particular period are not sold in that period. The input tax on all purchases in a period is deductible from the output tax, irrespective of whether the goods have been sold. In the case of the supply of services (which are also subject to VAT) it is difficult to recognise anything that represents the concept of value added.

2 Tax points and tax periods

An important principle of VAT in terms of its impact on the book-keeping is known as the 'tax point'. This is the point at which the taxable supply is considered to have been made, or received. In general terms, the tax point on outputs is the same as when the revenue is recognised in the books and in most cases this will be the date of the sales invoice – we will look at this again in Section 5 of this chapter. Consequently, a trader selling goods on credit terms might have to pay VAT to Customs and Excise before the tax is actually received from the customer. This cash flow problem is improved by being allowed to offset the input tax when the goods are purchased, and this could be in advance of when the supplier's account is actually paid.

The tax point is important because it determines the 'tax period' for which the supplier must account for VAT, and the date by which it must be paid. The period covered by a VAT return is called a 'tax period' (often called 'the prescribed accounting period' on official documents). The normal tax period is three months, and every business will be allocated a specific set of quarterly accounting dates when it registers for VAT. In order to spread the flow of returns to Customs and Excise over the year, there are three separate sets of quarterly tax periods. The VAT return, together with any payment due, must reach the VAT Central Unit within one month of the end of the trader's tax period.

Activity 1	

Ratna Patel is registered for VAT and has been allocated tax periods ending on the last day of July, October, January and April. In the three months to 30 April 1993, a summary of her accounting records (in so far as they concern VAT) are as follows:

	Total amounts including VAT	Amount of VAT included
	£	£
Credit sales	11,750	1,750
Cash sales	5,875	875
Purchases of trade goods (all on credit)	7,050	1,050
Purchase of office equipment	940	140
Operating expenses	3,750	175

Calculate the following for Ratna Patel:
1. The amount that must be paid to Customs and Excise for this quarter

2. The amounts that will appear in the financial statements for this quarter for:

> Sales
> Purchases
> Additions to office equipment
> Operating expenses

If you review the VAT-exclusive amounts for Ratna Patel (the figures that will appear in her financial statements, shown in the Key to Activity 1) for sales, purchases and additions to office equipment, you will notice that the VAT charged in respect of these items is 17.5% of the value of the supply. For example, the amount of VAT charged on goods sold (£2,625) is 17.5% of the total sales of £15,000. The same applies to purchases and the new equipment.

Activity 2	The VAT on operating expenses is £175. This is not 17.5% of the VAT-exclusive amount of £3,575. Make a note here of some of the reasons that may explain why this is so.

The VAT regulations are quite extensive, and provide the small trader with a number of different schemes for operating the tax. One of them allows VAT to be accounted for on a cash basis (as opposed to an accruals basis) if the trader's turnover falls below a certain limit (£300,000 in 1993). There are also several schemes for retailers who do not normally keep accounting records on a double-entry basis. The cash accounting scheme is discussed in Section 8, but it is not necessary for you to learn the various schemes available to retailers.

There are also options regarding the tax period. For example, a trader who is normally in a position to receive VAT repayments (i.e. input tax exceeds output tax) can ask for a monthly tax period. This will be appropriate for a trader whose outputs are zero rated (such as an exporter) but who has been charged VAT on various inputs. Where the annual value of taxable supplies (excluding VAT) is not more than £300,000, a trader can elect to use an annual accounting scheme. The annual accounting scheme requires the trader to make nine monthly payments on an estimated basis. A final adjustment is then made when the annual return is submitted.

There are also special schemes for traders who deal in second-hand goods such as antiques and second-hand cars. The details of these schemes are beyond the scope of this book.

3 The double-entry records

The double entry for the VAT element of each transaction is quite simple. The trader will open a ledger account called the VAT account. This is a personal account (in the sense that it is used to record transactions with a 'person' outside the business) but the account is normally kept separately in the nominal ledger. If this account has a credit balance, the business owes money to Customs and Excise. If it has a debit balance, Customs and Excise owes money to the business.

The VAT charged on outputs is credited to the VAT account. The VAT charged on inputs is debited to the VAT account. If there is a credit balance on the account, it shows the net amount due, and when this is paid the account is debited.

The complete double entry for output and input tax depends on whether the transactions are on a cash or credit basis. For example, the VAT charged on cash sales will be debited to bank and credited to the VAT account; whereas VAT charged on credit sales will be debited to debtors and credited to the VAT account as part of the double entry raised from the sales day book. A similar situation applies to the VAT on inputs. For example, the VAT on cash purchases will be debited to the VAT account and credited to bank; whereas VAT on credit purchases will be debited to the VAT account and credited to creditors.

<table><tr><td>**Activity 3**</td><td>A trader maintains the normal sales ledger control account and purchases ledger control account in his nominal ledger. All cash received is banked immediately. Transactions for tax period ended 31 December 1992 include the following:</td></tr></table>

	Sub-total	VAT added	Total
Cash sales	100,000	17,500	117,500
Credit sales	400,000	70,000	470,000
Credit purchases	300,000	52,500	352,500
Admin. expenses (all paid by cheque)	40,000	2,000	42,000

The balance owing to Customs and Excise at the beginning of the period was £25,000 and this was paid during the tax period.

Write up the VAT account set out below this box. Each entry in this account should identify the account to which the contra entry is posted.

VAT

Notice again that the normal trading items, such as sales, purchases and administration expenses, will be recorded at amounts that exclude the VAT element. For example, although the trader has charged £587,500 to its customers, £87,500 of this has been credited to Customs and Excise leaving £500,000 to be credited to sales.

4 Recording VAT in the books of prime entry

In order to accumulate the periodic totals for output and input tax, it will be necessary to include an additional column in each of the books of original entry (e.g. sales day book, purchases day book, cash received book and cash payments book). These columns are used to record the VAT element of each transaction.

In order to see how these additional columns are used, we will look at an invoice from Pronto Printers.

INVOICE	No. 876
	Pronto Printers Ltd
	347 Nowhere St
	Oxbridge
Ashford Traders	
743 High Street	
Favingbourne	1 January 1993

For supplying 20 reams of headed notepaper	£200.00
Less trade discount (10%)	£20.00
	£180.00
VAT 17.5% x (£180.00 - £1.80)	£31.18
	£211.18

Credit terms: 1 month. 1% cash discount on the invoiced price of £180.00 for payment within 14 days.

VAT No. 999 0000 11

Notice that the invoice price for the supply is £180.00 but because Pronto Printers is offering a cash discount of £1.80, VAT is charged on the discounted amount irrespective of whether the cash discount is eventually taken. Notice also that the cash discount being offered is based on the VAT-exclusive amount.

Looking at the transaction in the books of Ashford Traders, this is a credit purchase of stationery and will originally be recorded in the purchases daybook. The entry in this book will be as follows:

Purchases day book

Date	Name	Total	VAT	Purchases	Stationery	etc.
1 Jan	Pronto Printers	211.18	31.18		180.00	

The VAT of £31.18 will be included in the total input VAT on credit purchases to be debited to the VAT account. The account for Pronto Printers Ltd will be credited with £211.18. If Ashford Traders pay the account within 14 days, and take the £1.80 cash discount offered, the entry in the cash payments book will be as follows:

Cash payments book

Date	Name	Disc	Payment	VAT	Creditors	Purchases	etc.
14 Jan	Pronto Printers	1.80	209.38		209.38		

Notice that the VAT is not entered again (neither is the cost of the stationery) because *this payment is for the settlement of a creditor* and VAT would have been recorded at the time of purchase. The VAT column in the cash payments book is used to record any input VAT paid on cash transactions, such as the payment of motor expenses or cash purchases. The entries in the primary books of Pronto Printers Ltd will be a mirror image of those shown above.

If you are given the task of preparing financial statements from a trial balance, you might find that the trial balance includes an item described as 'VAT'. This will be the balance on the VAT account. It will either be a creditor or a debtor and should be presented as such in the balance sheet. A debit balance on this account will arise when the input tax exceeds the output tax. This can happen in several situations, for example, where a trader's outputs include exports which are chargeable to VAT at the zero rate. The debit balance represents an amount which will be refunded to the trader by Customs and Excise and so it should be treated as a debtor in the balance sheet in the normal way.

5 Tax invoices and self-policing

The VAT laws state that documentary evidence must be provided in respect of each taxable supply. This normally takes the form of a tax invoice showing the amount of the supply and the VAT charged. The invoice must state the VAT registration number of the supplier. If the recipient of the supply wishes to reclaim the VAT charged, the tax invoice must be retained as evidence of the amount of tax paid. The invoice must be produced for Customs and Excise if it is requested.

Activity 4

This system of tax invoices introduces an element of self-policing into the system. Try to describe how this works. It can be quite important for any staff involved on the purchasing side of the business.

This suggests that anyone involved in the purchasing side of the business should refuse payment until the relevant documentation has been provided. It also suggests that firms registered for VAT would prefer to deal with a supplier who is registered for VAT. Suppliers who are not registered for VAT will be suffering VAT on their own inputs which they cannot reclaim from Customs and Excise. The price that such traders charge for their supplies will take account of their input costs (including irrecoverable VAT) but these prices will not show VAT as a separate element in the invoiced price. Consequently, the recipient of such a supply will be unable to reclaim any of the VAT element that has been built into the invoiced price.

The tax invoice is probably the most important document in the VAT system. This is because a trader receiving the invoice might be asked to produce it by Customs and Excise in support of a claim to deduct the input tax. In view of this, the VAT regulations contain a number of rules regarding the information that must be included on a tax invoice if it is to be valid. A tax invoice must be provided if the supply is to another trader and includes items which have been charged at the standard rate. A tax invoice does not have to be issued to a final consumer (although it can be) nor does it have to be issued if the entire supply is zero rated. In general terms, the tax invoice must contain the following information:

- an identifying number for the invoice .

- date of supply

- name, address and VAT registration number of supplier

- name and address of recipient

- type of supply (sale, sale or return, hire purchase, etc.)

- adequate description of the supply

- amount charged (net of VAT) for each type of supply

- total amount charged, net of VAT

- rate of cash discount, if being offered

- amount of tax chargeable at each rate

- total amount of tax chargeable.

Some customers request a 'pro forma' invoice to enable payment to be made, or for a purchase order to be initiated. Care must be taken to ensure that the pro forma invoice is not construed as being a tax invoice. This can be achieved by ensuring that no VAT number is shown, and by excluding the charge for VAT.

There are a number of rules that allow a less detailed tax invoice to be provided in some cases. These rules apply where:

■   the supplier is a retailer

■   the value of the supply (inclusive of VAT) is less than £100.

In most of these cases the supply is on a cash basis, such as the purchase of petrol. The information to be included on the modified invoices is as follows:

■   name, address and VAT registration number of the supplier

■   date of supply and an adequate description of the supply

■   total amount charged for the supply (inclusive of VAT) and the rate of tax applicable.

In the case of supplies of petrol etc., if the amount is over £100, it is permissible to show the vehicle registration number instead of the name and address of the recipient. Details of the quantity supplied, and type of supply, can also be omitted.

As we mentioned in Section 2, the basic tax point is the point at which the supply is deemed to be made. There are a number of detailed rules regarding this and they depend on whether the supply made is a supply of goods or a supply of services. In general terms, the supply of goods is made when delivery commences; the supply of services is when the services have been completed. However, there is a rule (the 14-day rule) which allows the basic tax point to be ignored, providing the supplier issues a tax invoice within 14 days of making the supply.

In these cases, the basic tax point can be ignored and the date when the invoice is issued can be used instead. Quite often these two dates are identical. If required, the 14-day rule can be extended to 31 days to accommodate traders who issue invoices on a monthly basis.

Activity 5	The 14-day rule simplifies the way in which recording systems are set up in order to account for VAT. Try to describe the nature of this simplification.

There is nothing to prevent a trader using the basic tax point if this happens to be more convenient.

| **Activity 6** | The invoice shown below this box contains three mistakes. Two of them would make it invalid as a tax invoice, the third is an incorrect application of the VAT regulations. Describe the three points concerned.

1

2

3

|

| Pronto Parts Ltd |
| Unit 4 Pevron Industrial Park |
| Devmarket |

Hillmarton Traders
13 Hillmarton Road
Harling

INVOICE

For supplying 20 slave cylinders – part 0012234	£300.00
Less trade discount (10%)	£30.00
	£270.00
VAT at 17.5%	£47.25
	£317.25

Credit terms: 1 month. 1% cash discount on the invoiced price of £270.00 for payment within 14 days.

VAT No. 666 0000 123

6 Zero rating and exempt supplies

The VAT legislation defines a taxable supply by stating that any supply is taxable unless it is exempt. The types of supply that are exempt are then detailed in a list. The amount of VAT charged on taxable supplies is usually either the standard rate or 0%. There is a list of supplies that are taxable at the zero rate of tax.

Exemption and zero rating are two different aspects of the VAT system. A business that supplies nothing other than zero-rated goods must register for VAT and will be entitled to recover any VAT paid on supplies received. Such a trader will be constantly claiming a refund from Customs and Excise. Exemption is different; a trader whose supplies consist entirely of exempt supplies cannot register for VAT.

Activity 7	What are the VAT consequences for a trader who is unable to register for VAT because his supplies are made entirely of exempt supplies?

Sometimes a particular supply falls into both exempt and zero rating lists. In these cases, the supply is treated as zero rated. A trader whose total supplies are zero rated can apply to be exempted from registration. This relieves the trader of the burden of administration, but denies the right to recover VAT on supplies received.

Zero-rated supplies include: food, books, medical supplies and aids for the handicapped, children's clothing and footwear, transport of passengers, international transport of goods, exported goods.

The above list is by no means complete, and there are extensive regulations for each category mentioned. For example, food relates to items for human consumption not to items such as pet food. Supplies in the course of catering, e.g. restaurant meals, are not zero rated, neither are supplies of chocolate biscuits and similar snacks. Fuel and power for domestic use were changed from the zero rate in April 1994 to 8%, and from 8% to the standard rate in April 1995. Full details of zero rated legislation can be found in Leaflet 701/39 which can be obtained free from any VAT office.

Exempt supplies include: land, insurance, postal services, finance, education, health and welfare, burial and cremation, works of art, fund raising by charities. As with zero rating, this list is incomplete and it is essential to study the regulations for more information. For example, exemption for provision of education relates broadly to universities, colleges and schools as defined by the legislation. In some cases, suppliers of education who do not fall under the defined categories will be exempt, providing the supplies are made for purposes other than profit.

The health and welfare group includes supplies of services, and connected supplies of goods, by persons enrolled on certain registers, such as doctors, dentists, ophthalmic or dispensing opticians. It also includes provision of care (and connected goods) in hospitals or other approved institutions.

Registration with Customs and Excise is not required if the total supplies of a trader are exempt. A trader who has decided not to register for VAT because total taxable supplies do not exceed the threshold of £37,600 (for 1993/94) is not a 'taxable person' and so the supplies made by such a trader are not taxable supplies.

7 Partial exemption

There will be many instances where a trader is supplying both exempt and taxable supplies. This situation is not merely limited to businesses whose normal trade supplies are mixed (such as cosmetics and medicines) but virtually any type of trade where there may be an occasional exempt supply such as the sale of a part of the business premises. Sub-letting of business premises is another example because rents are exempt.

The problem that has to be addressed in these cases is related to the recovery of input tax. It will be necessary to analyse the input tax according to the use to which the supplies received are put. The VAT charged on supplies received might fall under one of three headings, namely:

- the input tax relates solely to taxable outputs, and is recoverable in full

- the input tax relates solely to exempt outputs, and cannot be recovered

- the input tax relates to business activities generally, and must be apportioned to the two types of output.

There are several types of input tax relating to general business activities, such as VAT paid on stationery and telephone bills. The VAT paid on these supplies must be apportioned between the two types of output. The normal basis of apportionment is the ratio of turnover on taxable outputs to turnover on exempt outputs. For example, a trader's turnover (excluding VAT) is £60,000 for taxable supplies and £30,000 for exempt supplies. The VAT charged on supplies received that cannot be directly attributed to either of these is £3,000. Two-thirds of the input tax (£2,000) will be attributed to taxable supplies and can be recovered; the remaining one-third (£1,000) will be attributed to exempt supplies and is, therefore, irrecoverable.

| **Activity 8** | Kim Polowski is registered for VAT and makes both taxable and exempt supplies. Some of the taxable supplies are charged at zero rate. An analysis of input tax for the period reveals the following: |

VAT directly attributable to taxable supplies   £2,000
VAT directly attributable to exempt supplies   £200
VAT that cannot be attributed to either   £1,000

Turnover for the period was £12,000 for taxable supplies and £4,000 for exempt supplies.

Calculate the total amount of input tax that can be set against Kim's output tax for this period.

This kind of calculation must be made for each tax period and then recalculated at the end of the year. Any adjustment is dealt with on the first return for the next year. As you can imagine, it is vital for partially exempt traders to keep a detailed analysis of all inputs. The VAT on supplies received which is attributed to making exempt supplies if is known as 'exempt input tax'. In the accounting records, the exempt input tax will have to be treated as part of the cost of the supply received. In the case of general inputs, this can involve making estimates in some cases. In order to cope with the double entry it might be necessary to have a VAT suspense account (colloquially known as 'the pot') to deal with the debits for VAT on general inputs until they are finally attributed to the relevant outputs.

8 Bad debts and cash accounting schemes

Bad debts

A trader who is registered under the ordinary VAT accounting scheme will be accounting for VAT on outputs for the period when they were made. In the case of a sale on credit terms, the trader might have to account for VAT even if the customer has failed to pay the amount due. A special kind of relief, known as 'bad debt relief', is available in these circumstances. It can be claimed when:

■ the debt has been outstanding for at least one year

■ the debt has been formally written off in the accounting records

■ certain records of the transaction are retained.

The claim is effected by simply including the amount of VAT not received as part of the input tax when completing the VAT return for the period (we will look at VAT returns in Section 12). If the debt is subsequently recovered, the VAT element must be repaid to Customs and Excise.

Cash accounting schemes

In the case of small businesses, a special scheme is available that permits the trader to account for VAT on a cash basis. This scheme (usually known as the cash accounting scheme) allows the trader to complete the VAT returns on the basis of payments received and payments made during the period. It is available to traders whose taxable turnover for the next twelve months is expected to be below £300,000. Any tax to be accounted for on imported goods must be dealt with outside the scheme.

The general effect is to defer payment of output tax until cash is received. The input tax cannot be claimed until the suppliers have been paid. The scheme also provides an automatic relief for bad debts. In many cases the scheme provides a cash flow advantage, although it can be a disadvantage.

Activity 9	It may be a disadvantage for a retailer whose sales are entirely on a cash basis to use the cash accounting scheme. Make a note here of why this may be so.

The same problem arises with a trader whose supplies are mostly zero rated. In the case of retailers there are a number of different accounting schemes (known as retailer schemes) that are designed to simplify administration of the tax. As mentioned earlier, it is not necessary for you to study the details of these schemes.

Traders taking advantage of the cash accounting scheme have to obtain a 'receipted' tax invoice for any inputs acquired on a cash purchase basis. Under the normal scheme, the tax invoice does not have to be receipted.

9 Non-deductible input tax

The input tax on most supplies received is deductible from the tax charged on supplies made. There are, however, a number of instances where the input tax on the supply received is not deductible, for example:

■ purchase of a motor car for use in the business

■ payments for business entertainment.

The input tax falling under these headings is known colloquially as 'blocked' tax, and has to be treated as part of the cost of the item concerned instead of being debited to the VAT account.

Another important category is goods acquired under a second-hand goods scheme. These schemes are designed to avoid an element of double-taxation when a consumer sells goods back into the business system. A trader who sells goods acquired from a consumer is only required to account for VAT on the profit margin (rather than the sales price) if the goods are eligible under one of the second-hand goods schemes. The trader selling such goods must not issue a tax invoice and, consequently, if the purchaser is a trader there is no opportunity of claiming the tax charged as input tax. The trader in second-hand goods can, however, sell them under the normal VAT system by charging tax on the full price.

10 VAT records

Because VAT is collected at the level of individual suppliers, it is vital that the supplier should keep a record of all transactions. In general terms, each supplier is obliged to keep the following:

■ a copy of all tax invoices issued

■ all tax invoices received

■ documentation relating to imports and exports

■ a copy of all credit notes issued for goods returned by customers (or for adjustments to amounts charged)

■ a copy of all debit notes issued (or the actual credit notes received) in respect of returns to suppliers (or adjustments to amounts charged)

■ a VAT account containing the information specified by regulations.

The VAT account must be divided to show the transactions for each tax period, and must differentiate between tax payable and tax allowable.

The tax payable portion must include the following:

■ output tax for the period

■ earlier output tax errors discovered during the period

■ retrospective adjustments (e.g. price adjustments on earlier supplies made)

■ other adjustments.

The tax allowable portion must include the following:

- input tax allowable for the period

- earlier input tax errors discovered during the period

- retrospective adjustments (e.g. price adjustments on earlier supplies received)

- other adjustments.

Examples of 'other adjustments' include the annual adjustment made for a partially exempt trader, and a claim for bad debt relief.

Here is the example VAT account that Customs and Excise use in The VAT Guide (HM Customs and Excise Notice 700):

Period from 1 April 1991 to 30 June 1991			
VAT deductible – Input tax	£	**VAT payable – Output tax**	£
VAT you have been charged on your purchases		VAT you have charged on your sales	
April			
May	2215.23	April	2780.23
June	1626.47	May	2305.81
	2792.01	June	3302.45
	6633.71		8388.49
VAT on imports	96.85	VAT due on postal imports	6.85
Net overclaim of input tax from previous returns	-125.50	Net understatement of output tax on previous returns	719.26
Bad debt relief	96.48	Annual adjustment: retail scheme D	91.69
Sub-total	6701.54	**Sub-total**	9206.29
Less:		Less:	
VAT on credits received from suppliers	-27.50	VAT on credits allowed to customers	-23.00
Total tax deductible	6674.04	**Total tax payable**	9183.29
		Less total tax deductible	6674.04
		Payable to Customs & Excise	2509.25

Note that 'VAT on imports' (i.e. imports from non-EC countries) only appears as input tax – this assumes that VAT has been paid at the border. However, many businesses defer payment of VAT on imports, and declare the tax as both input and output tax in the VAT account – as if the business were paying the tax on the import and reclaiming it simultaneously.

You can obtain a copy of The VAT Guide from any Customs and Excise office, and you are strongly advised to do so.

Activity 10	Ashok is registered for VAT and supplies goods that are taxable at both the zero rate and the standard rate. None of his supplies are exempt. His prescribed accounting periods are for the three months ended 30 June, 30 September, 31 December and 31 March. During the three months to 30 June 1993, the following transactions occurred:

Sales	Total excluding VAT (£)	VAT (£)
April	20,000	3,000
May	22,000	3,500
June	25,000	4,300

Purchases and expenses	Total excluding VAT (£)	VAT (£)
April	16,000	2,000
May	14,000	1,800
June	15,000	2,200

A debt for £235 has been written off after it had been outstanding for 18 months. The debt consisted of £200 for the supply made plus £35 VAT. You discover that the expenses shown for June include entertaining expenses. The total amount for entertaining expenses (including VAT at 17.5% on all items) was £470. Wages and salaries paid during the period were £14,000 and drawings by Ashok were £4,000.

Ashok has also issued the following credit and debit notes during the three months to 30 June 1993:

	Total excl. VAT (£)	VAT (£)
Credit notes issued for the quarter	400	70
Debit notes issued for the quarter	600	105

Draw up Ashok's VAT account for the period in the blank account that follows this box. Do not calculate the amount payable to Customs and Excise – we will do that in the next Activity.

VAT account for the period from 1 April 1993 to 30 June 1993	
£	£

11 The Single Market

On 1 January 1993 the single European market came into being. The main idea behind the single market is that the concept of imports and exports of goods between the 12 member states will disappear. Only goods received from outside the EC will be treated as imports for VAT purposes, and only goods despatched to countries outside the EC will be treated as exports.

When a VAT-registered trader in one EC country despatches goods to a VAT-registered trader in another EC country, the supply will normally be zero rated. No VAT will be paid at the frontier. The customer acquires the goods when they are supplied to him, and will account for VAT on his VAT return at the rate in force in the country of receipt.

When a VAT-registered trader in one EC country despatches goods to an unregistered trader in another EC country, in most cases the supplier will charge VAT at the rate in force in the country of despatch.

All traders have to use a country prefix to their VAT number to identify from which member state they are trading:

BE	Belgium	GB	Great Britain
DE	Germany	IR	Ireland
DK	Denmark	IT	Italy
EL	Greece	LU	Luxembourg
ES	Spain	NL	Netherlands
FR	France	PT	Portugal

The 12 member states have agreed a minimum standard rate of 15%, and the UK's zero rate will be retained.

There are certain requirements you need to satisfy before zero rating your exports:

■ you must obtain your customer's VAT number

■ you must show it on the sales invoice (including the country prefix)

■ the goods must be despatched to another EC country

■ you must hold commercial documentary evidence that the goods have been removed from your country.

As well as this main point, the removal of import and export duty between member states, there are three special schemes which we will not cover here:

■ distance selling

■ new liability

■ purchases of new means of transport.

Nor will we cover the effects of the single market on freight and transport suppliers. If you are particularly interested in any of these topics, contact your local Customs and Excise office for further information.

Process and return

If you send goods to another EC country for process and return, this will be treated as a supply of goods. No tax will be due when you send the goods for processing, but you will still have to record the movement of the goods on your EC Sales List (we will look at this later in this section) and show the value of the goods on your statistical declaration.

VAT will be due on the value of the processing work on return of the goods to the owner and will be accounted for by the owner as an acquisition on receipt of the goods. You must account for VAT on the value of the processing work and show the total value of the goods, including the processing price, on your statistical declaration.

Repair and return

If you send goods to another EC country for repair and return, the work will be treated as a supply of services. No VAT will be due. The movement of these goods need not be recorded on your EC Sales List, but the total value of the goods should be included on the statistical declaration, both when they are sent out and when they are returned.

Transfer of goods

Transfer of your own goods will count as a supply of goods – you need to be VAT registered in both countries, and fulfil all the requirements for zero rating. In all cases, you should retain the relevant commercial documentary evidence.

Goods received

If you are a trader registered for VAT and you acquire goods from a VAT-registered trader in another EC country, you must:

■   keep records of the goods acquired from other EC countries

■   hold commercial documentation, such as your supplier's invoice

■   calculate the VAT due on the acquisition of the goods and enter it on the 'tax due' side of your VAT account

■   include the VAT due in the appropriate box on your VAT return for the tax period in which the tax point of the acquisition occurs.

For goods acquired in the UK from another EC country, the VAT which you include on your VAT return as tax due may also be deducted as input tax, provided:

■   the goods have been or are to be used for business purposes

■   the goods are not items on which tax is non-deductible

■   the normal partial exemption rules, if they are applicable, are observed.

On 1 January 1993, two additional boxes were added to the VAT return (we will look at VAT returns in the next section). There is a box for the VAT due on acquisitions from other EC countries, and a box for the total of the tax due on sales and on EC acquisitions. VAT deductible on acquisitions is included in the existing input tax box.

The liability to pay VAT will be triggered by the acquisition or receipt of the goods by the customer. The VAT will become due either

- on the fifteenth day of the month following that in which you acquired the goods, or

- on the date of issue of an invoice from the supplier (including an invoice which is issued before the goods are sent to you)

whichever is earlier. Remember to supply your VAT number so that the supplier can show it on the invoice.

The EC Sales List

You will have to complete an EC Sales List if you are a trader registered for VAT in the UK and you:

- make supplies of goods to a person registered for VAT in another EC country

- send goods to a person registered for VAT in another EC country for process

- return goods after processing them to a person registered for VAT in another EC country

- transfer your goods from the UK to another EC country in the course of your business.

There are two exceptions to this – you do not need to complete an EC Sales List if:

- your total annual taxable turnover does not exceed the VAT registration threshold by 35,000 ECU or more (i.e. in the UK 35,000 ECU + £37,600, about £62,000)

- the annual value of your supplies to other EC countries is no more than 15,000 ECU (about £11,500) *unless* those supplies include new means of transport (boats, aircraft, motorised land vehicles).

On your EC Sales List, you must show:

- your own VAT number

- your name and address

- the date of submission

- the period covered

- your customers' VAT numbers, including the two-letter country prefix

- the calendar quarterly total value of the goods and associated freight and transport services which you have supplied to each customer

- an indication, where appropriate, that you have sent goods to another EC country for process

- an indication, where appropriate, that you have returned goods to another EC country after processing them, together with the value of the process.

Your EC Sales List can be in any of these forms:

- a pre-printed return provided by Customs and Excise, VAT 101

- a plain paper return

- magnetic media, e.g. computer tape or disk

- electronic data interchange (EDI).

The pre-printed form, VAT 101, will contain boxes for the registration numbers of your EC customers (including the country identifier) and for the total value of your sales to them. There will also be a box for you to show that goods for process have been sent or returned.

If you make monthly or quarterly VAT returns, you will have to send in an EC Sales List for each calendar quarter: 31 March, 30 June, 30 September and 31 December.

If you make annual VAT returns, you may be able to send in your EC Sales List once a year. Under certain circumstances, you may be able to send in your EC Sales List once a month.

In all cases, your completed EC Sales List must reach Customs and Excise within six weeks of the end of the period it covers.

| **Activity 11** | Below is Ashok's EC Sales List for the three-month period ended 30 June 1993. Ashok sends very few supplies abroad, and so chooses to write out his EC Sales List rather than complete a form. Make sure that Ashok has supplied all the necessary information.

Ashok has made no purchase from other EC member states in this quarter. Return to the VAT account that you wrote up in Activity 10, and add in any details that you think should be included from Ashok's EC Sales List. Calculate the amount that is payable to Customs and Excise. |

Ashok's Saris and Fine Fabrics
VAT Reg. No. GB 615 8180 24

Proprietor: Ashok Kandahar
31, High Street,
Oakby,
Leicester.
LE5 6JS

7 July 1993

EC Sales List for the period 30 April 1993 to 30 June 1993

Yves San Moritz, Paris	*VAT no. FR 234 8763 90*	*Supplies: £1,600*
Ruud van der Link, Amsterdam	*VAT no. NL 741 9472 74*	*Supplies: £2,300*

---

12 The VAT return

If you are VAT registered, the VAT Central Unit (VCU) will send you a VAT return (VAT 100) each tax period. You must fill in this return and send it back to the VCU by the due date shown on the form. This will be no later than one month after the end of the tax period covered by the return. At the same time you must pay the tax due in full. If you fail to send in the return and pay the tax due in full by the due date, you could be liable to a default surcharge.

You can pay by cheque, postal order or credit transfer. If you want to pay by credit transfer, tell your local VAT office and they will arrange for you to be sent a supply of special forms. When you send a payment, make sure to quote your VAT registration number on the back of the cheque, giro transfer form, etc.

VAT leaflet 700/12 *Filling in your VAT return* will help you complete your return correctly. If you don't already have a copy of this leaflet in your organisation or at your college, any VAT office will be able to supply you with a copy.

An example of a blank VAT return is shown on the following page, and the explanatory notes are shown on the page following that. Read through the explanatory notes carefully, as you will need to know how to complete a VAT return for the next Activity.

| Activity 12 | Using the information given in Activity 10, and your calculations from Activities 10 and 11, complete the blank VAT return form. Read through both the form and the explanatory notes before attempting to do this. |

HM Customs and Excise

Value Added Tax Return

For the period
01 04 93 to 30 06 93

For Official Use

199 615 8180 24 211 06 93   W10565
Ashok Kandahar
Ashok's Saris and Fine Fabrics
31, High Street
Oakby
Leicester
LE5 6JS   073344/25

Your VAT Office telephone number is 0533 801700

Registration number	Period
615 8180 24	06 93

You could be liable to a financial penalty if your completed return and all the VAT payable are not received by the due date.

Due date: 31 07 93

For Official Use

REMEMBER
You must include VAT due on EC transactions in boxes 2 & 3 if they occur on or after 1.1.93.

Before you fill in this form please read the notes on the back and the VAT leaflet "Filling in your VAT return". Fill in all boxes clearly in ink, and write 'none' where necessary. Don't put a dash or leave any box blank. If there are no pence write "00" in the pence column. **Do not** enter more than one amount in any box.

For official use			
	VAT due in this period on **sales** and other outputs	1	
	VAT due in this period on acquisitions from other **EC Member States**	2	
	Total VAT due **(the sum of boxes 1 and 2)**	3	
	VAT reclaimed in this period on **purchases** and other inputs (including acquisitions from the EC)	4	
	(Difference between boxes 3 and 4)	5	
	Total value of **sales** and all other outputs excluding any VAT. **Include your box 8 figure**	6	00
	Total value of **purchases** and all other inputs excluding any VAT. **Include your box 9 figure**	7	00
	Total value of all **supplies** of goods and related services, excluding any VAT, to other **EC Member States**	8	00
	Total value of all **acquisitions** of goods and related services, excluding any VAT, from other **EC Member States**	9	00

Retail schemes. If you have used any of the schemes in the period covered by this return, enter the relevant letter(s) in this box.

If you are enclosing a payment please tick this box.

DECLARATION: You, or someone on your behalf, must sign below.

I,_____ declare that the
(Full name of signatory in BLOCK LETTERS)
information given above is true and complete.

Signature_____ Date_____19_____

A false declaration can result in prosecution.

CD 2859/N3(04/92)   F3790 (JANUARY 1993)

VAT 100

Y

Notes

These notes and the VAT leaflet *Filling in your VAT Return* will help you fill in this form. You may also need to refer to other VAT notices and leaflets.

If you need help or advice please contact your local VAT office. Their telephone number is shown over the page.

If you are using the 'cash accounting scheme', the amounts of VAT due and deductible are for payments you actually receive and make, and not on invoices you receive and send out.

If you put **negative figures** in boxes 1 to 4, put them in brackets.

Amounts not declared correctly on previous returns

1.   If any of your previous returns declared too much or too little VAT that has not yet been accounted for, you can correct the position using boxes 1 and 4 for net amounts of **£1000 or less**.

2.   If the net amount is **over £1000**, tell your local VAT office immediately. Don't include the amount on this return.

If you do not follow these instructions you could be liable to a financial penalty.

How to pay your VAT

Cross all cheques and postal orders "AC Payee Only" and make them payable to "H M Customs and Excise". In your own interest do not send notes, coins, or uncrossed postal orders through the post.

If you wish to pay by 'credit transfer', ask your local VAT office. Pre-printed booklets of credit transfer slips will then be sent to you.

Please write your VAT registration number on the back of all cheques and credit transfer slips.

Where to send this return

You must make sure your completed form and any VAT payable are received by the 'due date' (shown over the page) by:

**The Controller
VAT Central Unit
H M Customs and Excise
21 Victoria Avenue
Southend-on-Sea X
SS99 1AA**

CD 2859/R/N3(04/92)

Box 1

Show the VAT due on all goods and services you supplied in this period.

Box 2

Show the VAT due (but not paid) on all goods and related services you acquired in this period from other EC Member States.

Box 3

Show the total amount of the VAT due ie the sum of boxes 1 and 2. This is your total **Output** tax.

Box 4

Show the amount of VAT deductible on any business purchases including acquisitions of goods and related services from other EC Member States. This is your **Input** tax.

Box 5

If this amount is under £1, you need not send any payment, nor will any repayment be made to you, but you must still fill in this form and send it to the VAT Central Unit.

Boxes 6 and 7

In box 6 show the value excluding VAT of your total outputs (supplies of goods and services). Include zero rated, exempt outputs and EC supplies from box 8.

In box 7 show the value excluding VAT of all your inputs (purchases of goods and services). Include zero rated, exempt inputs and EC acquisitions from box 9.

Boxes 8 and 9

EC TRADE ONLY

Use these boxes if you have supplied goods to or acquired goods from another EC Member State. Include related services such as transport costs where these form part of the invoice or contract price. The figures should exclude VAT.

The other EC Member States are: Belgium, Denmark, France, Germany, Greece, Netherlands, Ireland, Italy, Luxembourg, Portugal and Spain.

You must tell your local VAT office about any changes in your business circumstances (including changes of address).

Printed in the U.K. for H.M.S.O. 10/92 Dd. 836001 C108800 13110

Summary

The important learning points in this chapter are as follows:

- VAT is intended to be a tax on the final consumer, not on the business community

- the business community is required to collect the tax by keeping a record of all VAT charged on outputs and all VAT charged on inputs

- VAT is accounted for on a quarterly basis

- there is a basic tax point to identify when the supply is made, but in most cases the date of the invoice is used instead of the basic tax point

- there are regulations regarding the form of a valid tax invoice and the type of accounting records that each trader must keep

- there are two rates of tax: the standard rate (17.5% in 1993) and the zero rate

- some supplies are exempt

- traders who are partially exempt are required to apportion input tax where it cannot be attributed to specific outputs

- bad debt relief can be obtained in certain circumstances

- there are various schemes for small businesses, including the cash accounting scheme

- some input tax is 'blocked' and cannot be deducted from output tax

- the introduction of the single market has effectively removed the concept of imports and exports between EC countries

- all VAT-registered traders must return a VAT return form and pay the tax due in full or they will have to pay a default surcharge.

Key to Chapter 1 activities

Activity 1

1. VAT on outputs (£1,750 + £875)   £2,625
    VAT on inputs (£1,050 + £140 + £175)   £1,365
    Amount due to Customs and Excise   £1,260

2. Sales (£11,750 + £5,875 - £2,625)   £15,000
    Purchases (£7,050 - £1,050)   £6,000
    Additions to office equipment (£940 - £140)   £800
    Operating expenses (£3,750 - £175)   £3,575

Activity 2

There are several explanations. Some of these expenses will not be subject to VAT, for example the cost of employees' wages. Some of the inputs might also be exempt, such as bank charges, and some might be zero rated, such as text books. Some supplies may have been made by traders who are not VAT-registered.

Activity 3

Here is our completed VAT account.

VAT					
1992		£	1992		£
31/12	Purchases ledger control account	52,500	1/12	Balance b/d	25,000
			31/12	Bank (output VAT)	17,500
31/12	Bank (input VAT)	2,000	31/12	Sales ledger control account	70,000
31/12	Bank	25,000			
31/12	Balance c/d	33,000			
		112,500			112,500
			1/1/93	Balance b/d	33,000

Activity 4

A trader who wishes to be able to claim a deduction for input VAT will insist on being provided with a tax invoice to support the claim. Without this invoice the deduction might be denied by Customs and Excise. These tax invoices provide Customs and Excise with a means of checking on the returns made by the supplier.

Activity 5

It is easier to set up a recording system that operates by reference to the date of the invoice rather than the basic tax point.

Activity 6

The invoice is not dated. The invoice has no identifying number. The amount charged for VAT should have been calculated on the amount net of cash discount, i.e. 17.5% of (£270 - £2.70) = £46.78.

Activity 7

The trader will be unable to reclaim any VAT paid on supplies received (input tax).

Activity 8

VAT attributed to taxable supplies   £2,000
Proportion of unattributed VAT £12,000/£16,000 x £1,000   £750
                                                                                           £2,750

Activity 9

The retailer will already be accounting for VAT on outputs on a cash basis. If the cash accounting scheme is adopted, the claim to offset input VAT will be delayed until the bills are paid.

Activity 10

Here is our completed VAT account.

VAT account for the period from 1 April 1993 to 30 June 1993			
VAT deductible – Input tax	£	**VAT payable – Output tax**	£
VAT charged on purchases and expenses		VAT charged on sales	
April	2,000	April	3,000
May	1,800	May	3,500
June (see working)	2,130	June	4,300
	5,930	**Sub-total**	10,800
Bad debt relief	35	Less:	
Sub-total	5,965	VAT on credits allowed to customers	(70)
Less:		**Total tax payable**	10,730
VAT on credits received from suppliers	(105)		
Total tax deductible	5,860		

Working:
The 'blocked' input tax on entertaining expenses is $17.5/117.5 \times £470 = £70$.

Wages and drawings are not taxable inputs.

Activity 11

Ashok has supplied all the necessary information on his EC Sales List. Because Ashok has only supplied goods to other EC member states, and not acquired goods from other EC member states, there is no alteration to be made to the VAT account you prepared in Activity 10. Ashok's exports to EC member states are zero rated (assuming that he satisfies all the requirements for zero rating). VAT is due only when he acquires goods from other member states.

The amount payable to Customs and Excise is therefore:

Total tax payable less total tax deductible = £10,730 - £5,860 = £4,870.

Activity 12

Box 1   £10,730
Box 2   None
Box 3   £10,730
Box 4   £5,860
Box 5   £4,870
Box 6   £67,000 - £400 + £3,900 = £70,500
Box 7   £45,000 - £600 + £70 = £44,470
Box 8   £3,900
Box 9   None

Note that in Box 7, the 'blocked' input tax of £70 is treated as a part of the cost of the items concerned.